France's Relationship with Subsaharan Africa

France's Relationship with Subsaharan Africa

Anton Andereggen

PRAEGER

Westport, Connecticut
London

Library of Congress Cataloging-in-Publication Data

Andereggen, Anton.
    France's relationship with subsaharan Africa / Anton Andereggen.
        p. cm.
    Includes bibliographical references and index.
    ISBN 0-275-94756-4
    1. France—Foreign relations—Africa, Sub-Saharan. 2. Africa, Sub-
Saharan—Foreign relations—France. 3. France—Foreign
relations—1945- 4. Africa, Sub-Saharan—Foreign relations—1960-
I. Title.
DC59.8.A35A64   1994
327.44067—dc20   93-5446

British Library Cataloguing in Publication Data is available.

Library of Congress Catalog Card Number: 93-5446
ISBN: 0-275-94756-4

First published in 1994

Praeger Publishers, 88 Post Road West, Westport, CT 06881
An imprint of Greenwood Publishing Group, Inc.

Printed in the United States of America

The paper used in this book complies with the
Permanent Paper Standard issued by the National
Information Standards Organization (Z39.48-1984).

10 9 8 7 6 5 4 3 2 1

Contents

Tables

Preface

The African empire that France acquired in the 19th and 20th centuries developed without any clearly established plan. The French people in general did not have any interest in overseas possessions or in large-scale emigration to populate the newly acquired lands. Only Algeria attracted about 1 million French immigrants, with the negative consequences that led to the Algerian war of liberation.

When the European scramble to partition and occupy Africa began in the 1870s, an interested French minority consisting of politicians, merchants, and military officers did not want to be left out of the race for annexing African lands. The politicians recognized that France would be able to restore its pride, lost in the Franco-Prussian War, by acquiring an overseas empire. An extended overseas empire would provide the secure source of tropical raw materials and assured markets for the manufactured goods that the French merchants were seeking. The military officers saw in the acquisition of a large empire the possibility of military intervention and subsequent promotions in military ranks and social status. Therefore, politics, financial gains, and national ambition were equally important in the conquest for a French empire.

France granted independence to its former colonies in West and Central Africa in the early 1960s. Thanks to a network of formal and informal agreements with these countries, France continues to wield considerable power and influence politically, economically, socially, and culturally. Through the various governments of the Fifth Republic, the African policy of France has been exceptionally constant and stable. My goal in writing this book is to inform a general audience, in particular students in African Studies, about the special Franco-African relations as they have developed during colonial times and evolved ever since. Recent important changes that have developed in this relationship are being analyzed, and suggestions are being made for its direction in the future. Emphasis is given to the cultural component of this relationship. The publications regarding postliberation French African policies deal almost exclusively with neocolonialism, economics, politics, and military matters of individual countries. To the cultural component they give only minor importance; many works do not even mention it. The present publication is intended to fill this literary gap.

My interest in Franco-African relations grows out of my past research and publication on the more general concept of contemporary Francophone Africa and from my preparations for the French Area Studies Program at Lewis and Clark College. When the administration of that college agreed to my request for leading a six-month overseas study program and a subsequent one-year sabbatical leave, I continued my research at the *Université des sciences humaines* in Strasbourg and the *Université d'Avignon et des Pays du Vaucluse*, where I received generous support form the library personnel and the teaching staff in Francophone African Studies. My visits to the libraries of the *Université de Provence* in Aix and Marseille, as well as the discussions I had with several former *coopérants* who taught for extended periods of time in West and Central Africa deepened my knowledge of, and appreciation for, Francophone black Africa.

Certain official and university publications specializing in Franco-African relations—such as the journal *Maghreb-Machrek; Monde Arabe*, published in Paris by the Fondation Nationale des Politiques et Direction de la Documentation (Documentation française, under the auspices of the prime minister's office); *l'Annuaire de l'Afrique du nord*, published by the Centre d'Études et de Recherches sur les Sociétés de la Méditerranée (CERSM) in Aix-en-Provence; the journal *Grand Maghreb*, published by the Institut d'Études Politiques de Grenoble—consider Mauritania a member of the Maghreb states. On the other hand, the president of the republic and le Ministère de la Coopération et du Développement classify Mauritania as a member of the Francophone black African states. In this work Mauritania is treated as a member of the black African states since it was a member of the French West African Federation.

Two chapters provide background and a historical perspective on French West Africa and French Equatorial Africa to the general reader. They are limited to those features that are significant for the French colonial rule and for the present dominance/dependency situation. To give the reader a view from a different angle, the last chapter describes the special Franco-African relationship and analyzes how the attitudes of the French people toward the Africans have developed.

Abbreviations

AAPC	All African Peoples Conference
ACP	African, Caribbean, and Pacific States
AEF	Afrique Équatoriale Française [French Equatorial Africa Federation]
AOF	Afrique Occidentale Française [French West Africa Federation]
APD	Aide Publique au Développement [Public Development Assistance]
BA	Bloc Africain
BCAEC	Banque Centrale des États de l'Afrique Équatoriale et du Cameroun
BCEAO	Banque Centrale des États de l'Afrique de l'Ouest
BDG	Bloc Démocratique Gabonais
BDS	Bloc Démocratique Sénégalais
BEAC	Banque des États de l'Afrique Centrale
BSAP	Bulletin de la Société d'Anthropologie de Paris
CA	Convention Africaine
CACEU	Central African Customs and Economic Union [Union Douanière et Économique de l'Afrique Centrale]
CAPES	Certificat d'Aptitude Professionnelle à l'Enseignement Secondaire
CAR	Central African Republic
CCCE	Caisse Centrale de Coopération Économique
CCFOM	Caisse Centrale de la France d'Outre-Mer
CEAO	Communauté Économique de l'Afrique de l'Ouest [West African Economic Community]
CFA	Colonies Françaises d'Afrique *or* Communauté Financière Africaine
CFAO	Compagnie Française de l'Afrique Occidentale
CFI	Canal France International
CGT	Confédération Générale du Travail

CMRN	Comité Militaire pour le Renouveau National
CMSN	Comité Militaire de Salut National
CNLCI	Comité National pour la Libération de la Côte-d'Ivoire
CNT	Comité National de Transition
CR	Comités Révolutionnaires
CSC	Confédération Syndicale Congolaise
CSON	Conseil Supérieur d'Orientation Nationale
CUT	Comité de l'Unité Togolaise
DOM	Département d'Outre-Mer
	[Overseas Department]
ECU	European Currency Unit
EDF	European Development Fund
EEC	European Economic Community
EMS	European Monetary System
FAC	Fonds d'Aide et de Coopération
FAO	Food and Agriculture Organization
	[Organisation pour l'alimentation et l'agriculture]
FIDES	Fonds d'Investissement et de Développement Économique et Social
FIDOM	Fonds d'Investissement pour les Départements d'Outre-Mer
FLN	Front de la Libération Nationale
	[National Liberation Front]
FP	Front Populaire
FPI	Front Populaire Ivorien
GDP	Gross Domestic Product
GNP	Gross National Product
GPRA	Gouvernement Provisoire de la République Algérienne
IBRD	International Bank for Reconstruction and Development
ILO	International Labor Organization
IMF	International Monetary Fund
INED	Institut National d'Études Démographiques
INSEE	Institut National de la Statistique et des Études Économiques
IOM	Indépendants d'Outre-Mer
MNC	Mouvement National Congolais
MND	Mouvement National pour la Démocratie
MNSD	Mouvement National pour une Société de Développement
MPS	Mouvement Patriotique du Salut
MSA	Mouvement Socialiste Africain
MT	Mouvement du Travail
OAS	Organisation de l'Armée Secrète
OAU	Organization of African Unity
OCAM	Organisation Commune Africaine et Malgache
ODP	Organisation pour la Démocratie Populaire
OPEC	Oil Producing and Exporting Country
ORTF	Office de Radiodiffusion-Télévision Française

PAI	Parti Africain de l'Indépendance
PCF	Parti Communiste Français
PCT	Parti Congolais du Travail
PDCI	Parti Démocratique de la Côte-d'Ivoire
PDG	Parti Démocratique de Guinée; Parti Démocratique Gabonais
PFA	Parti de la Fédération Africaine
PPD	Parti Progressiste Dahoméen
PPM	Parti du Peuple Mauritanien
PPN	Parti Progressiste Nigérien
PRA	Parti du Regroupement Africain
PRD	Parti Républicain Dahoméen
PRPB	Parti de la Révolution Populaire du Bénin
PS	Parti Socialiste
PSS	Parti Socialiste Sénégalais
PUF	Presses Universitaires de France
RAMSES	Rapport Annuel Mondial sur le Système Économique et les Stratégies
RCA	République Centrafricaine [Central African Republic]
RDA	Rassemblement Démoctratique Africain
RDC	Rassemblement Démocratique Centrafricain
RDC	Rassemblement Démocratique Centrafricain
RDD	Rassemblement Démocratique Dahoméen
RDPC	Rassemblement Démocratique du Peuple Camerounais
RFA	République Fédérale Africaine
RFD	Rassemblement des Forces Démocratiques
RND	Rassemblement National Démocratique
RPF	Rassemblement du Peuple Français
RPR	Rassemblement pour la République
RPT	Rassemblement du Peuple Togolais
RSDG	Rassemblement Social-Démocratique Gabonais
SAA	Syndicat Agricole Africain
SCOA	Société Commerciale de l'Ouest Africain
SDF	Social Democratic Front
SFIO	Section Française de l'Internationale Ouvrière
SHO	Société du Haut Ogooué
SOFRES	Société Française d'Études par Sondages
TOM	Territoire d'Outre-Mer
UAM	Union Africaine et Malgache
UAMCE	Union Africaine et Malgache de Coopération Économique
UDEAC	Union Douanière et Économique de l'Afrique Centrale [Central African Customs and Economic Union]
UDPM	Union Démocratique du Peuple Malien
UDR	Union des Démocrates pour la République

UDSR	Union Démocratique et Socialiste de la Résistance
UFD	Union des Forces Démocratiques
UGTAN	Union Générale des Travailleurs d'Afrique Noire
UJSC	Union de la Jeunesse Socialiste Congolaise
UMOA	Union Monétaire Ouest Africaine
	[West African Monetary Union]
UNC	Union Nationale Camerounaise
UNDP	Union Nationale pour la Démocratie et le Progrès
UNESCO	United Nations Educational Scientific and Cultural Organization
UP	University Press
UPC	Union des Populations du Cameroun
UPS	Union Progressiste Sénégalaise
URAC	Union des Républiques de l'Afrique Centrale
URFC	Union Révolutionnaire des Femmes Congolaises
US	Union Soudanaise
WAEC	West African Economic Community
	[Communauté Économique de l'Afrique de l'Ouest]
WAMU	West African Monetary Union
	[Union Monétaire Ouest Africaine]
ZOPAC	Zone de Pacification du Cameroun

1

History of French West Africa Until World War II

CONQUEST AND "PACIFICATION" OF THE TERRITORIES

The earliest substantial and sustained French contact with Africa involved the slave trade. Beginning in the 17th century, circumstances encouraged the buying and transporting of slaves to the New World. French slavers, along with their colleagues from many other nations, set up collection stations along the west coast of Africa. The three best-known slave collection and embarkation points were Gorée (Senegal), El Mina (Ghana), and Ouidah (Dahomey). Gorée, a small island off Cape Verde, was prized and fought over by other European powers with West African interests because it was not only a center for the export of slaves to the New World but also a staging post on the voyage around Africa to the Indian Ocean.[1] In 1638, agents of the Compagnie Normande, a charter company created under policies laid down by Louis XIII's prime minister, Cardinal Richelieu, established a small trading post on an island near the mouth of the Senegal River. In 1659 this modest establishment was moved to the present site of Saint-Louis, becoming the first permanent French installation on the coast of black Africa.[2] Here began the remarkable experiment of personal assimilation of Africans into French culture that was to become an important theme in French colonial philosophy. By the time of the capture of Saint-Louis by the British during the Napoleonic Wars, the town had a mixed Franco-African population of 7,000. Of these, a sizable number were of mixed blood and had adopted the French way of life; they described themselves as French and also acted in that capacity. Until the 1830s, interests in the Senegal Basin were limited to trading in gum arabic and slaves through a series of trading posts *(comptoirs)* located along the banks of the river. In 1837, a French merchant named Jaubert living in Gorée introduced the peanut as a viable cash crop. The oil from the crushed nuts supplied the soapmakers in Marseilles with a secure source of vegetable fat.

In 1854, during the Second Empire, General Louis Faidherbe was appointed governor of Senegal. He was an energetic and imaginative young officer in the Army Corps of Engineers; the birth of France's modern black African empire can be dated from his governorship. He established a French protectorate over a third of Senegal's hinterland, and in Saint-Louis he streamlined the administration, founded a bank, and organized the famous Senegalese riflemen *(tirailleurs sénégalais)*.[3] These African troops, under the command of French officers, were the main instrument for the conquest of the rest of France's huge West African empire. Faidherbe's concept was not based on simple military conquest or imperial expansion; instead, he focused on the commercial advantage to be gained from reorienting the traditional trans-Saharan caravan trade to French-controlled posts on the west coast. At the same time, he tried to prevent commerce from falling into British hands; the English had also established trading posts on the coast of Senegal and were eager to expand trade with the interior. Along the coast, Faidherbe succeeded in reinforcing the original enclave usually referred to as the Four Communes, consisting of Saint-Louis, Gorée, Dakar, and Rufisque. In 1848, these had been accorded special status, and their inhabitants enjoyed full French citizenship. Faidherbe was not able to realize his ultimate goal of linking the Upper Niger with the Senegalese coastal ports because Al Hadj Omar, the founder of the great Toucouleur empire of Ségou, had imperial ambitions, viewed the French as a potential threat, and prevented Faidherbe from controlling the upper reaches of the Niger Valley (today's Republic of Mali). (The Toucouleurs were a Moslem Peul people who originated in the Fuda-Toro region of Senegal.[4]) The French succeeded in unifying and pacifying the strategic Senegal River Valley, however, where the occupation of West Africa was to begin in the early 1880s. Faidherbe is therefore regarded as the real founder of French West Africa, which contained a great variety of peoples speaking many different languages and living under widely different political systems.

During the decade after the defeat of France in the Franco-Prussian War, affairs on the European continent dominated the thoughts of the Europeans. By the 1880s, however, the stage was again set for action in Africa. This renewed European expansion in Africa is attributed to a number of developments. The most prominent among them was the rise of industrial capitalism in Europe, which, to a large extent, increased the pace of colonial conquest. The advanced industrial nations desired to capture markets for finished products and to import primary agrarian and mineral commodities. The growth of industrial capitalism turned Europe into the prime center for global politics and increased the rivalries between the major European countries such as Great Britain, France, Germany, and Belgium; the scramble for Africa was a reflection of such rivalries. The process of colonization also symbolized an assertion of the supremacy on the part of advanced industrial nations over the underdeveloped societies of Africa. The systematic conquest of Africa can be attributed to the Berlin Conference on African Affairs of 1884–85, arranged by German chancellor Otto von Bismarck and the French prime minister Jules Ferry. On the positive side, the conference provided for freedom of navigation on the Congo and Niger, free trade in the Congo Basin, and abolition of slavery and the slave trade. On the negative side, it encouraged effective occupation of the African territories claimed by the European powers.

Like most Europeans, the French were convinced of the implicit superiority of their own civilization and saw the imposition of their culture as their responsibility toward humankind. Many of the best French officers who opted for overseas service during the period came to believe in this *mission civilisatrice*.[5] By spreading French culture in its overseas territories, France wanted to absorb the colonies into the French system. The expression *France outre-mer* or "Overseas France" conveyed the same desire. In fact, the policy of assimilation gave theoretical justification to the integrationist approach of France. Assimilation in essence meant that the colony was to become an integral—if noncontiguous—part of the mother country. The idea of assimilation also appealed to the French love of order, belief in people's equality, and desire to spread French culture in different parts of the world. This concept was typical of the *esprit encyclopédique* of the 18th century.[6] Even today the commitment to a civilizing mission is very much alive in France.

The renewed French conquest under Captain (later, General) Joseph Gallieni followed mostly the direction established by Faidherbe, that is, eastward along the Senegal River to the Niger. In general, France occupied large tracts of commercially useless land, whereas Britain conquered much smaller but commercially more valuable areas in West Africa. Geographically, West Africa can be broadly divided into three zones: desert, savanna, and forest. Mauritania and Niger were essentially desert territories, while Sahara lands comprised much of Soudan (Mali). Only the Ivory Coast and Guinea were situated in the forest, and their northern areas were savanna, as were Senegal, Upper Volta (Burkina Faso), Dahomey (Benin), and Togoland. The whole area of French West Africa was roughly eight times larger than France. It had a common frontier with British colonies like the Gold Coast, Nigeria, Sierra Leone, and Gambia. The Portuguese possession, Guinea, and Spanish Sahara also shared common frontiers with the French territories. The dominant groups in Senegal, Mauritania, Guinea, Soudan, and Niger were all Moslem and were deeply opposed to French control. Among and alongside these Moslem rulers lived a large number of Africans who adhered to their traditional religions. They generally collaborated with the French to obtain their independence from the Moslems. The French exploited and even encouraged the chronic divisions among Africans. Therefore, France's conquest of the savanna lands can also be seen as the conflict of two imperialisms, Afro-Islamic and Euro-Christian. Effectively, each French colony was occupied by the following dates: Senegal, 1890; Soudan, 1893; Dahomey, 1893; Guinea, 1898; Niger, 1906; Mauritania, 1910; Ivory Coast, 1914. (Upper Volta was not created until 1920, when it was formed from parts of Niger, Ivory Coast, and Soudan; it was dismembered in 1932 but re-created in 1947.) Broadly speaking, all opposition to French rule in Francophone colonies was put down by the end of World War I. The political boundaries established by the Europeans by 1898—though usually not surveyed or demarcated on the ground until much later—determine the political map of West Africa even today. The only subsequent significant change occurred after the British and French conquest of the German colonies during World War I. It took the European powers twenty years to partition West African lands among themselves. At least another twenty years were needed to establish colonial regimes that were effective throughout the vast territories claimed by the colonizers. The following letter written by "Her Britannic Majesty's Government" and addressed to the "Gouvernement de la République Française," dated August 5, 1890, illustrates how—during the scramble to partition and occupy African territory—the borders were drawn between the French and British spheres of influence:

> The Government of Her Britannic Majesty recognizes the sphere of influence of France to the south of her Mediterranean possessions, up to a line from Say on the Niger, to Barruwa on Lake Chad, drawn in such manner as to comprise in the sphere of action of the Niger Company all that fairly belongs to the Kingdom of Sokoto; the line to be determined by the Commissioners to be appointed.
>
> The Government of Her Britannic Majesty engages to appoint immediately two Commissioners to meet at Paris with two Commissioners appointed by the Government of the French Republic, in order to settle the details of the above-mentioned line. But it is expressly understood that even in case the labours of these Commissioners should not result in a complete agreement upon all details of the line, the Agreement between the two Governments as to the general delimitation above set forth shall nevertheless remain binding.
>
> The Commissioners will also be intrusted with the task of determining the respective spheres of influence of the two countries in the region which extends to the west and to the south of the Middle and Upper Niger.[7]

THE ESTABLISHMENT OF FRENCH WEST AFRICA AS AN ADMINIS-TRATIVE UNIT

France was now faced with the problem of administering the empire that the enthusiasm of its soldiers, sailors, and merchants had won. The complexity of administering this vast colonial empire suggested the need for the establishment of a colonial ministry in Paris. (Previously the Ministry of the Navy had been the traditional protector of the scattered coastal trading posts in Africa.) No French control could be exercised without the cooperation of large numbers of Africans. Just as the French officers had relied on Africans to fill the rank and file of their expeditionary forces to "pacify" the territories, so did the administrators depend on a host of Africans employed as clerks, messengers, craftsmen of all kinds, and laborers. To ensure an efficient labor force, the colonial administration began to supplement and develop the schools begun by the missionaries.

To organize the administration on the local level, there was a model at hand that Faidherbe had devised for the portion of Senegal outside the Four Communes—to govern indirectly through the traditional hierarchy. Being a practical man, Faidherbe had signed treaties of protection with the traditional rulers. These treaties acknowledged French sovereignty while allowing the members of the native hierarchy to continue to rule over their fellows with only loose supervision by French officials. Faidherbe recognized this system of indirect control as the least disruptive, the least expensive, and therefore the most practicable means of governing at minimum cost. His pragmatic approach to African reality was later dignified with the term *association*. But this approach was subverted by Faidherbe's successors, who were usually less sensitive to the administrative utility and the social value of preserving the authority of the traditional chiefs. Instead, they created a hierarchy of French administrators who too often imposed French values on their subjects without regard to cultural differences. Logically, local authorities in the colonies could not be granted a larger role than was given those in France. The place of the metropolitan *préfet* was filled in the colonies by the governor, and the *sous-préfet* by the *commandant de cercle*. With few exceptions, this administrative model was ultimately imposed on all African territories conquered by France.

As territories were conquered and pacified, they were organized into colonies. Governors were named, and the territory was divided into what became the classic subdivision, the *cercle*.[8]   It was not until 1895, however, that the various colonies established in West Africa were brought under a governor-general. Thus the colonial federation of *Afrique Occidentale Française* (AOF), French West Africa, was formed. At the beginning its governor-general was substantive governor of Senegal and administered the federation from the Senegalese capital of Saint-Louis. When the capital of AOF was moved to Dakar in 1904, the office of governor-general was separately constituted. AOF ultimately grew to include all eight colonies of West Africa. The governor-general's principal objective was described as the rational development of the federation as a whole. He was not subject to local legislative councils as in British West Africa. Neither he nor the lieutenant-governors had any legislative powers; they could only propose legislation to the minister of colonies in Paris, who then would issue the necessary decrees. The governor-general controlled all senior appointments other than those of the lieutenant-governors of the constituent colonies and certain other specified senior posts. He controlled the defense forces, postal and telegraph services, public works, and sanitary services; he had the right to collect the lucrative customs and excise taxes; he had an independent budget. A Federal Advisory Council called *le conseil du gouvernement* was formed, but the governor-general was not obliged to take its advice. Each constituent colony had *le conseil administratif*, by whose advice the lieutenant-governors were similarly not bound. With such powers the governor-general stood at the apex of a highly centralized administrative pyramid. Whereas the National Assembly in Paris might pass laws and the president of the republic might proclaim decrees, the governor-general held the crucial power to implement both law and policy. Only in the critical area of finance was the governor-general required to submit his budget to the minister of colonies, who might suggest certain changes. At the same time, the lieutenant-governors in the various colonies were left with limited autonomous administrative authority. They were, in effect, the principal resident subordinates of the governor-general, who could oblige them to refer to him in all important matters of local policy.

In Senegal, as a result of the early experiments in assimilation (acculturation) in that colony, a *conseil général* was established for the *quatre communes* of Saint-Louis, Gorée, Dakar, and Rufisque.[9] The members of this council were elected by popular vote of the inhabitants of the *quatre communes.* These inhabitants enjoyed the status of French citizenship, which gave them the right to form political parties and other voluntary associations.[10] The *conseil général* had the key legislative function of controlling the budget for the whole of Senegal, not just for the *quatre communes,* which each had its own mayor and municipal budget. Since 1848, except during the period of the Second Empire (1852–71), they had sent one representative to the National Assembly in Paris. (A few scattered dependencies with French connections dating back to the *ancien régime* shared this privilege with the *quatre communes.*) This deputy could, if so inclined, directly criticize the minister of colonies in the assembly. In 1914 Blaise Diagne was elected as the first African deputy.[11]

In contrast to the four communes of Senegal, the rest of the people in West Africa were subjects. They had no right to send representatives to the metropolitan institutions; they became victims of the system of forced labor and *indigénat.* The latter referred to the special provisions in the penal code that permitted administrators to take speedy punitive action against African subjects. The administration was also in charge of recruiting Africans for the French army; they had to serve for three consecutive years. Maurice de Saxe, Maréchal de France, was reportedly the first French leader to recognize the Africans' ability to fight. During the War of the Austrian Succession (1740–42) he formed a regiment of Africans as part of a foreign legion.[12]

From the early 20th century on, the colonies were required by law to be self-supporting except in national defense and in the financing of public works of imperial interest. Therefore, one of the principal reasons for the establishment of a federation was to subsidize the administration and the development of the poorer colonies through a system of taxation, which fell most heavily on the richer coastal territories. Inevitably, resentment started to grow among the relatively affluent coastal states. This resentment became especially strong in Ivory Coast, which, with the help of conservative French business interests, ultimately destroyed the federation just before independence. In AOF most major development projects undertaken before the end of World War II were financed through the governor-general's budget. The surplus of that budget was routinely redistributed to those colonies that showed a deficit, to meet ordinary administrative costs.[13]

The size of AOF, coupled with communication difficulties, required a great deal of administration on the local level. This made continuation of the policy of assimilation impractical. Few problems arose when the areas involved were small and the numbers to be assimilated were relatively insignificant; it was now realized that the task of implementing a full-scale policy of turning Africans into French citizens, with the same rights and duties, would no longer work. Also, given the scarce resources of AOF, it was considered impossible to give each African the necessary education. As late as 1939, there were only 63,200 students in primary schools throughout AOF, which—at that time—had a population of 14.7 million.[14] The great majority of those students were in village schools, which gave no more than a two-year literacy course. At the top of the educational pyramid were the few *Grandes Écoles;* the most illustrious of these were the medical school at Dakar and the École William Ponty at Gorée.[15] At a less-elevated level were the veterinary school at Bamako (Soudan) and the teachers college in Ivory Coast. There were two *lycées* in Senegal that granted certificates corresponding to the French *baccalauréat.* All other forms of school were discouraged, including the Koranic schools in the Moslem territories. It seemed equally impossible to assimilate the African tribes who were so fiercely and proudly attached to their traditional culture. Therefore, Jules Harmond, a well-known French intellectual, proposed the policy of association. To him, tolerance, respect for native customs and laws, and cooperation were the main elements of association. He emphasized the need for variation in colonial practice and for the cultural evolution of natives along their own lines. According to Remond F. Betts, the great virtue of the policy of association was its simplicity, flexibility, and practicality as against the rigidity of universalism in the doctrine of assimilation.[16] Association and assimilation became the principal philosophic themes that dominated French colonial thought and practice during most of France's colonial empire from 1880 to 1960. Indeed, echoes of these competing doctrines continue even today to animate discussion of the nature of France's relations with its former colonies. Finally, the policy of association became acceptable to most political parties in France. The supporters of the French right regarded it as an instrument to dominate inferior people; the supporters of the French left accepted it as a concession to the existing conditions. Under this new concept, the colonies were administered at the local level through chiefs who had no formally recognized powers of their own, only those specifically accorded to them by the French administration. These chiefs were deprived of their traditional criminal and civil powers, which were henceforth based on French models; they were placed in charge of collecting taxes, rounding up forced labor, recruiting for the army, and supervising compulsory crop cultivation for the French colonizers.[17] Their authority was supported by paramilitary *gardes de cercle;* through them the French administration was able to maintain control over the local people, who were obliged to accept French law or, in the eyes of the French, were placed under its protection.[18] Large chieftaincies were simply broken up, and small ones were grouped together under a single chief;

tribes without chiefs were given them for the sake of administrative uniformity. A key role was played by the administrators' interpreters; since administrators moved so frequently from post to post, they rarely, if ever, learned the local language. The fact that only slightly more than 12 percent of the administrators during the period from 1887 to 1939 spoke an African language did not help to improve understanding and appreciation of African cultures.[19] Thus, the interpreters, controlling negotiations between the impermanent administrators and permanent chiefs, could gain much influence and power.

ECONOMIC CONSIDERATIONS IN FRENCH WEST AFRICA

The principal preoccupation of the administration in AOF during the colonial period was the development and exploitation of economic resources. French strategy was initially to open up and develop its West African empire from a base in Senegal along the same Senegal-Niger river axis along which it had been conquered. As early as 1882 work was begun on a railroad to link the leads of navigation of the two rivers at Kayes and Bamako (both located in the Soudan), but this line was not completed until 1906. At that time it had been realized that Saint-Louis, located at the mouth of the Senegal River, was not capable of development into a modern port. In addition, the Senegal was really suitable for navigation for only three months in the year. Therefore, a railroad was completed in 1885 from Saint-Louis to the new harbor of Dakar. During 1907–24, a line was built directly from Dakar (since 1904 the federal capital for French West Africa) to Kayes in order to bypass the Senegal River altogether. The construction of an effective west-east transportation system from the coast to the Upper Niger thus took some forty-four years to complete.[20] The only part of it that was profitable was the one serving the peanut-growing areas of Senegal. There was a lag of some twenty years after 1924 before the thinly populated and impoverished Soudan could respond to its improved communication system with the outside world. The only major crop developed for the world market in this colony was cotton, but only after considerable investments in irrigation.[21] Ultimately, the main economic role of the Soudan was to provide foodstuff for Senegal, whose peasant farmers found it more profitable to concentrate on growing peanuts for export. Indeed, by 1914, French economic strategy had shifted from the concept of opening up the inland territories of the Soudan, Upper Volta, and Niger, to the encouragement of agricultural production in the coastal colonies. Just as the economy of Senegal had become largely dependent on the export of peanuts, that of French Guinea became dependent on bananas and that of Dahomey and of Togo (after World War I) on palm produce.[22] Only Ivory Coast was not dependent on a single cash crop; it developed a considerable export of coffee, cocoa, bananas, and lumber. Railroads were built from suitable points on the coast to facilitate the export of these crops.

The form of exchange between France and its colonies was noncompetitive and complementary; to such a relationship was given the name of "colonial pact."[23] This pact involved no element of agreement on the part of the colonies; it subordinated the interests of the subject territories to those of the mother country. The colonies were obliged to finance the development projects through their own resources. The pact effectively bound the colonies to France, with the development of import and export trade being placed in the hands of two major companies, the *Société Commerciale de l'Ouest Africain* (SCOA), and the *Compagnie Française de l'Afrique Occidentale* (CFAO). The latter was associated with six banks, steamship lines, and industry in Marseille and Bordeaux. By means of cross-representation on boards, pricerings, and local area monopolies, these companies deprived the peasants of the benefits of competition. They even forced the Africans to abandon their traditional economy, which had been limited to their own village and their own needs.[24] The welfare of the colonies and their peoples was thus subordinated to private interests and the enrichment of the big French trading companies that generally failed to invest in the economy outside the export-oriented enclaves. With the development of communications along the coast and the introduction of money, these companies were mainly concerned with the encouragement of cashcrop production for sale overseas and the importation of consumer goods for sale at high prices to the Africans who could afford them. Thus, the trading companies were linking African economies with the metropolis, on the one hand, and establishing themselves as independent powercenters, on the other. This reflects France's traditional attitude in its relationship with the colonies, namely, putting its own interests first. As far as the trade pattern was concerned, Francophone Africa was closely integrated with France. The administration even stimulated the economic activity of the companies in several ways. They received government subsidies in the form of preferential prices for African crops that they sold in France; they profited from government restrictions on the importation of manufactured goods from outside France into French-speaking Africa; they sent the major share of their profits back to France while the Africans were being heavily taxed. Due to the restrictions on purchases from non-franc countries, AOF was a high-price area. Africans paid higher than the world prices for the imported goods they bought. In turn the French trading companies sold their goods at higher than the world prices on the French market. The market between France and its colonies was strictly protected by tariffs, quotas, and exchange controls. This system forced peasants in those areas that grew no cash crops to migrate into areas that did. This accounts for the large-scale migration of labor from the three inland colonies of Upper Volta, Soudan, and Niger into Senegal, Guinea, Ivory Coast, and Gold Coast.[25]

During the precolonial period, the Africans had controlled the middleman trade between the French exporter and the African peasant producer. During the colonial period, this position was in large measure wrested from them by the

Lebanese, who were satisfied with lower profit margins. By the outbreak of World War II, there were no African middlemen of any significance in AOF.[26]

NOTES

1. Philippe Boggio, "Soleil noir sur Gorée," *Le Monde,* Mar. 21, 1992, 25, 27.

2. Pierre Biarnes, *Les Français en Afrique noire de Richelieu à Mitterrand* (Paris: Colin, 1987), 33–44.

3. William B. Cohen, *The French Encounter with Africans: White Response to Blacks, 1530–1800* (Bloomington: Indiana University Press, 1980), 229–32.

4. E. E. Beauregard, "Toucouleur Resistance to French Imperialism," *Présence Africaine* (Paris), no. 131 (1984), 144–54.

5. For the French, *la mission civilisatrice* meant to send thousands of teachers to help Africans evolve from what was perceived to be a nonhistorical, savage human condition. Official rhetoric spoke of waiting a thousand years for the Gaulles to become civilized, but one hoped that, with France's aid, Africans would not have to wait quite so long.

6. Raymond F. Betts, *Assimilation and Association in French Colonial Theory, 1890–1914* (New York: Columbia University Press, 1961), 8.

7. Henri Brunschwig, "French Exploration and Conquest in Africa," in L. H. Gann and Peter Duignan, eds., *Colonialism in Africa: 1870–1960,* Vol. 1 (New York: Cambridge University Press, 1969), 137–38.

8. Robert Cornevin, *L'Afrique noire de 1919 à nos jours* (Paris: PUF, 1973), 70.

9. Jean Delcourt, *L'Île de Gorée* (Paris: Clairafrique, 1984).

10. By 1936 there were only 80,509 *citoyens français indigènes* (French citizens of African origin) in all of AOF. Of these, only 2,136 were from colonies other than Senegal. Even in Senegal the citizens from the Four Communes made up a large majority of African citizens.

11. Blaise Diagne was elected on a radical platform but soon after cooperated with the administration. In 1918 he acted as high commissioner for the recruitment of troops from French black Africa for the European front. In 1931 he became French under secretary of state for the colonies. (See Amady Aly Diagne, *Blaise Diagne: premier député africain* [Paris: Africa, 1990].)

12. Eugène Fieffé, *Histoire des troupes étrangères au service de France depuis leur origine jusqu'à nos jours, et de tous les régiments levés dans les pays conquis sous la Première République et l'Empire,* 2 vols. (Paris: Dumaine, 1854), Vol. I, 280–83.

13. Virginia Thompson and Richard Adloff, "French Economic Policy in Tropical Africa," in L. H. Gann and Peter Duignan, eds., *Colonialism in Africa, 1870–1960,* Vol. 4 (New York: Cambridge University Press, 1975), 128–30.

14. Lord Hailey, *An African Survey: A Study of Problems Arising in Africa South of the Sahara* (London: Oxford University Press, 1938), 192.

15. Peggy Sabatier, "Did Africans Really Learn to Be French? The Francophone Elite of the École William Ponty," in G. Wesley Johnson, ed., *Double Impact: France*

and Africa in the Age of Imperialism (Westport, CT: Greenwood Press, 1985), 179–87.

16. Betts, 106.

17. Jacques Lombard, *Autorités traditionnelles et pouvoirs européens en Afrique noire* (Paris: Presses de la Fondation nationale des sciences politiques, 1967), 210–12.

18. Catherine Coquery-Vidrovitch, "Le Travail forcé en Afrique," *L'Histoire* (Paris), no. 69 (1984), 100–05.

19. William B. Cohen, *Rulers of Empire: The French Colonial Service in Africa* (Stanford, CA: Hoover Institution Press, 1971), 126.

20. Jacques-Henry Gbenou, *Urbanisation et colonisation en Afrique occidentale française, 1900–1940* (Lille: A.N.R.T., Univ. de Lille III, 1986), 186–213.

21. Moïse M. K. Akle, "Sécheresses récurrentes de l'Afrique contemporaine et analyse critique de quelques programmes internationaux de lutte: le cas des grands bassins fluviaux de l'Afrique de l'ouest soudano-sahélienne," Thèse de doctorat, Univ. Louis Pasteur, Strasbourg, 1988, 233–70.

22. In French Guinea, toward the end of the colonial period, European and American capital began the successful exploitation of considerable deposits of bauxite and iron ore.

23. Virginia Thompson and Richard Adloff, *French West Africa* (London: Greenwood Press, 1958), 249.

24. Hubert Deschamps, "France in Black Africa and Madagascar Between 1920 and 1945," in L. H. Gann and Peter Duignan, eds., *Colonialism in Africa, 1870–1960,* Vol. 3 (London: Cambridge University Press, 1971), 226.

25. René Dumont, *Paysans écrasés, terres massacrées* (Paris: Laffont, 1978), 294–325.

26. *The Cambridge History of Africa,* A. Roberts, ed. (New York: Cambridge University Press, 1986), Vol. 7, 329–98.

2

History of French Equatorial Africa Until World War II

EXPLORATION AND CONQUEST OF EQUATORIAL AFRICA

The origin of the vast French Equatorial African possessions go back to a treaty that was signed in 1839 with the local chiefs of the Gabon coast. There, the French had established a small trading station. Using freed slaves as settlers, Libreville was founded in 1849, becoming the administrative center of the Gulf of Guinea settlements. It was not from Senegal, the center of virtually all earlier French colonial activity, that the exploration and conquest of the large territory of Equatorial Africa was organized; instead, it occurred in Gabon. The earliest exploration of the interior was undertaken in 1867 by a French naval expedition under the command of Lieutenant Commander Aymes. In 1875 the minister of the navy, Admiral de Montaignac, entrusted a young Italian-born aristocrat, Pierre Savorgnan da Brazza, with a mission of exploration.[1] Da Brazza had only recently become a naturalized French citizen and been commissioned in the French navy. During his first journey, between 1875 and 1878, da Brazza went up the Ogooué River and reached a point near the present site of Franceville in southwestern Gabon. He and his party then proceeded across the treeless Bateke Plateau and found a tributary of the Congo. Thus da Brazza had found a route that bypassed the falls and rapids in the lower Congo River and had reached the vast network of streams that drain the whole of Central Africa. The people whom da Brazza encountered on this expedition were mostly Bantu-speaking peoples who lived in relatively small villages. They were hunters and gatherers and often practiced a primitive slash-and-burn agriculture. Generally, these Bantu tribes were friendly and welcomed the French with curiosity. Unlike the members of expeditions in West Africa, da Brazza did not face any militarily strong, tightly organized states, but other dangers decimated his party considerably: the tropical diseases, like yellow fever and malaria, and the physical dangers of penetrating the dense rain forests. Subsequent French claims in the Congo Basin were based on da Brazza's success in finding a route from Gabon to the navigable waters of the Congo River upstream from the present sites of Kinshasa and Brazzaville. Aside from the climate and the impenetrable jungle, the most serious challenge to the French occupation of Equatorial Africa came from the competition posed by other European colonizers. Leopold II, king of Belgium, and his two private organizations, the International Association for the Exploration and Civilization of Central Africa, founded in 1876, and the Comité d'Études du Haut Congo, founded in 1878, were the source of the most effective competition for the French in the Congo Basin.[2] In 1878 Leopold hired an Englishman, Sir Henry Morton Stanley, to lead his expeditions to lay claim to as much of this vast region as possible and to establish stations along the way. (Failing to enlist British interests in the development of the Congo, Stanley accepted Leopold's invitation.) Stanley was the most knowledgeable and experienced explorer of the Congo Basin at that time.[3] He had crossed the continent in 1876–77, demonstrating that the great Congo River network was navigable for thousands of miles above the impassable rapids and falls near the west coast. To Leopold this meant that the conquest of the Congo Basin was now possible from the west, without having to face the well-armed Zanzibari slave traders who then dominated East Africa and the African great lakes region. Fearful that Stanley would succeed in laying claim to large portions of the Congo Basin, da Brazza took it on himself, without permission from the Ministry of the Navy, to launch a second expedition (1879–82). In 1880 he succeeded in establishing a small post on the right bank of the lower Congo River, at the site of modern Brazzaville. He hastily signed a treaty with Makoko, chief of the Téké, to prevent Stanley from extending his territorial acquisitions beyond the Congo River. The treaty ceded sovereignty to France over vast, though ill-defined, territories, including the strategic pool above the Congo River rapids and falls. (At that time the pool was considered to be the gateway to the Congo Basin.) Although da Brazza had been delegated no authority by the Ministry of the Navy to sign such an agreement with Chief Makoko, it was ratified by the French National Assembly. In the subsequent race between Stanley and da Brazza for control of the Congo Basin, the French ultimately occupied the poorest parts of the region. However, these new conquests could be most easily joined to their subject territories farther north in the Sudan.[4] In time, the division between the French and English claims (at the line of the Oubangui, a tributary of the Congo River) was ratified at the Conference of Berlin in 1884–85.[5] Thereafter, French exploration in Africa was oriented north toward the Sangha, Lake Chad, and the Anglo-Egyptian Sudan.

The accession of new territory to French rule necessitated administrative adjustments. Between 1886 and 1888 Gabon and Congo were divided and given financial autonomy. By a decree the whole area was renamed the French Congo in 1891. In 1894 the territory of Oubangui was established as a separate administrative area. From 1897 on, the French Congo and Oubangui were each governed by lieutenant-governors.

New expeditions were meanwhile launched as the European scramble for Africa continued. French claims were advanced as far as the Nile. The last confrontation between the French and the British in this part of Africa took place in what was then the western part of the Anglo-Egyptian Sudan. Captain Jean Baptiste Marchand was dispatched to the Upper Nile in 1896 with the aim of putting pressure on the British in Egypt's Sudanese hinterland. The aim of the Marchand mission was to link the French West and Central African empire with the Red Sea by a trans-Saharan railroad. However, British victory under General Sir Herbert Kitchener against the Mahdist fundamentalists at Omdurman in 1898 ended these dreams and undercut Marchand's goal. After countless delays and hardships, Marchand reached the Nile at Fashoda (present Kodok) and established himself there. There ensued the most acute crisis in Anglo-French relations during the whole pre World War I period. When faced with an overwhelming British force, the French gave up discussing their claims and evacuated the oasis of Fashoda, thus avoiding the risk of a more serious confrontation with the British.[6] The French government, at that time harassed by the Dreyfus affair, found itself ill-prepared for war. In 1899 the French were obliged to renounce all territory along the Nile in return for worthless districts in the Sahara. The boundaries of Franco-British interests were defined as the watershed between the Nile, Chad, and Congo basins.[7]

French sovereignty over Chad had been recognized by Franco-German agreements in 1894, but the territory had yet to be conquered. In 1890 a three-pronged military expedition headed for the Chari River; the first column came from central Africa via Soudan, the second came from Algeria across the desert; the third contingent came from the Congo, which had already fought its way through the area of future French Equatorial Africa. The scale of the operation was truly colossal. Moreover, it had to face some of the most inhospitable terrains and climatic conditions that exist anywhere on the globe. The combined forces of the three units defeated the forces of Sultan Rabah, an increasingly powerful leader from the eastern Sudan.[8] In 1900 at the battle of Kousseri on the banks of Lake Chad, he was cornered and killed. The "military territory of the land and protectorate of Chad" was proclaimed; the decree also abolished the lieutenant-governorship of Oubangui. The northern half of Chad was desert land with a few scattered oases; it was peopled by Moslem nomads. The southern third, on the other hand, was relatively fertile; it was peopled by sedentary, black African peasant farmers. Before the arrival of the French, they had suffered regular slave raids by the nomad warriors from the northern desert. With the arrival of the French the disruption of their society was ended; the traditional power system even turned around. The southern farmers quickly grasped opportunities to cooperate with the colonizers and became their indispensable supporters. The wider significance of the Kousseri victory was that the three blocks of French African territories—the Algerian Sahara, West Africa, and Equatorial Africa—were now geographically linked. France now exerted sovereignty over a vast contiguous piece of Africa stretching from the Mediterranean to the Congo;

however, the "pacification" of the indigenous tribes in the newly acquired territories proved a lengthy and difficult process. Rabah's followers continued to challenge French sovereignty in the region. The credit for ending tribal resistance fell to Colonel Largeau in 1911–12. By 1913 the French had completed a network of forts throughout the territory.[9] The French Congo now constituted a vast territory, bordering on Spanish Guinea and Portuguese Guinea, formed in 1900 and 1901, respectively.

THE CREATION OF FRENCH EQUATORIAL AFRICA

The colonial federation of French Equatorial Africa was slower to evolve than AOF. Under the constitution decreed in 1902, a commissioner-general was appointed to govern the whole French Congo from Libreville, assisted by a lieutenant-governor resident at Brazzaville, and a chief administrator for the district of Chad. (The latter was no longer called a "military territory.") In 1903 and 1906 decrees were issued on the organization of the general headquarters for the "possessions and dependent territories of the French Congo." The favorable governmental conditions prevailing in AOF, however, persuaded the French government to decide in 1908 on "the creation of the federal government of *Afrique Équatoriale Française* (AEF), formed by the alignment of Gabon, the Middle Congo, and Oubangui-Chari-Chad."[10] At the federal level, the governor-general, assisted by a nominated Governmental Council, had a monopoly of civil and military power. Each of the three constituent colonies enjoyed financial and administrative autonomy under a lieutenant-governor, assisted by a nominated Administrative Council. This highly centralized federal system survived with only minor changes down to the eve of independence. In 1916 Chad ceased to come under the authority of Oubangui and was given the status of a colony in 1920; its borders with the colony of Niger and with Oubangui-Chari-Chad were delimited.

In 1884, during the European scramble to partition and occupy Africa, Chancellor Bismarck proclaimed a protectorate (a different word for "colony") over the coast of Togoland and over the Cameroon coast. The boundary between Dahomey (Benin) and Togoland was defined in the Franco-German agreement of 1897. The new 1911 Franco-German agreement provided for some territorial adjustments in AEF. Germany renounced its rights to Morocco but, in return, received 272,000 square kilometers of AEF. The annexed area, designated New Cameroon, also encompassed Spanish Guinea in the south. During the first month of World War I, most of the German colonies were seized by the British and the French; this brought renewed suffering to the indigenous population. Togoland and Cameroon were divided between the two powers in separate agreements of 1914 and 1916, respectively. In 1916 the French part of Togoland was attached to AOF, while French Cameroon was attached to AEF in 1917. After the war, the Allies were somewhat embarrassed by the contrast between their proclaimed principles and the old-fashioned haggling over the fate of the former German colonies. The result was the establishment of the Mandate System under the supervision of the new League of Nations organization. Britain became responsible for those parts of Togoland and the Cameroons that bordered its existing colonies of the Gold Coast and Nigeria. France took the other parts of Togoland and the Cameroons that bordered its colonies of Dahomey and Gabon, respectively. There was no formal obligation to advance these territories toward independence. The mandatory power was required only to provide good and humane government, to refrain from exploitation, and to suppress remnants of the slave trade. The mandatory power was to send regular reports to the League of Nations Mandates Commission.

In response to the economic crisis of the 1930s, administrative reforms were implemented. The expense of maintaining a governor-general and four governors for a population of only 3 million was considered excessive, and the federation was transformed into a unitary colony of twenty departments grouped into regions that corresponded to the former federal colonies. The regions were administered by delegates of the governor-general; however, this new arrangement proved to be inefficient, and the four federal territories were reconstituted in 1937.

DEVELOPMENT PROBLEMS IN FRENCH EQUATORIAL AFRICA

Right from the start, AEF faced enormous development problems. The hinterlands were found to be mainly poor, undeveloped, and semiarid.[11] As in the case of AOF, the legislators in Paris quickly resolved that the administration and development were not to be subsidized by the French treasury; rather, the colonies must be self-sufficient. In AEF there were no affluent colonies to provide surplus revenue to be redistributed. Therefore, the French followed the model of King Leopold's Congo Free State. Initially the Ministry of Colonies in Paris chose the dangerous expedient of granting concessions to private companies to develop and administer large tracts of land. Between 1898 and 1900 the French Congo was shared out among forty concessionaires. These companies were granted rights of tenure and exploitation—normally for thirty years—over about 250,000 square miles, in exchange for a fixed annual payment plus 15 percent of profits. Unfortunately, most of these concessionaires were grossly undercapitalized, and none made any meaningful investment in basic infrastructure. Instead they traded and bought raw rubber and ivory at the lowest possible prices from the local African population. Because of the enormous size of the country and the difficulties in transporting supplies and reinforcement, it was constantly necessary to requisition native porters. A poll tax, imposed in 1902, added to the suffering of the Africans. Again the welfare of the indigenous population was subordinated to private interests. This exploitation of the Africans by the concessionaires led to public denunciation, which greatly embarrassed the

French government officials. Da Brazza was sent to the Congo to make an on-the-spot investigation.[12] His report forced the Ministry of Colonies to regroup the companies showing a deficit, to institute a tighter regulation of the system of concessions, and to rescind some of the leases. The concessionaires' profitability was now guaranteed by vertical integration and conversion into trading companies. One of the biggest of these companies, the *Société du Haut Ogooué* (SHO), extended its activities to all facets of negotiation and business, which led to renewed scandals. French writers like René Maran and André Gide exposed those scandals in their publications, namely in *Batouala* and *Voyage au Congo,* respectively. (René Maran received the Prix Goncourt in 1921 for *Batouala.*) A widely read press article in *Le Populaire* on the French companies' abuses in the Congo, coupled with the campaign of the socialist leader, Léon Blum, also added to the publicity. Finally the pressure of the French people's opinion was such that the colonial minister committed himself before Parliament not to renew or extend the leases of the companies.

The period between the two world wars can be considered as an era of lost opportunities for the French in Africa. Doctrinal wrangling combined with a chronic shortage of money led to economic stagnation. An integrated economic development plan providing for the creation of infrastructure—to be financed with credits guaranteed by the *métropole*—was proposed in 1921 by Albert Sarraut, minister of colonies. Although a majority in the National Assembly voted to accept the plan, the same majority also refused to appropriate funds to carry it out. Instead, the colonies were even taxed to aid France with its own postwar financial problems. The result of this situation was a very modest development both of human resources for assimilation and of governmental structures for some form of eventual association with the mother country.

The four AEF colonies were even less well endowed with educational facilities than AOF or the mandated territories of Togo and Cameroon. In 1935 the first college on the territory of AEF was founded in Brazzaville to improve conditions for African officers. Parts of AEF profited from the construction of the Congo-Océan railroad. Because the interior of AEF (except in Gabon) was accessible only by the Belgian railroad from Matadi, the French decided in 1924 to construct a railroad across French territory from Brazzaville to Mayombé. Difficulties in labor recruitment due to constant reduction of manpower because of illness and desertion slowed down construction. The railroad was finally completed in 1934 and opened the way for the development of the port of Pointe-Noire.

The economic development that took place in AOF and AEF during the period between the two world wars was concentrated on the production of export crops and their transportation to overseas markets, mainly in France. As a matter of policy, priority was given to the production of raw materials needed by French industry. The experiences gained in World War II would somewhat change France's attitude toward its colonies in Africa.

NOTES

1. Napoléon Ney, ed., *Conférences et lettres de P. Savorgnan de Brazza sur ses trois explorations dans l'Ouest africain de 1875 à 1886* (Brazzaville: Bantoues, 1984).

2. Leopold's International African Association was transformed later into the Association Internationale du Congo, out of which grew the Congo Free State.

3. Pierre Guillaume, *Le Monde colonial: XIXe-XXe siècle* (Paris: Colin, 1974), 111–13.

4. Jacques Denis, *L'Afrique centrale et orientale* (Paris: PUF, 1971), 108–12.

5. Henri Brunschwig, "French Exploration and Conquest in Africa," in L. H. Gann and Peter Duignan, eds., *Colonialism in Africa, 1870–1960*, Vol. 1 (New York: Cambridge University Press, 1969), 157.

6. Pierre Guillen, *L'Expansion: 1881–1898* (Paris: Imprimerie Nationale, 1985), 407–13.

7. Henri Brunschwig, *Le Partage de l'Afrique* (Paris: Flammarion, 1971), 94.

8. Joseph Amegboh, *Rabah: le conquérant des pays tchadiens* (Paris: Afrique biblio club, 1980).

9. Winfried Baumgart, *Imperialism: The Idea and Reality of British and French Colonial Expansion, 1880–1914* (Oxford: University Press, 1982), 1-90.

10. Pierre Biarnes, *Les Français en Afrique noire de Richelieu à Mitterrand* (Paris: Colin, 1987), 194-95 (author's translation).

11. Pierre Vennetier, *L'Afrique équatoriale* (Paris: PUF, 1972), 7–13.

12. Brazza fell seriously ill during the mission; on September 14, 1905, on his way home, he died at Dakar.

3

World War II and Reorganization

WORLD WAR II AND THE *RÉSISTANCE*

The Great Depression of the 1930s came as a shock to European self-confidence. Trade and production shrank, and millions of Europeans had no work. Economists of the period began to argue that a remedy lay in more active development of the overseas territories controlled by the colonizers. If more European capital and skills were directed to the colonies, so that they could produce more raw materials for European industry more efficiently, both Europe and the colonies would gain. As the colonies themselves became wealthier through the exploitation of their resources, the people of the colonies would buy more goods imported from Europe. This concept was broadened shortly before World War II. Transport and currency problems made it urgent for France to develop strategic raw materials in its colonies.

World War II was a turning point in the colonies of AOF and AEF. The members of the two key groups in the colonies, the army and the administration, were both by tradition conservative and patriotic. By the nature of their institutions, officers and colonial administrators were disciplined and respectful of hierarchy. For many of these loyal Frenchmen there could be no question of disobeying a clear order from one of France's most respected soldiers of World War I, Maréchal Henri Pétain. Others were anguished and uncertain when the government in Vichy gave orders to cease all hostilities and to respect an armistice with Hitler. A third group of Frenchmen stationed in Africa had the inclination to fight against a traditional enemy. Thus, French colonial society was divided and faced with a desperate dilemma. As a result, the French colonial empire south of the Sahara split into two. AOF, under the leadership of Governor-General Pierre Boisson, remained loyal to the Vichy government; AEF sided with the black governor of Chad, Félix Éboué,[1] and joined forces with General Charles de Gaulle in the struggle for a *France libre*.[2] Éboué was the first French official in charge of a colony to defy the Vichy government and to announce his territory's decision to join the Free French. With the help of Capitaine (later Général) Leclerc and some other senior military leaders stationed in Chad, Éboué was able to enroll the whole of AEF, including Cameroon, for the Free French cause. In return, de Gaulle named him governor-general over the entire federation and further honored him in 1944 by holding the Brazzaville Conference (to discuss postwar colonial reforms) in his capital. Given his background and personality, Éboué enjoyed great respect and influence in Gaullist councils on colonial policy. Although his own career was a symbol of successful assimilation to French culture and career patterns, he devotedly studied the languages and cultures of the Africans. As an administrator he advocated respect for the authority of chiefs and African civil servants and for traditional customs. He opposed assimilation, which he considered a mindless effort. Therefore, as governor-general he issued a decree defining a new status for the *notables évolués,* the new name for the members of the African elite. It offered them a social and civil status comparable to their educational and local social level. Therefore, the new status was conferred on Africans who had attained a significant level of French education and culture. Unlike full French citizenship, *évolué* status did not require the holder to relinquish important aspects of African culture. Prior to Éboué's innovation, many well-educated Africans had refused French citizenship because of the social and legal problems it posed for them and for their families. For instance, they were not willing to give up polygamy (often expected at the time among Africans), inheritance practices very different from Western concepts, and certain other customary habits.[3] Éboué's innovation amounted to a grant of social justice, giving legal recognition to an important new class within African society.[4]

For two years AOF remained under a pro-Vichy regime, which isolated it from the main currents of the war. In Dakar, Governor-General Pierre Boisson[5] followed a difficult political line of combining respect for Maréchal Pétain's authority and, at the same time, resisting the efforts of Pierre Laval[6] and his German cooperators to gain greater control of AOF. When an Anglo-American army invaded and took control of French North Africa, AOF joined the Allies and became with AEF de Gaulle's first base and vital link in the allied strategy. From the beginning of 1943 to the end of the war, AOF became a major source of supply of men and materials on a compulsory basis for the Free French.

Following his assumption of power in Algiers in 1943, de Gaulle's vision of a fighting France rallying its forces and carrying on the battle from its overseas territories was becoming a reality. There was a lot of resistance, however, from the United States and, to a lesser extent, from England, to granting him the enlarged role he sought in Allied councils. In addition, American anticolonial attitudes as expressed in the Atlantic Charter of 1941 further strained de Gaulle's relations with the Allies.[7] In fact, to gain status with the Allies, de Gaulle relied on support from the French overseas possessions, particularly those in Africa, whose future existence was in question. De Gaulle was also under acute pressure from within the French Community outside occupied France to demonstrate his leadership of the territorial possessions now free of Vichy control.

THE BRAZZAVILLE CONFERENCE OF 1944

In response to both international and internal French needs, de Gaulle called the famous Brazzaville Conference in January 1944, at which political, social, and economic reforms were to be outlined for France's colonies.[8] These reforms were in large measure a recognition of the major role that Francophone black Africa, in particular AEF, had played in keeping the Free French movement alive. Brazzaville was the ideal place for such a conference. It was the capital of the first major territory to rally to the Free French cause in 1940 and was under the firm control of one of de Gaulle's oldest and most faithful supporters, Governor-General Félix Éboué. In addition, Brazzaville was far removed from the political intrigues then taking place in Algiers. The conference was attended by forty-four delegates including the governor-general and governors from all African colonies and the representatives of the Consultative Provisional Assembly from Algiers under the leadership of de Gaulle himself. In his opening speech, de Gaulle stated that the French nation alone would make reforms in the structure of its overseas empire when the time was right. This was a clear warning to the anticolonialist declarations made in the Atlantic Charter of 1941. (There were no representatives of the French nation present when this document was signed.) Such a public defense of French sovereign rights at a time when France was occupied by Germany was aimed at further establishing de Gaulle's credentials as the leader of the French National Committee of Liberation. Aside from his opening remarks, de Gaulle took no further part in the conference, which was chaired by the colonial minister René Pleven.[9] The deliberations in the different working groups, however, followed guidance given by de Gaulle himself.

The proposed reforms provided for African representation in the National Assembly, the Senate, and the Assembly of the French Union. It also provided for the establishment of local councils, such as Senegal had had, for all the constituent colonies of AOF and AEF. These councils would be composed of African and European members elected on the basis of universal suffrage. A controversy arose among the delegates relating to the postwar constitutional connections between France and the colonies. Governor-General Éboué, the only African delegate in the conference, proposed the establishment of federal institutions that could harmonize the social, economic, and cultural differences between the French and the Africans. On the other hand, René Pleven preferred centralized institutions under French control. For the first time an official French body discussed the possibility of a federation being formed between France and its colonies. From here on French colonial policy was a constant search for a compromise between two extremes. On one hand, there was a formula that would conserve the unity of Greater France by retaining ultimate political control in Paris. On the other hand, there was the idea of allowing a degree of local autonomy both compatible with the idea of centralization of power and yet sufficient to turn African politicians' attention away from the ideas of independence. The delegates also discussed certain important social and economic problems. They stood for the abolition of the system of forced labor and replacement of the system of *indigénat* by a unified penal code independent of the administrative system as well as of native customs. The conference participants also recommended that Governor-General Éboué's newly established status of *notable évolué* be adopted in all colonies. In order to assure the growth of this elite, the delegates recommended the establishment of advanced training centers and educational facilities in all territories. On the economic side, provisions were made for the development of the infrastructure, the industrialization in the colonies, and direct interterritorial trade.

The conferees in Brazzaville were mainly colonial servants who had no decision-making, but only consultative, powers. Nevertheless, the conference played a far from negligible role in the process of decolonization. In fact, the conference is now considered as the first step in the process that led to independence sixteen years later. Of all the recommendations emerging from the conference, the one with the greatest long-term significance is the one suggesting the establishment of locally elected assemblies in each territory. Eventually these institutions, once established, became the centers that politically mobilized the African elites and ultimately shaped the demands for independence.

THE FOURTH FRENCH REPUBLIC AND THE FRENCH UNION

After the conference, Africans were given representation in the First Constituent Assembly of 1945 to draft a new constitution for the French Republic. The representatives in this assembly were elected on the basis of a double college system. French citizens of Africa voted on a separate roll called the first college, while the African subjects voted in the second electoral college. Most of the elected representatives were personalities from the *Résistance* and from the Free French with a strong and well-organized communist group.[10] When put to a vote in a referendum, the proposed constitution was defeated. In the Second Constituent Assembly of 1946, a resurgent right-wing group was able to claim its share of seats and to confront the communists' demands. In addition, a colonial lobby called the *États généraux de la colonisation française* was successful in removing many of the earlier more liberal constitutional proposals affecting colonial issues. But all was not lost in terms of constitutional change and a liberalization of the colonial regime. The assembly ratified the abolition of forced labor and of the *indigénat* and granted citizenship to all inhabitants of the colonies without affecting their civil status. No other twentieth-century colonial power was willing to make such a liberal gesture, which helped bind Francophone Africans to France long after the formal dissolution of the French empire. The assembly also established the *Fonds d'investissement et de développement économique et social* (FIDES), administered by the *Caisse centrale de la France d'outre-mer* (CCFOM), for badly needed economic and social development. The prosperity of the war years had proved illusory; it was no longer possible to gather rubber, and cotton cultivation was promoted only by inhuman methods. The territories were still creating wealth, but the Africans at the base of society remained in poverty. The creation of FIDES was an attempt to promote the harmonious development of all economic sectors in the territories. A negative by-product was the proliferation of French administrators and technicians throughout French black Africa.

The Fourth French Republic came into being in 1946. It established the French Union,[11] a federal association, consisting of metropolitan France, the existing *département d'outre-mer* (Algeria),[12] the newly created overseas departments (Réunion, Guadeloupe, Martinique, and Guyana), and the overseas territories. The latter also included the African territories and Madagascar, considered to be integral parts of an indivisible republic. Those countries that were too distinctive to be fitted into the union, Indochina, and the "Protected States" of Morocco and Tunisia became "Associated States" with internal autonomy but with France still exercising control over their foreign policy. (See Appendix 1, *Constitution of the Fourth Republic,* "The French Union.")

The adoption of the new constitution gave the African territories the right of representation in the three metropolitan legislative bodies, the National Assembly (lower house), the Council of the Republic (Senate or upper house), and the Assembly of the French Union. The latter was a legislative unit without clear directions and powers; it had its sessions in Versailles. With this, a new step on the road to decolonization had been taken. The new constitution also provided for the creation of a legislative body, called *Grand conseil* (Federal Council), in each of the two federations of AOF and AEF. Each territory was represented by five deputies in the Federal Council: the Council of AOF was composed of forty members, the Council of AEF, sixteen members. They were chosen in direct elections by the partially elected territorial assemblies, which were established in each colony. Membership in the territorial assemblies was complex; some members were elected, some were appointed by the governor, and others were ex officio members.[13] The elected members were chosen in direct elections, but the electorate was divided into two colleges in imitation of the provisions in the First Constituent Assembly of 1945. The first college was made up of French residents and the most educated Africans who had assumed French civil status *(citoyens de statut français).* The second was composed of the large masses of enfranchised Africans *(citoyens de statut local).* Although smaller in absolute numbers, the first college was far larger than the second, relative to the number of voters in each college. This complex process, however, did involve direct popular elections for the first time in black Africa, which marked the beginning of a political process leading to independence. For the future, the most important legislative innovation in this pyramid of assemblies is the fact that black African deputies sat as full and equal members in the National Assembly, representing the African territories. From now on, the territories began to be the focus of political activity rather than to continue to be mere subdivisions for the convenience of colonial administrators. The direct and indirect elections to fill the seats in the different legislative bodies had the effect of increasing the number of the African political elite and encouraging growing political awareness in each territory, which, in turn, led to the formation of political parties and associations. The ten-year (1946–56) experience in parliamentary practice under the new constitution also gave rise to the assertion of a degree of African national consciousness.

In reality the French Union was a medium to perpetuate French influence in Africa by treating the African territories as integral parts of the mother country. Despite the innovations on the local level in AOF and AEF, the focus of attention was Paris. African politicians interested themselves primarily with securing the deputyships in the French National Assembly, for glamour, excitement, and real power were located in Paris, not in the local councils. Indeed, the slender margins by which the unstable postwar governments of France held power meant that the votes of African deputies could often be vital. The African deputies allied with, or formally joined, metropolitan parties, while building up their own parties at home. Although it was requested that, on arrival in Paris, the African deputies join one or the other of the metropolitan parties, in practice only the *Parti Communiste Français* (PCF) showed any real readiness to welcome the first postwar generation of African politicians into its parliamentary ranks. Thus they not only ensured reelection to the deputyship but also managed to control the local councils and the *Grand conseil* in Dakar and Brazzaville.

THE ESTABLISHMENT OF AFRICAN POLITICAL PARTIES

African political organization began shortly before the two constitutional conventions held in 1945 and 1946. Because of the continuous fluctuations in the price of their commodities, French plantation owners in Ivory Coast sought to establish an economic organization to safeguard their interests as planters. For this purpose, Félix Houphouët-Boigny, himself a rich planter, organized the *Syndicat Agricole Africain* (SAA) in 1944.[14] Houphouët succeeded in grouping about 200,000 rich and relatively poor farmers for the SAA, which paved the way for the establishment of the *Parti Démocratique de la Côte-d'Ivoire* (PDCI) in 1946. It advocated greater control of the administration by Africans, extension of suffrage, a liberal revision of the taxation system, and elimination of the system of dual college. This program was essentially reformist; it strove to improve the position of Africans within the framework of the French Union. This concept not only was acceptable to the French rulers but even encouraged the growth of political parties in the territories, as long as they could be regulated. This encouragement led the African parliamentarians to call a meeting in Bamako (Soudan) in October 1946, to form a united front and develop a common strategy. The conference was dominated by the more extreme nationalist elements encouraged by French communists, the only metropolitan representatives to attend. The outcome of the conference was the foundation of the *Rassemblement Démocratique Africain* (RDA) under the leadership of Houphouët.[15] Its program was more or less an extension of the PDCI program. It basically opposed the exploitation of the black man by the white and advocated equality of rights in all spheres. The RDA was a multiethnic party with branches under a variety of names in all AOF and AEF territories. It was a loosely organized interterritorial organization with considerable territorial autonomy.[16] This foreshadows Houphouët's later move to undermine AOF. Because of multiethnic support and his strong organizational skills, Houphouët was able to lead a highly successful campaign of nonviolent resistance: strikes by railroad workers and domestic servants, hunger strikes in prisons, protest marches by women, and so on. With encouragement from François Mitterrand,[17] Houphouët led the RDA in 1950 to break with the Communist party; it was clear to him that the communist connection undermined his party in an increasingly conservative France.[18] From that point on, the more radical elements began to move away from Houphouët and from his more moderate colleagues in the RDA. In 1954 Houphouët and his party entered into an alliance with the *Union Démocratique et Socialiste de la Résistance* (UDSR), whose major architect was Mitterrand.[19] The UDSR was a centrist group that faced stiff opposition from the communists on the left and the Poujadists[20] on the right. Under these conditions the centrist forces would have failed to remain in power without the support of African deputies. This situation placed the RDA in a comfortable bargaining position. Due to his collaboration with the administration and alliance with important French commercial interests, Houphouët became French Africa's most influential politician in the decade before independence.[21]

In 1947 the RDA founded a branch in Guinea known as the *Parti Démocratique de la Guinée* (PDG). The PDG did not become a significant territorial mass movement until the emergence in the early 1950s of Sékou Touré.[22] Guinea was undergoing rapid economic growth, largely as a result of a boom in bauxite, iron ore, and diamond mining. This increased the industrial labor force, which in turn increased the importance of trade unions. Touré organized a successful sixty-six-day strike for higher wages and shorter working hours. He was a strong proponent of social reform and a determined opponent of the ethnicism that dominated Guinean politics at the time. In the battle against ethnicism Sékou used two different concepts in establishing good relations among the many African tribes. First, there was his trade union experience, which had enabled him to establish many contacts among communities in different parts of the country; second, the philosophy of the *Confédération Générale du Travail* (CGT) of workers' solidarity rose above ethnicity. In 1957 the PDG decided to abolish chieftaincy in the interests primarily of democracy; however, this decision also helped to promote ethnic integration by destroying a traditional center of ethnic-based power. (The constitution of newly independent Guinea made ethnic particularism illegal.) The French administration actively encouraged ethnic unions and their transformation into ethnic political parties. The strategy of balkanization was always prevalent in France's relations with black Africa.[23]

The dominant African political party in Senegal in 1945 was the *Section Française de l'Internationale Ouvrière* (SFIO), led by Lamine Gueye, who had fused his *Parti Socialiste Sénégalais* (PSS) with the SFIO in 1938.[24] During the preparations for the two constitutional conventions held in 1945 and 1946, Gueye organized and led the *Bloc Africain* (BA), an informal caucus that coordinated the activities of the African representatives. Gueye gained most of his active support from the *quatre communes* and the coastal ports, including Dakar. His policy was to persuade France to carry assimilation to its logical conclusion and grant full political and legal rights to all Africans in Senegal. Gueye and his party won the 1946 elections, but soon afterward the SFIO broke up because of conflicting internal disputes. Gueye's protégé was Léopold Sédar Senghor, who was one of the few Africans to complete his *agrégation* successfully during the early 1930s; he became French Africa's first fully qualified French university professor. Being a brilliant poet-philosopher, he represented the apogee of assimilation and personified the triumph of the French *mission civilisatrice* in West Africa. He became the theorist and literary exponent of *négritude*, a literary movement of the 1930s, 1940s, and 1950s, as a protest against French rule and the policy of assimilation.[25] Although the political impact of *négritude* was negligible, it served as a major psychological, cultural, and intellectual movement.[26] Senghor proved also to be an adept politician. He began his political career as a member of the SFIO in the First Constituent Assembly. In 1948 he broke with Gueye over the question of African subservience to the SFIO metropolitan hierarchy. Senghor had also become increasingly dissatisfied with the dictatorial tendencies displayed by Gueye within party councils in the SFIO. Thus Senghor led the intellectuals and the vast majority of the newly enfranchised ex-subjects of the countryside in a revolt against Gueye's leadership in founding the *Bloc Démocratique Sénégalais* (BDS). This new party established an African form of socialism and requested autonomy for Senegalese political parties from French control. In the French National Assembly of 1951 Senghor linked the BDS with a number of ethnic parties representing other territories in French black Africa. They formed an alliance known as the *Indépendants d'Outre-Mer* (IOM). This was a loose bloc of parliamentary representatives in Paris of various party and ideological persuasions; their common trait was refusal of membership in Houphouët-Boigny's dominated RDA. A major African politician needed both a parliamentary bloc in Paris and a power base in Africa; Senghor and Houphouët acquired both. (On an individual basis, Senghor was the only real competition for primacy among African politicians in preindependent Francophone black Africa.) Both differed in their perception of politics.
. Senghor was committed to a more formal socialism while Houphouët, the tribal

aristocrat and rich planter, was more attuned to "laissez-faire" economics and private ownership.[27]

The rise of African political leaders like Senghor and Houphouët and their active involvement through African political parties within the framework of the French Union were an important landmark in the evolution of AOF and AEF. The government under Guy Mollet, a coalition of the socialists, radicals, and the UDSR-RDA, became a symbol of Franco-African cooperation.[28]

NOTES

1. In 1932 Éboué was appointed secretary-general and later acting governor of Martinique; in 1936 he was made a full governor in Guadeloupe, where he introduced many reforms associated with the *Front Populaire* government in France. His sudden transfer to Chad in 1939 was fortuitous for the Allied cause, especially for France. A good biography is Brian Weinstein's *Éboué* (New York: Oxford University Press, 1972).

2. M. Crowder, "The Impact of Two World Wars on Africa," *History Today* (London), 34 (Jan. 1984), 11–18.

3. Jean de La Roche, *Le Gouverneur-général Félix Éboué, 1884–1944* (Paris: Hachette, 1957), 159–61.

4. Shortly after the Brazzaville Conference, Éboué died in Cairo in 1944. In 1949 he became the only black to be buried in France's Panthéon of heroes in Paris.

5. After de Gaulle and his officers had pushed aside the American favorite, General Henri Giraud, who commanded the French forces in North Africa, Boisson was imprisoned for his cooperation with the Vichy government. He died in 1943 in prison while awaiting trial.

6. Pierre Laval led the Vichy government in policies of collaboration with Germany, for which he was ultimately executed as a traitor to France.

7. The Atlantic Charter is a joint declaration issued in 1941 by Winston Churchill and Franklin D. Roosevelt stating that England and the United States respected every people's right to choose its own form of government and wanted sovereign rights and self-government restored to those forcibly deprived of them.

8. Jean-Louis Miège, *Expansion européenne et décolonisation de 1870 à nos jours* (Paris: PUF, 1973), 310–11.

9. René Pleven is best known for his sponsorship of the Pleven Plan, from which the North Atlantic Treaty Organization evolved.

10. When the *Front Populaire* assumed power in 1936, French socialists and communists went to Africa to take up assignments as teachers, civil servants, and physicians. They propagated that the emancipation of Africa would not take place without the French left. (See Jacques Kergoat, *La France du Front populaire* [Paris: La Découverte, 1986]; Nicole Racine and Louis Bodin, *Le Parti communiste français pendant l'entre-deux-guerres* [Paris: Presses de la Fondation nationale des sciences politiques, 1972], 205–13.)

11. The term *Union Française* was first used officially in March 1945 in the announcement of the French government's intention that the Indochina Federation

would form, with France and other parts of the community, a French Union whose external interests would be represented by France. For the significance of this statement, see P. Mus, *Le Destin de l'Union Française, de l'Indochine à l'Afrique* (Paris: Seuil, 1954), 82–85.

12. Algeria was unique in the French empire in that it alone had attracted any significant number of French settlers. France had first become involved with Algeria in 1830, when the last Bourbon king, Charles X, mounted an expedition to flush out the Barbary pirates who still preyed on shipping in the Mediterranean. The French soon found out that it was easier to get into, than to get out of, such an involvement. In the 1830s and 1840s they were drawn into the conquest of the whole of Algeria despite the strenuous resistance of Arab nationalist leaders. Napoleon III (1852–70) was attracted by the idea of "military colonists" (time-expired soldiers) on the Roman pattern to provide a French presence in Algeria. French policy toward Algeria was never consistent, least of all in the treatment of the majority population, the Arabs; however, more than any other area, it was increasingly treated as genuinely a *département* of metropolitan France. This made ultimate decolonization all the more difficult. Whatever they might be promised under the French Union, the nationalists were not happy to see the continuation of a situation in which economic and political dominance remained with the settlers who made up only about one-sixth of the population.

13. For an instructive account of the position of the *commandant de cercle* in relation to African members of the Territorial Assembly, see Maurice Méker, *Le Temps colonial* (Dakar: Nouvelles éditions africaines, 1980).

14. Marcel Amondji, *Félix Houphouët et la Côte-d'Ivoire: l'envers d'une légende* (Paris: Karthala, 1984), 75–85.

15. Kenneth E. Robinson, "Colonialism French-Style, 1945–55: A Backward Glance," *Journal of Imperial and Commonwealth History*, 12 (2) (1984), 24–41.

16. Marcel Amondji, *Côte-d'Ivoire: le P.D.C.I. et la vie politique de 1945 à 1985* (Paris: Harmattan, 1986), 25–29.

17. After the end of the war Mitterrand served in the government of Charles de Gaulle as secretary-general for prisoners of war. He was first elected deputy to the National Assembly in 1946. From the late 1940s he held a succession of ministerial posts, including minister for Overseas Territories (1950–51). (See François Mitterrand, *Présence française et abandon* [Paris: Plon, 1957].)

18. As a member of the First Constituent Assembly, Houphouët did not, unlike many African members, associate himself with the French socialists, but with a small group of "fellow travelers," the *Mouvement Unifié de la Résistance*, closely allied with the communists.

19. Paul Henri Siriex, *Félix Houphouët-Boigny, l'homme de la paix* (Paris: Seghers, 1975), 141.

20. The Poujadists were the disciples of Pierre-Marie Poujade. In 1953 Poujade organized a successful local storekeepers' strike to protest heavy taxation. Expanding his activities to other towns in southern France, he enrolled 800,000 members in his *Union de Défense des Commerçants et des Artisans* (Union for the Defense of Tradesmen and Artisans). Poujade's support came largely from discontented peasants and small merchants. The Poujadists succeeded in reducing tax collection drastically in the south of France, paving the way for various tax concessions granted by the National Assembly in 1955. The peak of Poujadisme occurred during

the elections of January 1956, when Poujadist candidates won 52 of 595 assembly seats. Because of Poujade's fascistic and anti-Semitic tendencies, his influence waned; his candidates won no seats in the elections of November 1958.

21. Léo Hamon, *Les Partis politiques africaines (II)* (Paris: Librairie générale de droit et de jurisprudence, 1961), 20–36.

22. Sékou Touré, a great-grandson of the Mandinka emperor Samori Touré, was the leader of the Guinean branch of the French communist *Confédération Générale du Travail* (CGT). One of the best biographies on Sékou Touré is Ibrahima Kaké Raba, *Sékou Touré: le héros et le tyran* (Paris: Jeune Afrique, 1987).

23. Hamon, *Les Partis politiques,* 37–50.

24. Catherine Coquery-Vidrovitch and Henri Moniot, *L'Afrique noire de 1800 à nos jours* (Paris: PUF, 1974), 229–32.

25. Along with Aimé Césaire from Martinique and Léon Damas from French Guiana, Senghor began to examine Western values critically and to reassess African culture. The group's quarrel with assimilation was that although it was theoretically based on a belief in the equality of man, it still assumed the superiority of European culture and civilization over those of Africa. They became increasingly aware, through their study of history, of the suffering and humiliation of blacks first under the bondage of slavery and then under colonial rule. These views inspired many of the basic ideas behind *négritude:* that the mystic warmth of African life, gaining strength from its closeness to nature and its constant contact with ancestors, should be continually placed in proper perspective against the soullessness and materialism of Western culture; that Africans must look to the richness of their past and of their cultural heritage in order to choose which values and traditions could be most useful to the modern world; that *négritude* itself encompasses the whole of African cultural, economic, social, and political values; that, above all, the value and dignity of African traditions and peoples must be asserted. (For a detailed analysis of *négritude,* see Sébastien-Okechukwu Mezu, *Léopold Sédar Senghor et la défense et illustration de la civilisation noire* [Paris: Didier-Érudition, 1968]; A. I. Luvai, "Négritude: A Redefinition," *Busara* [Nairobi], 6 [2] [1974], 79–90.)

26. Irving Leonard Markovitz, *Léopold Sédar Senghor and the Politics of Négritude* (New York: Atheneum, 1969), 50.

27. Léo Hamon, *Introduction à l'étude des partis politiques de l'Afrique française* (Paris: Librairie générale de droit et de jurisprudence, 1959), 154–64. (Excerpt from *Revue juridique et politique d'outre-mer,* 2 [Apr.–June 1959], 150–96.)

28. Janet G. Vaillant, "African Deputies in Paris: The Political Role of Léopold Senghor in the Fourth Republic," in G. Wesley Johnson, ed., *Double Impact: France and Africa in the Age of Imperialism* (Westport, CT: Greenwood Press, 1985), 141–52.

4

Loi-cadre Reforms and Charles de Gaulle's Return

REORGANIZATION AND REFORMS

France gave little serious prewar consideration to eventual independence for the African colonies. For most French, the suggestion that colonial peoples be given civic status equal to that enjoyed by metropolitan French was considered the climax of liberality. Few French would have expected the population of a subject territory to choose independence over membership in, or association with, the French nation. But World War II irreversibly altered the political context in which the French colonial empire existed. The ten years after the war saw rapid political developments in the neighboring British West African territories, culminating in self-government and independence for Ghana. By contrast, the more farsighted politicians in France began to discuss how best to preserve the colonial system while altering it to meet the demands of a changing world.[1] Their solution was to seek a closer association with the African colonies through the metropolitan political process in a Franco-African Community. On the other hand, in de Gaulle's opening speech at the Brazzaville Conference of 1944, the possibility of eventual independence was carefully hedged with the condition that it take place within a "French context." In Francophone black Africa, the main focus of debate during the second half of the 1950s was the nature of future relations with the *métropole* as well as relations between African territories themselves and the continuation of the two federations. The young African political parties formed in the postwar period were now put to a crucial test.

Certain important events took place during the middle of the 1950s that influenced France's relations with its colonies in Africa. In Indochina, Ho Chi Minh organized an armed struggle against the French; the battle of Dien Bien Phu in 1954 marked the end of French influence in Southeast Asia. At the Bandung (Indonesia) Conference of 1955, the leaders of the newly liberated countries pledged their determination to put an end to colonialism elsewhere; they extended their support to the liberation movements in Algeria, Tunisia, and Morocco. The pace of events accelerated with the Suez Crisis of 1956, which proved to be a turning point in the history of postwar decolonization.[2] As a result of this conflict, France lost its control over the North African territories, which culminated in independence for Tunisia and Morocco in 1956. In Algeria the war of independence gathered fresh momentum. To block the advance of the Algerian nationalists, France was compelled to wage a war that resulted in a heavy drain on human and material resources.[3] The continuation of this struggle began to undermine the confidence of the French people in successive governments that functioned under the Fourth Republic. These events in North Africa, coupled with the constitutional advance of British colonies in West Africa, made the French colonies in black Africa restless. Against this background the French politicians had no intention of allowing violence to decide the issue in France's Sahel.

In the elections for the French National Assembly in 1956, the RDA was the big winner while Senghor's IOM and the SFIO suffered heavy losses. This brought Houphouët-Boigny to new prominence as minister of state in the narrowly based Guy Mollet socialist coalition government. Mollet charged his minister for overseas France, Gaston Defferre,[4] with Houphouët's assistance, to prepare a proposal for constitutional and administrative reforms for the black African territories. In his new prestigious position, Houphouët was now able to exercise a major influence on the destiny of Subsaharan French Africa. The result of Defferre and Houphouët's common work was the passage of the *loi-cadre* reforms in June 1956.[5] With its implementing decrees, the new law came into full force in April 1957. It provided for changes without involving constitutional reforms, which, during the last few years of the Fourth Republic, had become politically impossible. It also changed the structure of relations between France and its colonies; indeed, it represented the end of the power and unity of AOF and AEF. It also marked the end of the greater French republic, which lumped the overseas territories in a unified state with the mother country. The new law provided for the transfer of a substantial block of enumerated powers over local affairs to popularly elected territorial governments. For the first time, Africans were granted universal suffrage. The system of dual electoral colleges was abolished, and French citizens were placed on the same footing with the Africans.[6] The reforms also provided for the Africanization of the administration; it was intended that eventually some 50 percent of the students of the *École Nationale d'Administration* should come from overseas territories.

For each territory, the *loi-cadre* established a Governmental Council in which executive powers were invested. The council was composed of twelve members; all of them were elected by the popularly elected Territorial Assembly. The leader of the council was named *vice-président,* who became, in all but name, a prime minister. By instituting the Governmental Council, the French introduced a parliamentary system in AOF and AEF. The colonial governor continued to preside over the colonies but lost much of his authority over day-to-day governmental operations. The federal governments in Dakar and Brazzaville lost much of their authority, which was simply transferred to the individual territories. The *Grand conseil* was transformed into an advisory body. It made only recommendations regarding the coordination and unification of territorial legislations and fiscal regimes.

The *loi-cadre* reforms provided for two broad categories of government services, territorial services and state services. By passing some important services to the territorial level, France's policy was cautious in avoiding African participation in important matters such as defense and external affairs. The six groups of state services left under the control of the *métropole* were as follows:

1. External affairs (diplomatic and consular, frontier control, external trade and exchange control, immigration, and cultural relations).

2. External communications (aviation, including air safety and meteorology, radio communications and submarine cables, international lighthouses and beacon ships, *inscription maritime* and harbor masters).

3. Defense and security (armed forces, *gendarmerie*, customs, security police, ciphers, civil defense, and economic mobilization).

4. Civil liberties (courts of French justice, excluding courts of customary law in private law matters; administrative courts, *police judiciaire*, and labor inspection).

5. Solidarity and economic, social, and cultural expansion (treasury, financial supervision, supervision of state companies and "mixed" companies, central development projects financed by FIDES, distribution among territories of products that may need to be subject to quotas, university education, broadcasting and television stations, map and survey service, geological map service, and atomic energy).

6. Representation of central power (high commissioners and governors, heads of provinces and administrative districts, and their secretaries and cabinets).[7]

The state services were controlled by the High Commissioner, who was a representative of the French government; he was nominated by the president of the French republic and reported directly to the minister for overseas territories. It was the high commissioner's duty to maintain the solidarity of the constituent units and to coordinate territorial and state services; through him the French government protected French interests in the colonies. Thus, there were three important centers of power in each territory: the Territorial Assembly, the Governmental Council, and the High Commissioner. The territorial services were controlled by the Governmental Council. The areas over which legislative power was transferred to the territorial assemblies were land, soil, conservation, agriculture, forestry, fisheries, most mineral rights, internal trade, customary law, primary and secondary education, health, cooperatives, urbanization, and so forth. The Territorial Assembly communicated all decisions to the High Commissioner for execution within thirty days. If the commissioner considered any decision a danger to national defense, public order, security, or civil liberty, he could report to the minister for overseas territories and request a cancellation of the decision by a cabinet decree.

REACTION TO THE *LOI-CADRE* REFORMS

François Mitterrand (as minister of the interior) commented that, on one hand, the *loi-cadre* reforms symbolized France's spirit of progress, and, on the other, gave the African states a chance for a quiet and harmonious evolution. In view of some French politicians, the *loi-cadre* reforms could be regarded as constitutional only by a somewhat generous interpretation of the provisions of the constitution.[8] The trade unions in all the territories denounced the *loi-cadre* reforms as a pretext for the continuation of the French colonial regime. The *Union Générale des Travailleurs d'Afrique Noire* (UGTAN), which controlled over 80 percent of the African organized labor, advocated the creation of strong federal executive councils for AOF and AEF. Even Houphouët's own RDA proposed a strong government for both federations. The radical wing of the RDA went to the extent of opposing Houphouët's participation in the French cabinet and disapproved of the Europeans he proposed as candidates for the RDA. The RDA leaders also initiated a dialogue with the two inter-territorial parties, namely the *Mouvement Socialiste Africain* (MSA) and the *Convention Africaine* (CA). Seeking an area of agreement among the three parties, the RDA leaders suggested that the minority party in each territory should take the title of the majority party. Each section would then be called a territorial section of the RDA, however, the negotiations among the leaders of the three parties failed to secure these objectives. Senghor became the spokesman for the federalist cause and opposed the *loi-cadre* reforms in the French National Assembly. He asserted that France wanted to perpetuate its colonial regime by a "divide and rule" tactic. It was his belief that the twelve small colonies would individually be too weak to make a success of independence and would therefore remain dependent on France. He further accused France of wanting to balkanize the two great federations along tribal and ethnic lines in order to maintain greater colonial influence.[9] Senghor wanted to create a strong West African Federation (probably under his leadership), linked with France but developed along African, rather than European, lines. He accused Houphouët of being the instrument of France in continuing the colonial regime in Africa. Surprisingly, Sékou Touré and his associates sided with Senghor in proclaiming that AOF needed a strong federal executive. He even introduced a resolution in the Territorial Assembly of Guinea advocating a federal executive for AOF, which was passed in July 1957.

The following formal statements give a good perception of the two political positions in Francophone black Africa:

> The only goal the political process is supposed to have is to lead the peoples towards self-government and democratic decision-making. In order to attain this objective, Title VIII of the Constitution must be revised in order to create a Federal Republic and a Confederation of free and equal peoples. This revision will make it possible for the overseas departments, overseas territories, and territories under trusteeship to choose their own political status, that is, the status of a politically autonomous State or the status of an Associated State. This revision can be worked out only through the combined effort of all the different African political parties . . . and by regrouping and fusing the African parties into a large unified party which, inspired by Socialist ideas, maintains the autonomy of the African negro ideology and integrates the cultural values of black Africa. Therefore, the members of the African Convention request that all parliamentarians of the overseas territories . . . fight for a revision of the Constitution in the above mentioned sense and see to it that the political autonomy of each territory of AOF and AEF be assured, but within the framework of *two Federations*. The latter will be endowed with common services and will constitute *two States* qualified to be integrated into the *Republic*. The African Convention assures the French people of trust and lasting friendship. It also asks the people of France to have confidence in the peoples overseas who are eager to form political, economic, and cultural ties with France based on the concept of irreplaceable human values. This will be possible after all the peoples overseas have received a status conforming to their legitimate aspirations (Political resolution of the African Convention, January 11–13, 1957).

> The Congress values the great victories won over the last eleven years that mark the way towards political, economic, social, and cultural emancipation of the black African population. The Congress considers the elections and subsequent participation of black Africans in the legislative and executive branches of the French Republic a crucial factor to achieve these goals. It also considers the *loi-cadre* reforms as an irreversible step in the direction of emancipation. The Congress considers the independence of peoples as an inalienable right permitting them to shape their own version of sovereignty according to the wishes of the majority of the people in each individual State. But the Congress takes into account that independence forms the basis of the peoples' life manifesting itself in the 20th century through the formation of big political and economic agglomerations. Therefore, the Congress considers membership of black Africa in a big political and economic entity a real factor of power and independence for each member of this entity. Thus, it proposes formation and subsequent strengthening of a democratic and fraternal Franco-African Community based on equality. The Congress urges its parliamentary groups to propose a law for the formation of a *Federal State composed of autonomous States* with a Federal Government and a Federal Parliament acting as the supreme institution of the unified State (Political resolution of the RDA, September 30, 1957).[10]

The antifederalist movement was led by Houphouët, backed by France. He supported the policy of self-determination for each territory, mainly because he did not wish his rich Ivory Coast to subsidize a federal executive in Dakar. (Ivory Coast provided about one-third of the total customs revenue for the eight territories of AOF.) He held the conviction that if Ivory Coast was allowed to develop independently, it would become the most prosperous territory in AOF. He was also aware of the importance of his territory for the French economy and expected additional economic benefits and technological aid from the *métropole*. Furthermore, he thought that the *loi-cadre* reforms would encourage further democratization of the French administration in black Africa and eliminate the superimposition of tutelage that had been created within the framework of the two federations. Léon M'Ba of Gabon found it advantageous to side with Houphouët for similar reasons.[11] Due to its natural resources in uranium, manganese, coal, and crude oil, Gabon was the richest territory in AEF. Thus the *loi-cadre* reforms gave rise to two antagonistic philosophies among the African leaders: federalism, supported by Senghor and Touré, and territorialism, backed by Houphouët, M'Ba, and France.[12] Paradoxically, Houphouët provided the incentive for both the creation of the most important federationwide political party, the RDA, and the eventual destruction of the two federations. Today, we realize that the *loi-cadre* reforms were indeed the decisive steps that led to the increased weakening of colonial ties, leading quickly to independence for all of French Africa; however, perceptions at that time were less clear.[13] Most French politicians and African leaders were still searching for some formula to maintain African association with France while satisfying growing demands for self-determination.[14] Even Sékou Touré at that time sought to sustain association with France on a voluntary basis. He asserted that the *loi-cadre* reforms would eventually destroy the two federations and leave each territorial unit isolated.[15] Pierre François Gonidec, an authority on law of the 1950s, observed that France's reforms greatly resembled the policy of autonomy followed by Britain. He correctly predicted that the territories of AOF and AEF would in the future become separate units, distinct from France.[16]

The elections of March 1957 for the new territorial assemblies diverted the attention of Africans from the final goal of political independence to lengthy debates on the relative merits and demerits of the *loi-cadre* reforms. As expected, the RDA emerged as the strongest party in these elections. Important RDA leaders became the heads of the Governmental Council in several territories while Houphouët was again elected president of the RDA. The elections, however, also increased the schism within the RDA, which led to a conference at Bamako (Soudan) in September 1957, in order to resolve those differences. The conferees discussed the nature of the RDA, the future of Franco-African relations, the cooperation between interterritorial parties, and the character of the two federal executives.[17] The delegates failed, however, to solve their differences and to propose a precise program for joint action. The conference even aggravated the rift among the African leaders, which left a noticeable imprint on the history of black Africa. Houphouët launched a massive campaign against the concept of a federal executive and emphasized his desire for building up Ivory Coast with the assistance of France. He urged the leaders of the other African territories to follow the same path while strengthening the edifice of the Franco-African Community.

While African leaders tried unsuccessfully to solve some of the problems created by the *loi-cadre* reforms, a series of events brought down the Fourth Republic. Instability of governments was the most prominent feature of the French political system under the Fourth Republic (1946–58). Its continuation depended on the ephemeral coalition of multiparty groups and factions. The problem of political instability became all the more complicated because of the war of independence in Algeria. The possession of Algeria was vital for France for several reasons. First, it was the link of communication with North Africa, the Middle East, and black Africa. Second, over 1 million people of French descent living in Algeria owned 40 percent of the land; they were French citizens who had lived there for up to four generations. Finally, French industry depended on Algerian oil fields. Thus, many *métropole* French and Algerian French regarded Algeria as an extension of France itself. The governments of the Fourth Republic became increasingly incapable of dealing with the *Front de la Libération Nationale* (FLN) of Algeria under the leadership of Ferhat Abbas.[18] By 1958 large areas in the countryside were controlled by the freedom fighters. Faced by growing resistance, France was compelled to send more than 500,000 troops into Algeria. This created additional problems for France within the North Atlantic Treaty Organization (NATO) and the United Nations (UN). It also began to strain France's relations with newly born countries such as Morocco and Tunisia. At that point the French army leaders became convinced that the Fourth Republic was in no position to resolve the crisis. On May 13, 1958, they joined hands with the army leaders in Algeria to overthrow the parliamentary system in France.[19] The Pierre Pflimlin government collapsed, and a radical change in the political realm became a necessity. This time the French aspired to replace a weak executive by a strong and stable one.[20]

THE FIFTH REPUBLIC AND THE FRENCH COMMUNITY

Charles de Gaulle represented the only hope to deal with the serious situation. Because of his extraordinary qualities of leadership and great popularity, both in France and in the overseas territories, he was summoned from retirement at Colombey-les-deux-Églises to govern France. De Gaulle was a keen observer of the developments in Africa. Even before the establishment of the Fourth Republic in 1946, he had envisioned the creation of a permanent link between the *métropole* and the colonies.[21] Furthermore, he aspired to build up France as a powerful unit against the hegemonic position of the United States. While highlighting the importance of *grandeur* for France, he stated: "France is not really herself unless she is in first rank."[22] In his endeavor he felt that the African colonies could assist France in attaining a position of an independent power center in global politics. He felt that power and prosperity had to be sought in large communities of nations unified at least in their diplomacy, their military defense, and their economic development. With these objectives in mind, he drafted a new constitution for consideration by the Constituent Assembly.

The final version of the new constitution created a community that replaced the French Union of the Fourth Republic. The concept of *la Communauté* is not clearly defined. The new constitution merely refers to the fact that its institutions are founded on the common ideal of liberty, equality, and fraternity and are designed to permit democratic evolution (see Appendix 2, *Constitution of the Fifth Republic,* Preamble and Art. 1). The community's powers were divided into two major categories. The primary powers were retained by the community without any restrictions. The powers of secondary importance, including administration of justice, education, and telecommunications, were entrusted to the member states. The community consisted of four major power blocs: the President of the Community *(Président de la Communauté),* the Community Senate *(Sénat de la Communauté),* the Community Executive Council *(Conseil exécutif de la Communauté),* and the Arbitration Court *(Cour arbitrale).* As president of the community, the president of France *(Président de la République française)* retained substantial powers *(droits du domaine communautaire)* over such matters as unified defense, external affairs, currency, economic policy, and strategic minerals.[23] The president could send personal representatives to any member state, act as chairman of the Executive Council, and summon and dissolve sessions of the Senate. In fact, the new position was only superficially different from what existed under the *loi-cadre* reforms. In general, the president's powers with regard to the community remained ambiguous over a fundamental question, that is, to whom he was responsible when acting as head of the community. Two provisions somewhat checked the presidential powers: the appointment of Africans to diplomatic positions and France's financial contributions to the economic development of a particular member state. Both had to be endorsed by the French Parliament. The community Senate was composed of delegates from the French Parliament and the legislatures of the member states, serving a five-year term. Each senator from a member state represented 300,000 inhabitants. The Senate performed legislative functions and advised the president on financial matters. The Executive Council was composed of the prime minister of France, heads of governments from member states, and ministers in charge of community affairs. It had the following main functions: to inform and advise the member states about France's position on foreign policy; to facilitate governmental and administrative cooperation between members of the community and to take into consideration proposals submitted to the community by the president on his own initiative. Members of the council could also participate in the debates of the Senate. The Arbitration Court consisted of seven judges who served for a six-year term and were selected from a college of magistrates. They settled disputes between members of the community. In order to partially accommodate the advocates of a French Commonwealth, provision was made for periodic ministerial meetings and for community agreement by treaty. The French Community greatly differed from the British Commonwealth. Even if the community conferred the status of self-government to all its members, they did not enjoy the status of sovereign states as did the members of the British Commonwealth. Furthermore, foreign policy of the community was not separate from the one of the Republic of France, whereas the British Commonwealth of nations did not have a common foreign policy. The self-governing member states no longer had the right to send representatives to the French Parliament.

Ratification of the new constitution was to be by referendum held in each individual territory by an unequivocal "yes" or "no" vote on whether the voters wished their territory to remain in the community as an autonomous republic *(État membre de la Communauté)* or to accede immediately to outright independence.

The African territories had barely absorbed the changes brought about under the *loi-cadre* reforms when an African electorate was again called on to vote on a vital question for the territories' future. In August 1958, just before the final version of the constitution was published, de Gaulle himself embarked on a tour of French Africa. He wanted to explain the significance of the community to the African leaders and to emphasize the seriousness of the choice to his African audience. He assured the people that a "no" vote would bring immediate independence but cautioned that consequently all French aid would cease. The terms were somewhat threatening for the Africans. They worried whether they would be able to stand on their own feet, considering the high level of economic integration with France; whether their educational system could survive the departure of French teachers; whether their communication and public transportation systems could still function if France called back its technicians and advisers. Furthermore, they were concerned about their welfare services, which were subsidized by France. All along, Francophone black Africans had relied on France as a guaranteed market for their products. The question whether adequate alternative markets could be found caused them much anxiety. In short, they questioned whether their nation would be viable at all. De Gaulle was aware of France's unchallenged hegemony in black Africa and was quite confident that all the territories would opt for membership in the community; thus an outburst of freedom struggle on the Algerian line would be averted. He even hoped that the "yes" votes in black Africa would persuade the Algerians to stay within the community. With the exception of Guinea he received an enthusiastic welcome in every territory. Since the Brazzaville Conference of 1944, de Gaulle had become a hero for many Africans. Due to his charismatic personality, most African leaders were receptive to his ideas and feelings. They were generally moderate leaders who believed in promoting economic liberalism and blocking the infiltration of communist ideas in Francophone Africa. De Gaulle had established personal rapport with some of the African politicians, who publicly referred to him as their father or godfather. Indeed, he was the godfather of some of the children of African political leaders. Moreover, de Gaulle's continuous emphasis on the economic, intellectual, and moral developments of people under a Franco-African Community created a feeling of brotherhood among the Africans and the French.[24]

The referendum in the *métropole* and in French Africa was held on September 28, 1958 (see Table 1 for voting results in Francophone black Africa). Only Sékou Touré's Guinea was bold enough to reject the community. Touré had become one of the staunchest critics of the French administration. His view carried weight with the workers' organizations such as the UGTAN, and his PDG was in firm control of the Guinean countryside. He believed that a strong and united AOF would serve two purposes: eradicate colonialism and consolidate the African unity movement. For Touré the French Community was nothing but a French Union under a different name. The community did not provide for equal status for African states and France, a point that Touré had advocated repeatedly. He made it clear, however, that Guinea would vote "yes" if its demand for independence and juridical equality with France were recognized. He even went to Paris to negotiate, but de Gaulle refused to enter into a dialogue with him. Exploitation of the rich mineral deposits in Guinea by non-French companies may have given Touré the feeling of being in a stronger position than most of his nationalist colleagues in other territories to assert his independence. He maintained that huge amounts of money were spent by France to influence the elections and, through his PDG, retaliated by launching a vigorous campaign against the French tactics of applying pressure. He declared that if the French government ignored the legitimate aspirations of the Africans, Guinea would refuse to join the community and proclaim itself an independent state.

After the results of the referendum were known, a somewhat contrite Touré attempted to mollify de Gaulle with an offer to join the community voluntarily. De Gaulle coldly rejected this proposal, and Guinea began to function as a sovereign nation outside the French Community. All French assistance to Guinea was immediately ceased, and all French personnel were abruptly withdrawn, as was all French equipment, including telephones. Eventually, the French army too was withdrawn. De Gaulle's harsh treatment was to have severe consequences for the Guinean people. Especially the withdrawal of aid under the FIDES harmed Guinean interests considerably. There can be no doubt that de Gaulle's harshness was intended as a deterrent to prevent further defections from the community.

To a certain extent, Touré's advent to power in independent Guinea affected the French economic interests in West Africa. France did have some public and private financial stakes in Guinea. When the radical regime of Touré threatened to nationalize all foreign capital, the *métropole* did not remain inactive. The French government refused to recognize Guinea as an independent sovereign

TABLE 1

Voting Results in Francophone Black Africa
(Referendum, September 28, 1958)

Territory	Registered	Voted	Yes	No	Percent yes votes
AOF					
Ivory Coast	1,639,017	1,607,558	1,606,752	224	99.9
Dahomey	771,415	431,017	418,709	9,237	97.0
Guinea	1,044,043	1,012,416	33,784	986,933	3.3
Upper Volta	1,622,194	1,215,045	1,194,286	8,153	98.2
Mauritania	224,559	190,768	178,000	10,918	93.2
Niger	1,149,328	415,746	316,251	88,921	76.2
Senegal	974,675	804,999	780,465	21,565	97.0
Soudan	1,517,536	702,380	684,513	16,199	97.5
AEF					
Gabon	229,869	182,062	167,560	12,877	92.0
Congo	433,259	342,389	339,504	1,962	99.1
Oubangui	610,894	488,060	478,667	5,731	97.0
Chad	528,352	363,283	335,912	5,149	92.5

Source: *Bulletin de l'Afrique noire* (Paris), no. 67 (Sept. 30, 1958), 1210–11.

nation. De Gaulle even announced that if the United States recognized Guinea, France would withdraw from NATO. In December 1958, when Japan and Iraq sponsored a resolution in an assembly of the United Nations for admission of Guinea, France abstained from voting.

Extreme support for the Franco-African Community came from Houphouët-Boigny's Ivory Coast. Through his well-drilled PDCI cadre, Houphouët was instrumental in mobilizing the Ivorian people in favor of the community. Due to Guinea's withdrawal from the community, France's dependence on Ivory Coast had increased, thus de Gaulle's friendship with Houphouët paid off. In October 1960, when Houphouët-Boigny organized a meeting in Abidjan to discuss and resolve the Algerian crisis, he invited all Francophone African states as well as the *Gouvernement Provisoire de la République Algérienne* (GPRA). Thus, he acknowledged the Algerian FLN while, at the same time, averting French animosity by giving official recognition to the GPRA.

In Niger the poll was relatively low (36.2 percent), and there was a significant percentage (21.4 percent) of negative votes. Niger's rather marginal voting result was due to the influence of Kwame Nkrumah, president of Ghana.[25] In April 1958 Nkrumah had convoked the first conference of independent African states at Accra. It was attended by Ethiopia, Liberia, Libya, Morocco, Sudan, Tunisia, the United Arab Republic, and representatives of the Algerian *Front de la Libération National* (FLN), who were accorded a nonvoting status. The main issues discussed by the delegates were the steps to be taken to safeguard the sovereignty and territorial integrity of independent African states, the future of dependent territories, and racial problems. Expressing solidarity with the Algerian people and the black population in South Africa, the conference declared war on colonialism and racism—it formally launched the pan-African movement on African soil. Seeking support for his movement for Africa's total liberation, Nkrumah put out feelers to French-speaking West African political leaders. He offered them assistance in rallying for the cause of voting in favor of independence.[26] In Niger he was able to influence Djibo Bakary, a Marxist-oriented politician and one of the main organizers of the communist-oriented trade union movement.[27] Nevertheless, Niger voted in favor of retaining the imperial link with France. In December 1958, when Nkrumah organized the All-African Peoples Conference (AAPC) at Accra, the leaders of all African nationalist parties from Cape to Alexandria were invited. With the exception of Sékou Touré's PDG, all Francophone black African parties declined to attend the conference. Furthermore, these countries did not join the rest of the African states in condemning French policies in Algeria, whereas the conference participants extended support to the Algerian people, who were forced to use violent means in their struggle against colonial subjugation and exploitation.

The people in Gabon voted to join the Republic of France as an overseas department; however, this request was not acceptable to de Gaulle. When Gabon's political leader, Léon M'Ba, proposed a national flag bearing a French tricolor in an effort to retain a symbolic close bond with France, the *métropole* dissuaded him from executing this project.

The outcome of the referendum also had an important indirect impact on the future of black Africa. The "yes" votes broke up the federations of AOF and AEF, a situation that contrasted with events in Nigeria, a territory roughly equivalent to the AOF, where the British made every effort to preserve unity. Throughout its colonial history, France continuously centralized its administrative authority and services in Dakar and Brazzaville. The need for budget subsidies by the poorer landlocked territories had been one of the principal reasons for establishing the federations. For reasons explained earlier, the most easily identifiable enemies of AOF were Houphouët-Boigny and his associates in Ivory Coast. As the ablest parliamentarian and best-placed African politician in the French system (he was minister of state), Houphouët was able to reach his goals in shaping French African policies. As president of the RDA, combined with his unrivaled political connections in Paris, he became the most outspoken enemy of the African federations. His ideas of balkanization had encouragement from powerful quarters in Paris. (Nkrumah identified balkanization with an

Africa divided into "small, weak, and unstable states."[28]) Continued French domination of the overseas possessions was made easier by splitting them up into many weak and financially dependent countries. Poor political units have far less bargaining power and are less adventurous in foreign policy matters than two large, financially secure federations.

There can be no doubt that the French government's *loi-cadre* reforms of 1956 favored the balkanization of Africa. Before 1956 economic planning and infrastructure developments were still based on two large federations rather than on a group of small, relatively poor independent states. Up to the period of the *loi-cadre* reforms, the French continued developing a federal infrastructure with little thought to the possible consequences of territorial autonomy and subsequent early independence. The *loi-cadre* reforms with focus on territorial autonomy at the expense of the autonomy of the two federations forced planners to shift priorities hastily, although many critics reasoned that it made little economic sense to grant theoretical autonomy to countries as deprived of resources as Chad, Upper Volta, Soudan, and Oubangui-Chari. De Gaulle's 1958 referendum narrowed the choice to either balkanized semi-independence within a French Community or balkanized independence outside the community. The lag in France's perception of the economic situation in black Africa supports the contention that balkanization was not a long-considered, carefully planned French plot; however, France's motives to terminate the federations before independence were probably intentional.

NOTES

1. Jean Lacouture, *De Gaulle: le politique,* Vol. 2 (Paris: Seuil, 1985), 568–87.

2. When Gamal Abdel Nasser was elected Egypt's president in 1954, the Soviet Union came to see Egypt as the place to begin its Middle East penetration. In the mid-1950s the first shipments of Soviet arms to Nasser took place, via Czechoslovakia. Nasser then began his attack on surviving vestiges of European control by nationalizing the Suez Canal Company in July 1956, an act that had far-reaching consequences. U.S. plans to give assistance in the construction of the Aswān High Dam were abandoned, while the U.S. president sought to devise a new international canal regime acceptable to the Egyptian, French, and British governments, which were the principal stockholders in the nationalized company. These conciliatory plans collapsed, however; without the knowledge of the U.S., the British and French governments began preparations to seize and reoccupy the canal by force. In October 1956 the Israeli army invaded the Sinai Peninsula, and two days later French and British planes attacked the Egyptian airfields. The U.S. condemned the Suez expedition as a violation of the UN Charter. The British and French retreated in humiliation from the Suez. Nasser emerged from the brief war with undiminished prestige throughout the Arab world.

3. The RDA deputies were against the repressive methods used by the French forces in Algeria, but they never took an anti-French stand since the RDA was a part of the French government.

4. During the German occupation Gaston Defferre was editor of the underground newspaper *L'Espoir*.

5. *Loi-cadre* has been translated invariably as "framework law," "enabling law," and "outline law." The word *cadre* appears only once in the original document (Loi no 56–619 du 23 juin 1956) in the following context: "il (le Gouvernement) fixera les conditions de création de cadres territoriaux et de détermination de leurs statuts et de leurs modes de rémunération" ["Loi no 56–619 du 23 juin 1956," *Recueil Dalloz* (Paris), 27e cahier (1956), législation, 216]. In this context *cadre* has the meaning of "trained personnel around which a larger organization can be built and trained." Since the law "enabled" the colonies to become sovereign states, "enabling law" is probably the happiest translation. The law is sometimes referred to by the name of its author, *loi-Defferre*.

6. Henri Grimal, *La Décolonisation, 1919–1963* (Paris: Colin, 1965), 346–52.

7. Kenneth E. Robinson, "Constitutional Reform in French Tropical Africa," *Political Studies* (London), 6 (1) (Feb. 1958), 56.

8. Dorothy Pickles, *The Fifth French Republic* (New York: Praeger, 1965), 37.

9. The partition of Africa has been compared with the creation of a number of weak states in the Balkans out of the European colonial possessions of the Ottoman empire (Turkey) in the late 19th and early 20th centuries (source: Joseph-Roger de Benoist, *La Balkanization de l'Afrique occidentale française* (Dakar: Nouvelles Éditions africaines, 1978), 9–10, 267–72.

10. Henri Grimal, "Les Deux Proposition politiques des Africains," in René Rémond, ed., *La Décolonisation, 1919–1963* (Paris: Colin, 1965), 385–86 (translation by the author).

11. In 1952 M'Ba was elected to the Territorial Assembly and in 1956 became mayor of Libreville. In 1957, after the victory of his party, the *Bloc Démocratique Gabonais* (BDG), he was elected president of the Gabon Executive Council (the highest post then held by an African).

12. Jean-Louis Quermonne, *Le Gouvernement de la France sous la Ve République* (Paris: Dalloz, 1980), 58.

13. For a description of the situation in June 1958, see Postscript to new edition of Dorothy Pickles, *France: The Fourth Republic* (Westport, CT: Greenwood Press, 1976), 231–38.

14. Raoul Girardet, *L'Idée coloniale en France, 1871–1962* (Paris: La Table Ronde, 1972), 258–84.

15. Sékou Touré, *Expérience guinéenne et unité africaine* (Paris: Présence africaine, 1960), 24–25.

16. Pierre François Gonidec, *L'Évolution des territoires d'outre-mer depuis 1946* (Paris: Librairie générale de droit et de jurisprudence, 1958), 81–84.

17. André Blanchet, *L'Itinéraire des partis africains depuis Bamako* (Paris: Plon, 1958), 36–52.

18. Son of a Moslem official in the Algerian civil service, Ferhat Abbas received an entirely French education in Algeria; as a result, he could not speak fluent Arabic. The "Manifesto of the Algerian People" of 1943, prepared by Abbas, not only condemned French colonial rule but also called for the application of the princi-

ple of self-determination and demanded an Algerian constitution granting equality to all inhabitants of Algeria.

19. Paul-Marie de La Gorce and Bruno Moschetto, *La Cinquième République* (Paris: PUF, 1979), 16–26.

20. Jean-Pierre Rioux, *La France de la IVe République,* Vol. 2 (Paris: Seuil, 1983), 128–31.

21. Robert Bourgi, *Le Général de Gaulle et l'Afrique noire: 1940–1969* (Paris et Dakar: Bibliothèque africaine et malgache, 1980), 7–15.

22. Quoted in Edward A. Kolodziej, *French International Policy Under de Gaulle and Pompidou: The Politics of Grandeur* (New York: Cornell University Press, 1974), 37.

23. Jean-Jacques Becker, *Histoire politique de la France depuis 1945* (Paris: Colin, 1988), 93–94.

24. André Passeron, *De Gaulle parle des Institutions, de l'Algérie, de l'armée, des affaires étrangères, de la Communauté, de l'économie et des questions sociales* (Paris: Plon, 1962), 451–83.

25. Opposed to British rule in his country, Kwame Nkrumah published *Towards Colonial Freedom* in 1947; in 1948 he began publishing the *Accra Evening News* as a vehicle for his views. In the first general elections in 1951, Nkrumah's Convention People's party won, and he became the first prime minister in 1952. He led Ghana to independence in 1957 and served as its first president when it became a republic in 1960.

26. Ibrahima Kaké Baba, *L'Afrique coloniale: de la Conférence de Berlin (1885) aux indépendances* (Paris: ABC, 1977), 87–88.

27. Virginia Thompson, "Niger," in Gwendolin M. Carter, ed., *National Unity and Regionalism in Eight African States* (New York: Cornell University Press, 1966), 162–63.

28. Kwame Nkrumah, "I Speak for Freedom," in G.C.M. Mutiso and S. W. Rohio, eds., *Readings in African Political Thought* (London: Oxford University Press, 1975), 214.

5

Decolonization

THE FRANCO-AFRICAN COMMUNITY

After the referendum twelve autonomous member states began to function within the Franco-African Community, which served as a useful, though short-lived, stepping-stone to political independence (see Table 2). It opened the way to a relationship between Madagascar and the African territories, on one hand, and between these two entities and the French republic, on the other. At that time, the French republic consisted of metropolitan France, Algeria (including the two Saharan *départements* formed in 1957), the four *départements d'outre-mer* (Guadeloupe, Martinique, Réunion, and Guyana), and five small *territoires d'outre-mer* (St Pierre et Miquelon, the Comoro Archipelago, French Somaliland, Polynesia, and New Caledonia).[1] All of them elected representatives to the National Assembly and to the Senate. Togo and Cameroon, as UN trust territories, were not members of the French republic. They did, however, send representatives to the French parliamentary assemblies. The 1958 constitution abandoned the assimilationist principle that had dominated French thinking since the beginning of colonization. It stated explicitly that any future change of status—including that of gaining independence—of any member state of the community could occur without revision of the wording of the constitution. For the first time, the word *independence* was used in a French constitution with reference to the organization of former overseas dependencies.

Some important decisions were taken by the community. The principle of free movement of goods within the community was established. In dealing with foreign countries, each state had the right to set up its own tariffs within the framework of established economic policies for the community. Key economic decisions on investments, prices to be paid for exports, and prices charged for French products sold in Africa were still routinely made in France. In contrast to

TABLE 2

Chronology of Decolonization of French Black Africa, 1958–61

	Internal autonomy (a)	Transfer of competence from Community	Procla- mation of indepen- dence	First cooper- ation accords (b)	Admission to the United Nations
ex-AOF					
Ivory Coast	12.04.58	07.11.60	08.07.60	Apr. 61	09.20.60
Dahomey	12.04.58	07.11.60	08.01.60	Apr. 61	09.20.60
Guinea			09.30.58		12.12.58
Upper Volta	12.11.58	07.11.60	08.05.60	Apr. 61	09.20.60
Mauritania	11.28.58	10.19.60	11.28.60	June 61	10.27.61
Niger	12.13.58	07.11.60	08.03.60	Apr. 61	09.20.61
Senegal (c)	11.25.58	04.04.60	08.20.60	June 60	09.28.60
Mali (Soudan) (c)	11.24.58	04.04.60	09.22.60	May 63	09.28.60
ex-AEF					
Gabon (d)	11.28.58	07.15.60	08.17.60	Aug. 60	09.20.60
Congo (d)	11.28.58	07.12.60	08.15.60	Aug. 60	09.20.60
CAR (d)	11.28.58	07.12.60	08.13.60	Aug. 60	09.20.60
Chad (d)	11.28.58	07.12.60	08.11.60	Aug. 60	09.20.60
UN trust territories					
Cameroon	12.30.58	04.04.60	01.01.60	Nov. 60	09.20.60
Togo	12.30.58	04.04.60	04.27.60	July 63	09.20.60

(a) After the referendum of September 28, 1958.

(b) Does not take into consideration the cooperation accords for technical person-nel concluded in 1959 and continued by each state after independence.

(c) Members of the Mali Federation from 01.17.1959 to 08.20.1960.

(d) Members of the *Communauté rénovée*.

Source: "Coopération entre la France, l'Afrique noire d'expression française et le Madagascar," *Notes et études documentaires* (Paris), Secrétariat général du gouverne-ment, no. 3330 (Oct. 25, 1966), 7.

the era before the French Union was established (1945), the last thirteen years of French colonial rule in black Africa were progressive in certain economic sectors. After World War II the French broke with their traditional insistence on colonial self-sufficiency and provided large-scale, direct development financing from the French treasury. The institutional vehicles chosen as conduits for the distribution of grants and loans on concessional terms were the FIDES and its disbursement branch, the CCFOM. This generosity was probably motivated by genuine feelings of gratitude for Africa's support of Free France during World War II. There is also the possibility that France wanted to share with its black African territories some of the assistance it received under the generous American-sponsored Marshall Plan. At the time of the formation of the community, all twelve African nations depended to some degree on French capital grants for development expenditures. Due to its generosity, France had accumulated a considerable deficit. The establishment of the community did not improve the balance of payments position immediately, but it did contribute toward the stabilization of the French economy.

All citizens of the community enjoyed equal political rights; discrimination on the basis of race and religion was abolished. The member states had the right to be represented in such organizations as the United Nations Educational, Scientific, and Cultural Organization (UNESCO) and the International Labor Organization (ILO). When crucial issues regarding the community were discussed, four minister councillors attended the cabinet meetings. They were appointed for a one-year term and had an important function within the community. The four councillors for the first term were Houphouët-Boigny (Ivory Coast), Sédar Senghor (Senegal), Gabriel Lisette (Chad),[2] and Philibert Tsiranana (Madagascar).[3] French relations with the more affluent states, in particular with Ivory Coast and Senegal, were considerably strengthened within the framework of the community. As chief of the French delegation in the General Assembly of the United Nations, Houphouët explained and defended the concept and goals of the Franco-African Community. Thus, he became the principal spokesman of the community in the United Nations.

Through the establishment of the community, France received some other political advantages. After attaining the status of self-governing members of the community, the African states failed to replace or to eliminate the colonial institutions. French settlers continued to hold key positions in industrial and administrative services. Some of them controlled the distribution of local products as well as the sale of imported French goods. Large numbers of French technicians and skilled workers continued to enjoy employment because too many of Africa's best and brightest students had little interest in the technical professions or in private business. Just before independence, management and technical services were almost completely controlled by whites. Virtually no barriers were posed to French metropolitan citizens settling in Francophone black Africa before independence. Frenchmen continued to dominate the top and middle levels of the administration. The ready supply of skilled Frenchmen willing to work in

Francophone Africa also diminished the chances for Africans to receive training and subsequent promotion into technically skilled managerial positions.

After the implementation of the *loi-cadre* reforms, the poorer landlocked countries could no longer rely on the traditional support of the richer coastal countries. Thus, Niger, Upper Volta, Soudan, Chad, and Oubangui-Chari became more and more dependent on France. In addition, the constitution of the Fifth Republic considerably influenced the constitutions of the African states. Having participated in French elections and institutions since the establishment of the French Union (1945), the African politicians and populations were well acquainted with French domestic politics, institutions, and political mores. It was therefore a natural process to choose the constitution of the Fifth Republic as a model for their own constitution. Often the advisers for the constitution of the Fifth Republic also assisted in drafting the constitutions of the Francophone African states. Moreover, the centralization of power in the French presidency was well suited to traditional African leadership concepts of the strong chief. It also provided a degree of national cohesion through its administrative network to loosely formed states with mostly artificial borders. Through all of these different aspects of France's presence in Africa, the French were able to create a network of dependence around each African member of the community. In some of the Francophone countries this tight pattern of dependence is still in place. The community also enhanced the stature of France in the world and placed it in a better bargaining position in relation with other industrialized countries.[4]

CONTINUATION OF THE FEDERAL SPIRIT

After the creation of the Franco-African Community, the federalists did not give up hope. In the wake of French withdrawal from Guinea, Sékou Touré was forced to look for support from other quarters. A limited measure of support came from the Soviet Union through the establishment of trade relations. Nkrumah realized Touré's situation and promptly made a grant of financial support to tide Guinea over during that initial period of independence. There existed some ideological affinity between the two political leaders. In the first place, both Ghana and Guinea had completely thrown off the yoke of colonialism and attained independent nationhood. Second, both leaders believed in promoting an African unity movement while launching an anticolonial struggle in Africa. Two months after Guinea's independence, the two leaders made formal moves to unite their countries. They described their union as a nucleus for a Union of African States and envisaged it as an alternative to de Gaulle's vision of the French Community. This would be an African association to rival the ties that France was forging with its former colonies and the British Commonwealth. In a joint statement issued in November 1958, however, Touré and Nkrumah stated that their union had not been founded to prejudice the present or the future relations between the Republic of Guinea and the French Community, on one hand,

and between Ghana and the Commonwealth, on the other.[5] Since the two African politicians intended to promote an African unity movement, they did not want to antagonize any of the member states of the French Community or of the British Commonwealth.

The tendency to form unions or federations transformed the concept of federalism into a complex phenomenon in West Africa for the following two reasons. First, in spite of the disintegration of AOF due to the *loi-cadre* reforms, the RDA retained its interterritorial character. Furthermore, in July 1958 the interterritorial *Parti du Regroupement Africain* (PRA) was created as a reaction against the autonomist forces led by Houphouët-Boigny and his RDA. Thus, the interterritorial parties, such as the RDA and the PRA, provided a platform, for the federalists, autonomists, and those striving for political independence, to influence the voters. Therefore, the idea of federalism and territorialism divided the interterritorial political parties into three opposing camps. At the same time, however, the promoters of federal ideas were encouraged to negotiate and to find common grounds by ignoring their respective territorial party loyalties. Second, there were three major divisions among the member states of the community on the issue of regional federation. France, Ivory Coast, and Niger stood for territorialism. Senegal and Soudan, under the leadership of Sédar Senghor and Modibo Keita, respectively, were attempting to build a regional federation. Senghor wanted to create the *République Fédérale Africaine* (RFA), a primary federation with equal representation of the territories and a central government responsible to the Federal Assembly. He intended to integrate it with the French republic to form a confederation.[6] The third group, Niger, Dahomey, and Upper Volta, had no clear-cut stand on the issue of federalism or territorialism. Therefore, the members of the first two groups began motivating the members of the third group for their ideology.

The trend for integration set by the Ghana-Guinea Union encouraged negotiations for the establishment of a federation between Senegal, Soudan, Upper Volta, and Dahomey. At the Constituent Congress of the Mali Federation at Dakar in January 1959, the territorial assemblies of these four countries formally endorsed the option of forming a federation within the French Community. At this point de Gaulle agreed that African states might negotiate independence and yet remain members of a modified community; however, Houphouët-Boigny had other plans and started to interfere in the internal affairs of Upper Volta. He pointed out that Ivory Coast provided employment for thousands of migrant workers from Upper Volta and stated that the Abidjan-Ouagadougou railroad linked Upper Volta with Ivory Coast while a Mali Federation would not provide such a link. He sent a delegation to Upper Volta to convince President Maurice Yameogo and the major trading centers of the advantage of Abidjan as a commercial outlet for Upper Volta's commodities. Yameogo found it difficult to antagonize Houphouët and his economically prosperous country and withdrew his intention to join the Mali Federation.[7] When Houphouët helped to detach Upper Volta from the proposed Mali Federation, he did not intend that poor Upper

Volta should link with relatively rich Ivory Coast and live off it. He wanted a strong French Community in which Upper Volta would live off France.

In Dahomey the leaders of the local section of the PRA, the *Parti Progressiste Dahoméen* (PPD), were divided into two camps. The youth wing of the PPD adopted a resolution proposing the creation of a United State of Benin, grouping together Cameroon, Nigeria, Dahomey, Togo, and Ghana. The second group supported close association with Senghor. At that time Dahomey lacked a viable deepwater port. Houphouët exploited the situation by promising Dahomey's president, Sourou Migan Apithy,[8] that he would sponsor a deepwater port in Cotonou with the assistance of France if Dahomey remained outside any federation. An important event further undermined Dahomey's desire to participate in a federation. Serious antialien riots in Ivory Coast resulted in the expulsion of several thousands of Africans, more than half of them Dahomeans. Dahomey, at that time, went through an economic depression and was therefore ill prepared to absorb this influx of people. This provided the Dahomeans with evidence of their relative dependence upon Ivory Coast. In February 1959 Dahomey officially decided not to join any federation. Thus, through his keen diplomacy, Houphouët succeeded in motivating the leaders of Upper Volta and Dahomey not to join the Mali Federation. His staunch opposition to any federation in West Africa earned him further sympathy and support from the *métropole*.

Thanks to Sédar Senghor and Modibo Keita, the opponents of a federation were ineffective in their respective states. The Mali Federation of Senegal and Soudan was established with a unicameral Federal Assembly composed of twelve members of the Legislative Assembly from each state. The president, elected by the majority of the assembly members, headed the federal government. He appointed a Council of Ministers (including the prime minister), which was responsible to the assembly. The Federal Court, representing the judiciary branch, was independent of the executive and the legislative branch. A federal party, the *Parti de la Fédération Africaine* (PFA), came into being. It included members from the *Union Soudanaise* (US) and the *Union Progressiste Sénégalaise* (UPS), the dominant parties of the two states. As expected, Keita began to function as chief of the new federal government and Senghor as president of the assembly. At the PFA conference in Dakar in July 1959, the political leaders agreed that the federation should negotiate with France for converting the community into a multinational confederation composed of independent states. As a consequence, in September of the same year, Senghor and Keita submitted to de Gaulle a formal request for the transfer of sovereign power from the community to the Mali Federation. De Gaulle's answer was positive; he was even willing to give economic support to the federation. In 1960 the Mali Federation succeeded in attaining independence from France.

Houphouët-Boigny did not want France to give recognition to the Mali Federation, but de Gaulle ignored his request for the following reasons. First, France was preoccupied with the Algerian question. Since Soudan shared the northeastern border with Algeria, France was not in a position to face yet another source of tension beyond the Algerian borders. Second, France did not want any other member of the community to follow Guinea's example. Third, since Senghor and Keita had repeatedly expressed their desire to remain inside the community, even though they had formed a federation, France did not wish to antagonize them. Therefore, the emergence of the Mali Federation induced certain modifications in the structure of Franco-African relations.[9] In spite of the fact that the constitution had provided for changes in status, including accession to independence, it proved necessary to revise the document to make independence compatible within a context of a French Community of nations. Article 86 of the constitution was therefore revised in order to enable a state to remain within the community after independence and, at the same time, to enable any other independent state to become a member of the community without thereby ceasing to be independent. Article 85 was also revised in order to make it possible to revise all the articles of Title XII (dealing with the community) simply by agreement between the member states. (See Appendix 2, *Constitution of the Fifth Republic*.) All eleven Francophone black African states signed agreements providing for closer cooperation with France in a number of fields, but only five—Senegal, Congo, Gabon, CAR, and Chad—decided to remain within the community. This *Communauté rénovée* (renewed community) of seven states, including the French republic and Madagascar, soon disintegrated. Formal independence was viewed by most French as a price to be paid to preserve the close cultural and economic ties forged over the previous century.

Senegal and Soudan drew certain economic benefits from the federation. The two countries also cooperated in building the Dakar-Niger railroad project from Dakar to Bamako. Despite these benefits, the Mali Federation proved short-lived, mostly due to two opposite doctrines of social and economic development.[10] There was no agency to coordinate their activities; generally, cooperation proved slow and inefficient. Senegal was a relatively richer state with a smaller population than Soudan. Moreover, the political leaders of Senegal and Soudan differed in their attitudes toward the federation. Keita wanted to concentrate supreme political power in one single individual, while Senghor encouraged a joint executive with collective responsibility. There were also differences in opinion regarding union membership. Soudan admitted only resident Senegalese to the US, while Senegal did not want to include Soudanese party workers in committees of the UPS. The Mali Federation collapsed in August 1960, with Soudan assuming the name of Mali and its leaders blaming Houphouët-Boigny and France for the failure. Houphouët had no immediate reaction to the independence of the Mali Federation nor to its discontinuation. He kept on emphasizing the need of economic cooperation between individual African states and France. He was now convinced that supraterritorial governments were not able to solve the fundamental economic and political problems of the African states. He was not opposed, however, to any kind of regrouping of the Francophone African states; he was only hostile to any form of territorial regrouping that prevented individual countries from direct association with the Franco-African Community.

To countercheck the federalist movement, Houphouët himself was forced by certain events to turn to federalism, though in a mild form. In order to prevent Senghor from dominating Francophone West Africa, Houphouët formed the Sahel-Benin Union, made up of Ivory Coast, Upper Volta, Dahomey, and Niger. The union was more of an *entente* than a formal federation; indeed, the union was generally called the *Conseil d'Entente*. It had no Federal Assembly, only a council of prime ministers and delegates. The first to join Houphouët's design was Niger, which witnessed a struggle for political leadership. As a result of a subtle political game on the part of the French administration, Hamani Diori[11] acceded to power. After having formed the government, Diori pursued his antifederal ideology by inviting France and Houphouët-Boigny to suppress his political opponents. Furthermore, because of frequent droughts, Niger's economy was on a fragile footing and depended on the Ivory Coast for assistance. In April 1959 Houphouët and Diori established a customs union for their countries and signed various accords of cooperation.

Dahomey joined the *Entente* because of its close ties with Niger. A large number of Dahomeans were employed in the Niger civil service; Dahomey's trade route went through Niger via the port of Cotonou. Diori and Hubert Maga,[12] premier of Dahomey's coalition government, were schoolmates at the École William Ponty in Dakar. After all this it was no difficult task for Diori to persuade Maga to join the council of prime ministers of the *Entente*. The economic dependence of Upper Volta on Ivory Coast was described earlier. In order to consolidate these economic links, the two countries formed a customs union in April 1959. A few months later Upper Volta joined the *Entente*. In all four *Entente* countries the local RDA branches were in power, which facilitated the dialogue between these states.[13]

The creation of the *Entente* in regrouping Dahomey, Niger, and Upper Volta reflects another diplomatic success of Houphouët. His goal was twofold: the establishment of a parallel group within the French Community to challenge the federalist forces in West Africa and closer economic and technical cooperation among the member states. He did not, however, envisage the establishment of a supranational political entity. Houphouët's new pseudofederal policy weakened when France decided to grant independence to states outside the *Entente*. In June 1960 they separately requested independence; however, the *Conseil d'Entente* continued its function after independence under Ivorian leadership.

Houphouët did not want the continuation of any vestiges of federalism in Francophone Africa. De Gaulle accepted his request and embarked on the negotiation of agreements that were to govern France's relations with all its former colonies in Francophone Africa except Guinea. This time there were no threats to critically important assistance projects or to future association with France. On the contrary, committees under the direction of de Gaulle improvised formulas that granted sovereignty to the African states while maintaining close association with France.

The leaders of the four territories of the former AEF—Léon M'Ba (Gabon), David Dacko (Central African Republic, CAR), Fulbert Youlou (Congo), and François Tombalbaye (Chad)—declared as late as February 1960 that the AEF was to become a united and internationally sovereign state, with internal autonomy for its constituent parts. They considered a separate independence for their countries as unviable, because these territories were too small and too poor for statehood. They were less evolved politically and economically and more closely tied to France than were their sister republics in West Africa. In spite of previous tensions between the political leaders, the four autonomous republics resolved to exercise their sovereignty jointly in the *Union des Républiques de l'Afrique Centrale* (URAC). The union, however, was never successfully established, and a few months later all four territories became independent states. Thus, territorialism again triumphed over federalism in Francophone Africa. By December 1960, de Gaulle realized that the French Community no longer existed; however, the historical conditions of the times left room for the community to survive in a new manner.

The community as originally conceived had ended almost as soon as it had begun. It remained in oblivion, because the provisions of Articles 82, 83, and 84 (see Appendix 2) and those of the organic laws dealing with the organs of the community were clearly no longer applicable yet had never been revised. The Executive Council had not met since March 1960; states had been notified early in 1961 that the Senate of the community, which had met only twice, was to be considered dissolved.

The UN trust territory of Cameroon under French administration became independent in 1960. In 1961 the southern half of the trust territory of Cameroon under British administration voted to join former French Cameroon and to form a federation. (The northern half of British-administered Cameroon joined the Republic of Nigeria.) The federal constitution of the United Republic of Cameroon *(République Unie du Cameroun)* conferred executive powers on the president, who is the head of the federal government; he is assisted by a vice president, who may not come from the same state as the president. Legislative power is held by a unicameral National Federal Assembly, whose members are elected by direct and secret universal suffrage. (One deputy is elected for every 80,000 inhabitants.)[14] Since unification the federal government of Cameroon has pursued a strategy of sound fiscal and monetary policy and political stability. Therefore, the Cameroonian economy has continued to display steady growth. This demonstrates that regions of varied colonial background can successfully unite into larger political units.

In June 1956 Togo had been chosen as the "pilot state" for the introduction of the *loi-cadre* reforms; it became the Republic of Togo with limited self-government. In UN-supervised elections in 1958, Sylvanus Olympio[15] became prime minister, leading Togo to complete independence in 1960. The political evolution of Togo toward independence was constantly marred by the question of the Éwé people. After World War II, manifestations, petitions, and appeals to the UN in favor of a reunification of the Éwé of Gold Coast, British Togo, and French Togo multiplied. The outcome of referenda held in 1956 in British Togo and in 1957 in French Togo was as follows: British Togo joined Gold Coast (which became Ghana in 1957), and French Togo became the autonomous Republic of Togo.[16] Unlike most of the other Francophone African countries, Togo refrained from extending preferential trade accords to France.

NOTES

1. Since 1958 there no longer exists a minister for overseas territories; their affairs come within the purview of a minister of states, who is also responsible for the four overseas departments.

2. Gabriel Lisette became president of Chad in 1958 and resigned in 1959. After the proclamation of independence in 1960, his political role came to an end.

3. In 1960 Philibert Tsiranana became the first president of the independent Malagasy Republic. He and his *Parti Social Démocrate* (PSD) remained in power until 1972.

4. Guy de Carmoy, *Les Politiques étrangères de la France, 1944–1966* (Paris: La Table ronde, 1967), 297.

5. Philippe Devillers et al., *Indépendance et relations internationales: quelques études de cas* (Paris: Centre d'étude des relations internationales, 1961), 74–76.

6. Ernest Milcent and Monique Sordet, *Léopold Sédar Senghor et la naissance de l'Afrique moderne* (Paris: Seghers, 1969), 170–73.

7. On the Mali Federation, the most authoritative source is Guédel Ndiaye, *L'Échec de la Fédération du Mali* (Dakar: Nouvelles Éditions africaines, 1981).

8. Sourou Migan Apithy was the founder of the *Parti Républicain Dahoméen* (PRD) and was regularly elected to the French National Assembly. In 1958 he became prime minister of Dahomey and in 1964 president of the republic. The military coup of 1972 interrupted his political career.

9. Rajen Harshé, *Pervasive Entente: France and Ivory Coast in African Affairs* (Atlantic Highlands, NJ: Humanities Press, 1984), 74–77.

10. Pierre François Gonidec, *L'État africain: évolution, fédéralisme, centralisation et décentralisation, panafricanisme* (Paris: Librairie générale de droit et de jurisprudence, 1970), 283–85.

11. Hamani Diori was one of the founders of the *Parti Progressiste Nigérien* (PPN), an affiliate of the RDA. He became the first president of independent Niger in 1960. Moderate and businesslike, he weathered a period of instability in the mid-1960s; in 1974 he was overthrown in a military coup.

12. Hubert Maga was a member of both the Dahomean Territorial Assembly (1947–1960) and the Grand Conseil of AOF (1947–1957), as well as the National Assembly in Paris in the 1950s. By January 1962 he was successful in establishing a one-party regime, but factional rivalry continued as the economy worsened. In 1963 the military intervened and deposed Maga.

13. André Jeudy, *Administrateur des colonies: essai d'autobiographie critique* (Lille: A.N.R.T., Univ. de Lille III, 1988), 382–461.

14. Jean Imbert, *Le Cameroun* (Paris: PUF, 1982), 48–67; Isabelle Grenier, *Résistances et messianismes: l'Afrique centrale au XIXe et au XXe siècle* (Paris: ABC, 1977), 106–08.

15. Sylvanus Olympio was elected president of Togo in 1961, under a constitution granting extensive presidential powers. Togo became a one-party state (*Comité de l'Unité Togolaise,* CUT), but its seeming stability was deceptive. In January 1963 Olympio was assassinated in the first successful army coup in postwar Subsaharan Africa. France declined to intervene because Togo did not have a mutual defense agreement with France at the time.

16. Robert Cornevin, *Le Togo* (Paris: PUF, 1967), 92–98.

6

Independence

FRANCE'S CONCEPT OF INDEPENDENCE

France's policy of decolonization was carried out with spectacular speed and smoothness and in a general atmosphere of cooperative comprehension.[1] Much credit for this must go to the government of Guy Mollet, in particular to his two ministers, Gaston Defferre and Houphouët-Boigny. With the *loi-cadre,* they provided for the basic administrative infrastructure on which effective independence could be built.

Samora Machel gives the following definition of decolonization: "To decolonize a state means essentially to dismantle the political, administrative, cultural, financial, economic, educational, juridical and other systems which, as an integral part of the colonial state, were solely designed to impose foreign domination and the will of the exploiters on the masses."[2] From this point of view, there was definitely no decolonization of the Francophone black African states. Although independence profoundly changed the formal nature of relationships between France and its former dependencies, the continuity of French assistance and presence was largely maintained. Sometimes political roles were simply exchanged. Thus, the former governors in Gabon and Niger became the French ambassadors assigned to these countries. Former French colonial civil servants stayed on as advisers. Indeed, there was little thought given among African leaders to speeding up the departure of the French; on the contrary, most were concerned with avoiding a breakdown in government and services and an economic stagnation. Only Mali, due to the strong Marxist influence in its ruling party, hastened the departure of the French.

At the time of independence the various Francophone African countries found themselves at different stages of social, political, and economic development. All were, to one degree or another, economically underdeveloped; some were clearly unprepared in any practical sense for independence and would never make much sense as viable nation-states. Their borders were mostly arbitrarily drawn, insensitively crossing ethnic and natural topographic lines. The resulting problem of divided tribes and divided loyalties has since plagued relations among African neighbors as well as the internal cohesion of many African states. The number and dispersal of ethnic groups in Africa could simply not adapt to the European model of nation-states. In Francophone black Africa in 1960, only Senegal, Ivory Coast, and Guinea were reasonably well prepared for immediate independence. Concerning the different levels of readiness for independence, at one extreme was Ivory Coast with its rich agricultural economy and substantial number of influential African planters and entrepreneurs, its sophisticated political leadership, and its well-disciplined mass political party under the leadership of Houphouët-Boigny. The most extreme case of hopeless political and economic inviability and national artificiality was Chad. The northern Moslem nomads who inhabited the few scattered oases largely ignored the arbitrarily drawn borders and continuously opposed their colonizers; they disdained foreign culture, education, and language. The southern black African peasants were sedentary and produced cotton as a cash crop. To further complicate the problem of national unity, these peasants were mostly Christians and animists who cooperated with the French. By the time of independence, the African contingent of the civil service positions in Chad was almost exclusively staffed by southern black Africans. Long-suppressed northern resentments quickly surfaced, leading to a refusal of accepting a largely southern-dominated government and administration. The chronic instability that has affected and is still affecting Chad is due to the conflict between the northern and southern population.

As a result of the assimilation policy, most Francophone states had a small, well-educated elite.[3] Some members of this elite had the invaluable experience of several years of training as deputies in various French legislative bodies and as members of advisory councils. After the implementation of the *loi-cadre* reforms, many African leaders had served as members of territorial governments. The French transferred power to this French-educated small elite at the time of independence. With the exception of Sékou Touré and Modibo Keita of Mali, all Africans who assumed the top political leadership in French African states were moderate socialists. They were experienced and well prepared to take over political power from the French. As we have seen earlier, however, the next level of administrators and technicians was often ill prepared and insufficient in numbers. Individual character of the different Francophone countries and their circumstances, especially differences in history, geography, and economic and political potential, were crucial in determining the future of the successor regimes.

As soon as the pattern for individual independence was established, de Gaulle started to devise ingenious means for preserving French interests in Africa. The extraordinary relationships that France still enjoys with its former African dependencies rest on the various bilateral cooperation agreements of the early 1960s. Through the linkages between the accession to international sovereignty and the signing of these model cooperation agreements, France managed to institutionalize its political, economic, and cultural preeminence over its former African dependencies. Thus, *coopération* was intended to provide more than just assistance or aid; its real aim was to maintain privileged links in spite of international sovereignty. In this context, the defense agreements were (and to some extent still are) an essential part of the complex network of economic, cultural, and political pacts concluded between the *métropole* and its ex-colonies (see Table 3). Agreements with Senegal, Ivory Coast, Dahomey, Niger, Mauritania, Gabon, Congo, CAR, Chad, and Togo included a full range of diplomatic, economic, monetary, and technical assistance and defense agreements. Arrangements with Mali included only economic and technical assistance. Those with Upper Volta and Cameroon embraced all except the common defense accords; they prevented France from stationing military security forces on their soil, but both countries signed military aid agreements.[4] The defense agreements also contained special provisions granting the French privileged access to strategic raw materials such as oil and natural gas, uranium, thorium, lithium, beryllium, and helium. These agreements provided in particular for priority sales to France and possible embargoes to other countries in the interests of common defense.[5]

In 1959 France was contributing more economic aid for Africa in proportion to its resources, than were the United States, the United Kingdom, or the Soviet Union. Over the years, relations between France and some Francophone African countries have declined while others have grown more elaborate. Not one of the former Subsaharan colonies ever decided to leave the system for good. Even Guinea took the initiative to negotiate cooperation agreements with France before the death of Sékou Touré in 1984.

The cooperation agreements between France and the African states have not been published. The same holds true, in general, for the revised 1973 and 1977 versions, which constitute (with the exception of Mauritania) mere adjustments to the 1960 agreements.[6] About fifty new agreements were negotiated; together they marked an important step in the "normalization" of relations within the French system of cooperation.[7] At times, what is known is far less significant than what is not known; there exists a certain secrecy, even an enigma, in these special relationships. The phenomenon cannot be explained merely by observing economic, political, cultural, and military factors. It amounts to much more than adding the benefits France and the various countries may gain in one area or another. Without generous aid and the honoring of certain security guarantees, France could not enjoy its trade and investment advantages for very long. In binational committees *(commissions mixtes),* the French and the various African partners jointly sort out the programs and problems involved in their bilateral relations. The network of cooperation agreements forms a solid framework within which these extraordinary relationships continue to exist and allows France to remain the dominant power in a large part of Africa. No other middle-sized power enjoys a similar status and international influence. In the post-

TABLE 3

Most Important Cooperation Agreements Concluded Between France and Francophone Black African States During the Period 1959–63

State	Political sector			Economic and financial sector			
	Foreign policy	Defense	Strategic raw materials	Monetary, economic, financial	Post and telecommunication	Civil aviation	Merchant marine
ex-AOF: Ivory Coast	---	04.24.61	---	04.24.61	04.24.61	04.24.61	04.24.61
Dahomey	---	04.24.61	---	04.24.61	04.24.61	04.24.61	04.24.61
Guinea	---	---	---	05.22.63	---	---	---
Upper Volta	---	04.24.61*	---	04.24.61	04.24.61	04.24.61	04.24.61
Mauritania	---	06.19.61	---	06.19.61	06.19.61	06.19.61	06.19.61
Niger	---	04.24.61	---	04.24.61	04.24.61	04.24.61	04.24.61
Senegal	06.22.60	06.22.60	06.22.60	06.22.60	---	06.22.60	06.22.60
Mali	---	---	---	03.09.62	---	---	---
ex-AEF: Gabon	08.17.60	08.17.60	08.17.60	08.17.60	---	08.17.60	08.17.60
Congo	08.15.60	08.15.60	08.15.60	08.13.60	---	---	---
CAR	08.18.60	08.13.60	08.13.60	08.11.60	---	---	---
Chad	08.11.60	08.15.60	08.15.60	08.15.60	---	---	---
ex-Trust: Cameroon	---	11.13.60*	---	11.13.60	---	11.13.60	---
Togo	---	07.10.63	---	07.10.63	---	---	---

*Technical military assistance only.

| | Juridical sector | | | Social and cultural sector | | Technical cooperation |
State	Justice	Agreement on governance	Diplomatic representation	Cultural cooperation	Post-secondary education	
ex-AOF: Ivory Coast	04.24.61	---	---	04.24.61	04.24.61	04.24.61
Dahomey	04.24.61	---	---	04.24.61	04.24.61	04.24.61
Guinea	---	---	---	05.22.63	---	05.22.63
Upper Volta	04.24.61	---	---	04.24.61	04.24.61	04.24.61
Mauritania	06.19.61	---	---	06.19.61	---	06.19.61
Niger	04.24.61	---	---	04.24.61	04.24.61	04.24.61
Senegal	06.14.62	06.22.60	---	02.04.60 08.05.61	06.22.60	09.14.59
Mali	03.09.62	---	03.09.62	03.09.62	03.09.62	03.09.62
ex-AEF: Gabon	12.31.59	08.17.60	---	11.18.59	08.17.60	11.18.59
Congo	05.18.62	08.15.60	---	08.15.60	08.15.60	07.23.59
CAR	07.12.60	08.13.60	08.13.60	08.13.60	08.15.60	07.17.59
Chad	07.12.60	08.11.60	---	08.16.60	08.15.60	11.29.59
ex-Trust: Cameroon	11.13.60	---	11.13.60	11.13.60	08.08.62	11.13.60
Togo	07.10.63	---	---	07.10.63	---	07.10.63

Source: "Coopération entre . . .," *Notes et études documentaires*, no. 3330 (Oct. 25, 1966), 45.

independence era, considerations of national image and influence continue to be the most important factor in forming French policy toward Francophone black Africa.

Many African nationalists considered the cooperation agreements with France neocolonialist.[8] In the French National Assembly and in the Senate many deputies felt that a federal institutional framework should have been preserved. They also questioned the advantage of signing individual, rather than multilateral, accords with the Francophone African countries. Many references were made to balkanization and the creation of micronations. Kwame Nkrumah of Ghana claimed that balkanization was a deliberate ploy that led to "neocolonialism." In his monograph by that title Nkrumah wrote:

> Neocolonialism is based upon the principle of breaking up former large united colonial territories into a number of small non-viable States which are incapable of independent development and must rely upon the former imperial power for defense and even internal security. Their economic and financial systems are linked, as in colonial days, with those of the former colonial ruler. . . . Balkanization is the major instrument of neocolonialism and will be found wherever neocolonialism is practised.[9]

Neocolonialism, Nkrumah argued, is economic exploitation. His monograph shows clearly how little of the profits of foreign companies in politically independent Africa filters through to the African masses. Some African workers benefit from the wages, although they are generally much lower in comparison with wages paid to European workers. But most of the rest of the population, especially the vast rural peasant group, does not enjoy any benefits. For example, minerals are exported from Africa in their primary state and, if repurchased in the form of finished goods, return to Africa at grossly inflated prices. Moreover, the Western countries dictate the price of primary products on the world market.[10] Sékou Touré emphasized that balkanization should be feared as a "Machiavellian plan" of the big powers aimed "at dividing Africa in order to remain master of the continent."[11] Further allegations of economic exploitation were made in March 1961 at the All-African People's Conference in Cairo, which defined neocolonialism as "the survival of the colonial system in spite of formal recognition of political independence in emerging countries, which become the victims of an indirect and subtle form of domination by political, economic, social, military, or technical means."[12]

AFRICAN UNITY MOVEMENTS

The African unity movements, initially led by Ghana and Guinea, encouraged other African states to defend and consolidate their position. Houphouët-Boigny, supported by France, strove to win over a large number of African states for his political ambitions. After Ivory Coast's declaration of independence in

August 1960, Houphouët arranged a series of meetings among the Francophone West African states in order to establish strong economic ties, a common currency, a customs union, and a common foreign policy in African affairs. Another reason for these meetings was to counterbalance the pan-African movement led by Ghana. With the financial support of France, Houphouët regulated development projects in the *Entente* states (Upper Volta, Niger, and Dahomey). The Ivorian leader made it clear that these projects were not intended as an incentive for the creation of a political confederation, which would infringe on national sovereignties. The close cooperation between France and Ivory Coast provided a platform for negotiation of the various issues and problems faced by the Francophone West African states.

Mostly in response to the Algerian crisis, a meeting was organized at Brazzaville in December 1960 to promote inter-African cooperation. The following countries were represented: Ivory Coast, Senegal, Dahomey, Upper Volta, Niger, Mauritania, Gabon, Congo-Brazzaville, CAR, Chad, Cameroon, and Madagascar.[13] At this time, with the formation of a government in exile under Ferhat Abbas, the Algerian crisis had taken a new turn. France made every effort to block UN discussion on the Algerian crisis on the grounds that Algeria represented an internal problem of France. In September 1960, de Gaulle declared that the Algerians should be allowed to decide their own destiny through suffrage. The twelve countries of the Brazzaville Conference endorsed de Gaulle's statement and proclaimed that the honest and democratic application of the principle of self-determination was the only solution to the Algerian crisis.[14] Ghana, Guinea, and Mali disapproved of this proposed solution on grounds that it was likely to strengthen neocolonialism and at the same time jeopardize the unity of Africa.

The members of the Brazzaville Conference also discussed the Congo-Léopoldville crisis. The origin of the crisis can briefly be described as follows. The path to independence of the Belgian Congo (Congo-Léopoldville at independence, and Zaïre from 1966 on) was marked by intense rivalry between regionalists and federalists and by a direct attempt of neocolonial forces to control the party politics. The Belgians, whose postwar policy in the Congo had emphasized economics and social progress without political development, could no longer isolate the Congo from events happening in neighboring countries. Léopoldville, the capital and largest city, faced French Congo and its capital Brazzaville across the river. De Gaulle's offer of independence to Congo-Brazzaville in 1958 was bound to cause a stir in Léopoldville. Moreover, at the Brussels World Fair in 1958 many Congolese delegates came into contact with a wider world and absorbed new ideas. A few days after independence in July 1960, there was a mutiny of the *Force publique* (the combined army and gendarmerie), caused not by the political aspirations of some of its officers but by the fact that the force had been under strain due to several months of political unrest. The Belgian commander refused to acknowledge that independence was to improve the Congolese soldiers' treatment, salary, and prospects of promotion. On the other

hand, politicians and civil servants enjoyed rapid promotion to wealth and affluence. The inexperienced government of Prime Minister Patrice Lumumba was
not able to control the situation. In the confusion, the mineral-rich province of
Katanga proclaimed secession. At that time the Katanga province was of vital
importance to the Congo as it contributed more than half of the country's total
revenues.[15] The apparent role of Katanga's prime minister, Moïse Tschombé,
as a puppet of Belgian mining interests gave the secession a broader significance.
Belgium sent in troops on the pretense of protecting Belgian nationals in the
disorder. But, in fact, these troops landed in Katanga primarily to sustain the
secessionist regime of Tschombé. Lumumba appealed to the UN to expel the
Belgians from the Congo and to put an end to the secessionist movement in
Katanga. The UN called on Belgium to withdraw its military forces; a UN
peacekeeping force, primarily composed of African troops, was sent to the
Congo to maintain law and order. In August 1960 Lumumba organized a
conference of independent African states in Léopoldville; thirteen states attended
it, including Guinea, Togo, Morocco, and the Algerian provisional government.
The participants were unable to find a solution to the crisis, but they did want to
keep cold war out of Africa.

The UN involvement in the Congo crisis posed new problems for France.
The French government disapproved of the UN intervention and proposed direct
negotiations between the concerned parties. The members of the Brazzaville
Conference, in their final official statement, were of the same opinion and
requested that no other state intervene in Congo's domestic affairs, neither
through the intermediacy of soldiers nor through that of diplomats. They
supported neither Tschombé nor Lumumba; they simply refrained from involving themselves on either side.

As a sequel to the Brazzaville Conference and in the wake of the Algerian
and the Congo crisis, the pattern of alliances and counteralliances continued. In
January 1961 Ghana, Guinea, Mali, Morocco, and United Arab Republic organized a conference in Casablanca. These states came to be known as the members of the Casablanca group. The heads of state attending the conference
proclaimed their determination to liberate the African territories still under
foreign domination in giving them aid and assistance. They agreed to resist
colonialism and neocolonialism in all their forms and to oppose the stationing
of foreign security forces on the continent and the establishment of military
bases that endanger the liberation of Africa. On the Algerian question, the
members of the conference recognized the right of the Algerian people to independence and self-determination. They adopted a critical resolution on
Mauritania, whose northeastern territory was being used by French troops in
their fight against the Algerian people. Their final resolution stated that every
assistance given to France in its repressive war in Algeria constituted an act of
hostility directed against the African people as a whole. It requested the immediate withdrawal of French troops from Algeria and called for the withdrawal of all
African troops serving under French command. It also denounced the military

assistance given to France by NATO. Concerning the Congo crisis, the members of the Casablanca group affirmed their recognition of the elected parliament and legally constituted government of the Democratic Republic of the Congo under the leadership of Lumumba. They urged the UN to change its ambiguous and unrealistic policy in the Congo and to eliminate from that nation all Belgian and foreign military and paramilitary personnel not belonging to the UN operational command. They even went as far as to propose that the respective governments represented at the conference should withdraw their troops and other military personnel placed under the UN operations command in the Congo. The members of the Casablanca group adopted a different attitude from that of the Brazzaville group. The former accused France, on the one hand, for its policies in Algeria, and, on the other hand, condemned Mauritania for allowing France to station troops on its soil to fight the Algerian FLN. Their stand directly affected the interests of France and of certain Francophone African leaders. The Congo crisis also made them critical of the UN operations. As a result, the Franco-Ivorian model of cooperation and the Brazzaville group came under severe criticism from the Casablanca group.[16]

In response to the Casablanca Conference, the members of the Brazzaville Conference under the leadership of Houphouët-Boigny called a meeting in Monrovia (Liberia) in May 1961. Uncommitted states such as Ethiopia, Liberia, Nigeria, Sierra Leone, Somalia, Sudan, Togo, and Tunisia also attended the conference. Thus, Ivory Coast began to operate both within and without Francophone Africa. The resolution passed in the conference called for recognition of the inalienable right of each state to exist and to develop its own personality. It also called for noninterference by all states in each other's affairs. It proclaimed the absolute equality of African states and condemned outside subversive activities by neighboring states. Houphouët had already gotten the principle of noninterference approved by the members of the Brazzaville Conference; now he was able to extend this principle for acceptance by other African states. In organizing the *Entente* states, Houphouët had been pursuing his own brand of federalism; now he was able to expand his concept of pan-Africanism. The accepted norms of interstate relations became imperative for the conference participants in view of the Ghana-Guinea Union's subversive activities. Ghana had supported the overthrow of the Diori regime in Niger and had encouraged secessionist movements in Ivory Coast. Guinea, on the other hand, had supported the members of the *Parti Africain de l'Indépendance* (PAI) in their attempt to challenge Senghor's policies. (The PAI was influenced by Marxist ideology.) Sékou Touré had also supported the *Comité National pour la Libération de la Côte-d'Ivoire* (CNLCI) and the *Union des Populations Camerounaises* (UPC); both were fighting the duly constituted governments in the respective countries. The conference participants welcomed the decision made by France and the GPRA to open negotiations in May 1961 and encouraged both parties to conclude an agreement to end the war in Algeria. This stand was consistent with the one adopted by the members of the Brazzaville Conference.

At a conference in Tananarive (Madagascar) in September 1961, fourteen Francophone states formed the *Union Africaine et Malgache* (UAM) with the following members: Cameroon, CAR, Congo-Brazzaville, Dahomey, Gabon, Ivory Coast, Madagascar, Mauritania, Niger, Rwanda, Senegal, Chad, Togo, and Upper Volta.[17] These countries wanted to cooperate in all domains of foreign policy in order to strengthen their solidarity, ensure collective security, and develop their economic resources. Houphouët-Boigny made sure that the charter of the UAM contained the principles of national sovereignty and noninterference in the internal affairs of member states. The UAM members signed a defense agreement that supplemented the defense pact that most of the members had signed with France. They also aimed at establishing closer ties between France and the Francophone African states. Thus the UAM offered a new platform for the continuation of Franco-African cooperation. In turn, active French support strengthened the UAM.

By the end of 1961 two rival groups had been formed in Africa, each defending its own version of pan-Africanism, the Casablanca group and the Brazzaville-UAM group. The split between the two groups became more marked with the aggravation of the Algerian and Congolese crisis. Originally both groups claimed to be the representatives of all African states and tried to define the concept of African unity. The members of both groups differed in their domestic political regimes and in their foreign policy orientation. The states of the Casablanca group were governed by homogeneous regimes that featured highly disciplined single-party rules. These countries promoted union through mergers within centralized unitary states or through uniform acceptance of the same fundamental ideology. As a consequence of these characteristics, these states were aggressive and expansionist and were prepared to subvert groups that opposed their concept of unity.[18] They opposed all forms of colonialism and neocolonialism; they were especially critical of those African countries that associated themselves with France, because this kind of association was based exclusively on economic imperialism that reduced the African nations to poverty. The Casablanca group was opposed to any agreement that used the unification of Western Europe as a disguise for perpetuating colonial privileges in Africa.[19] This objective could not be reached in the 1960s. Even if the members of the Casablanca group welcomed the cooperation with socialist countries, they generally continued to retain certain precolonial ties with the former colonizing country and sometimes established new economic ties with some other capitalist country in the West. For instance, Guinea did break away from France immediately after independence but established economic ties with the United States to pursue its economic development. Similarly, Ghana under Nkrumah continued to be a member of the British Commonwealth. The members of the Casablanca group were unable to take any positive steps to check the capitalist expansion in Africa, mostly because their concept of socialism permitted them to establish economic ties with socialist and capitalist countries simultaneously. There was a considerable gap between what they preached and what they practiced in their foreign policies.

The members of the Brazzaville-UAM group were essentially status quo-oriented and moderate in their approach to African questions. They kept a low profile on the issue of colonialism and neocolonialism. There were some states with single-party regimes like Gabon and Ivory Coast, but those regimes did not defend a radical ideology. The formation of the Brazzaville-UAM group strengthened Ivory Coast's position in African affairs. Houphouët-Boigny's fundamental principles in interstate policies—that is, noninterference in each other's affairs and respect for national sovereignty—were legitimized at the conferences in Brazzaville, Monrovia, and Tananarive. These principles became acceptable to a large number of newly created African states.

In May 1963 the Addis Ababa (Ethiopia) Conference led to the establishment of the Organization of African Unity (OAU), which brought together the rival groups advocating opposite approaches to African questions. A common determination to promote understanding and cooperation among the African peoples while transcending ethnic and national differences was the primary goal of the OAU. Its members wanted to safeguard and consolidate their recently won independence as well as the sovereignty and territorial integrity of their countries.[20] Houphouët-Boigny's concept of noninterference in the internal affairs of states and their inalienable right to independent existence was adopted by the OAU charter. Houphouët and Nkrumah strongly condemned political assassination as well as subversive activities on the part of neighboring states or any other state. On that basis both leaders agreed that the independence of some separate states was meaningless unless all of Africa became free and united. They both condemned colonialism, neocolonialism, and racial discrimination. On the economic side, the members of the OAU wanted to establish self-sustained forms of development, as distinct from the socioeconomic structures inherited from the former colonial power. The significant outcome of the Addis Ababa summit was the compromise reached between the Casablanca and the Brazzaville-UAM states. It gave recognition to the national boundaries of the African states, which were originally determined by the colonial powers at the Congress of Berlin in 1884–85.[21]

With the establishment of the OAU it was expected that the various regional groups would voluntarily dissolve themselves. Indeed, in consideration of the OAU charter, the Casablanca group disintegrated. In May 1964 the Brazzaville-UAM group also announced its intention to dissolve the organization in response to the good example of the Casablanca group and in deference to the OAU charter. The UAM was never totally dissolved, however; its members continued their cooperation on economic, technical, and cultural matters through the *Union Africaine et Malgache de Coopération Économique* (UAMCE), which was constituted in Dakar in 1964 in order to take over some functions of the UAM. (The political and military objectives of the UAM were abandoned in response to the OAU charter.) Fourteen Francophone countries joined this organization (Cameroon, CAR, Congo-Brazzaville, Dahomey, Gabon, Ivory Coast, Madagascar, Mauritania, Niger, Rwanda, Senegal, Chad, Togo, Upper Volta); its headquarters was in Yaoundé (Cameroon). Considering the close association of France with the former UAM members, the transition from UAM to UAMCE did not infringe in any way on France's economic, technical, and cultural ties with the Francophone African countries.

At the meeting of heads of Francophone African states at Nouakchott (Mauritania) in February 1965, the decision was made to transform the UAMCE into a new organization to be known as the *Organisation Commune Africaine et Malgache* (OCAM). The subsequent regrouping of the mostly Francophone African states was made in the context of the OAU charter. In order to accelerate the development in the economic, social, technical, and cultural field, cooperation and solidarity among the member states were reinforced. The charter of the OCAM provided for three institutions: the conference of heads of state, the council of foreign ministers, and the secretariat, which was located in Yaoundé. It also adopted Houphouët-Boigny's long-standing principle of respect for sovereignty and noninterference in the internal affairs of African states, which—according to Houphouët—constituted the only guarantee for peace and development on the continent.[22] He further stated that economically, socially, culturally, and even politically the Francophone African states formed a homogeneous unit, clearly different from non-Francophone African states. When the conference participants deliberated not to participate in the 1965 conference of the OAU in Accra, Houphouët's preeminent position in the OCAM became evident. An important issue of interstate politics was at the base of this deliberation. Ghana was accused of encouraging subversive activities in neighboring states. It was alleged that the Ghanian government had a hand in the attempted murder of Niger's president, Hamani Diori, in April 1965. Through Houphouët's influence the OCAM states unanimously endorsed the resolution to condemn Ghanian subversive activities and to boycott the OAU Accra Conference.

A second important issue of interstate policies discussed by the conference participants was the question of admission of the Democratic Republic of the Congo to the OCAM. Tschombé's government was besieged by rebel forces that were supported by the radical African states. Moreover, it was alleged that the People's Republic of China was also supporting the anti-Tschombé movement. While upholding the principle of noninterference, Houphouët-Boigny condemned China and the radical African countries and suggested that the Democratic Republic of Congo be admitted to the OCAM.[23] Moktar Ould Daddah,[24] president of Mauritania and of the OCAM, was the only delegate to oppose Houphouët's proposal. After prolonged deliberations, the Democratic Republic of the Congo was admitted to the OCAM; Mauritania withdrew its membership. France had openly supported the admission of the Democratic Republic of the Congo to the OCAM and promised substantial aid to that state, especially for the reorganization of its administrative structure.

The formation of the OCAM assured the continuation of good economic and cultural relations between France and the members of the organization. This proved Houphouët's thesis that it was possible to maintain and consolidate a pan-Africanist position within a framework of interdependence between the *métropole* and its former colonies. Keeping the group of like-minded African states intact after a new regrouping gave Houphouët much prestige in France as well as in Francophone Africa. As a result of political fluctuations over the years, some Francophone African states have quit the OCAM, and others have joined it. When Mauritius joined the OCAM in 1970, it changed its name to *Organisation Commune Africaine, Malgache et Mauricienne;* after Madagascar withdrew its membership in 1973, it took on its present name: *Organisation Commune Africaine et Mauricienne* (OCAM).[25]

NOTES

1. The word *decolonization* has not found a favorable acceptance by Africans; it can be taken to imply that the initiatives for decolonization, as for colonization, were taken by the *métropole.* Consequently, Africans prefer to speak of their "struggle for liberation" or their "resumption of independence."

2. Samora Machel, *Establishing the People's Power to Serve the Masses* (Dar Es Salaam: Tanzania Publishing House, 1980), 6.   Machel became the first president of independent Mozambique in 1975.

3. René Dumont, *L'Afrique noire est mal partie* (Paris: Seuil, 1973), 68–71.

4. Maurice Ligot, *Les Accords de coopération entre la France et les états africains et malgache d'expression française* (Paris: la Documentation française, 1964), 27–48.

5. Guy Martin, "The Historical, Economic, and Political Bases of France's African Policy," *Modern African Studies,* 23 (1) (June 1985), 197–98.

6. Albert Bourgi, *La Politique française de coopération en Afrique: le cas du Sénégal* (Paris et Dakar: Bibliothèque africaine et malgache, 1979), 76–88.

7. Jean Touscoz, "La *Normalisation* de la coopération bilatérale de la France avec les pays africains francophones," *Études internationales,* no. 5 (June 1974), 208–25.

8. René Dumont and Marie-France Mottin, *L'Afrique étranglée* (Paris: Seuil, 1980), 19–22.

9. Kwame Nkrumah, *Neo-Colonialism: The Last Stage of Imperialism* (London: Heinemann, 1965), xiii, 14.

10. Nkrumah, *Neo-Colonialism,* 39–49.

11. Quoted by Colin Legum, *Pan-Africanism: A Short Political Guide* (New York: Praeger, 1965), 254.

12. Legum, 254.

13. Hella Pick, "The Brazzaville Twelve and How They Came to Be," *Africa Report* (Washington), 6 (5) (May 1961), 2.

14. Edward A. Kolodziej, *French International Policy Under de Gaulle and Pompidou: The Politics of Grandeur* (New York: Cornell University Press, 1974), 458--59.

15. Jean Ziegler, *Sociologie de la Nouvelle Afrique* (Paris: Gallimard, 1964), 208–10.

16. Kwame Nkrumah, *Africa Must Unite* (London: Banaf Books, 1970), 174–79.

17. Ernest Milcent and Monique Sordet, *Léopold Sédar Senghor et la naissance de l'Afrique moderne* (Paris: Seghers, 1969), 208.

18. John Marcum, "How Wide Is the Gap between Casablanca and Monrovia?" *Africa Report* (Washington), 7, (1) (Jan. 1962), 1–3.

19. Nkrumah, *Africa Must Unite*, 186–88.

20. At its twenty-seventh annual summit of African heads of state, held in Addis Ababa in 1990, the OAU welcomed Namibia as its fifty-first member. The major practical achievements of the OAU, some of which have had only temporary effect, have included mediation in the Algerian-Moroccan dispute (1964–65) and in the Somali-Ethiopian and Kenya-Somali border disputes (1965–67); efforts to mediate in the civil war in Nigeria (1968–70) proved ineffective. In the early 1980s the OAU attempted mediation to halt the civil war in Chad and proposed economic sanctions against South Africa to protest that country's policy of racial segregation.

21. Philippe Decraene, "Problèmes et tensions entre états d'Afrique noire," *Études internationales* (Quebec), vol. 4 (Dec. 1979), 13.

22. Mirlande Hippolyte, "De Nouakchott à Niamey: l'itinéraire de l'O.C.A.M.," *Revue française d'études politiques africaines* (Paris), no. 34 (Oct. 1968), 36–42.

23. Albert Mabileau and Jean Meyriat, *Décolonisation et régimes politiques en Afrique noire* (Paris: Presses de la Fondation nationale des sciences politiques, 1967), 70–73.

24. Moktar Ould Daddah became Mauritania's first president after independence in 1961. He was noted for his progress in unifying his biracial (Moor and Negro), widely dispersed, and partly nomadic people under his authoritarian but enlightened rule.

25. At this writing, the following ten states constitute the core of the OCAM: Benin, Burkina Faso, CAR, Ivory Coast, Mauritius, Niger, Rwanda, Senegal, Seychelles, and Togo.

7

General de Gaulle
and His Successors

GENERAL DE GAULLE'S AFRICAN POLICY

De Gaulle's conception of France was based upon French international stature. Stressing the concept of *grandeur* for France, he stated that France was not really itself unless it was in first rank and that only vast enterprises were capable of counterbalancing the ferments of disintegration in its people.[1] He opted to achieve his objectives by playing a leading role within the European Economic Community (EEC) and by further strengthening France's position in Africa. Undoubtedly he felt that he had a special role to play in the destiny of the African countries he had helped to create. There are at least four ingredients to this commitment:

1. an economic element that seeks reliable sources of crucial raw materials and growing markets for goods and investments;

2. a cultural element that emphasizes the common cultural and linguistic heritage of French-speaking societies;

3. a power element that allows France to compete with the other industrial powers;

4. a moral element that translates the experience gained during the colonial years into a sense of ongoing responsibility.[2]

These are Gaullist ideas, upheld by all of de Gaulle's successors and still deeply rooted in French-African policy today.

All Francophone black African states maintain a close association with France. These ties take many forms and are present at many levels. Some have been institutionalized, as in the financial framework of the Franc Zone or the bilateral cooperation agreements. But many other ties are not easily defined or identified, even if they are known to exist. These special relationships came into being during the last period of colonial rule under Charles de Gaulle. The general's strong personality and the way he related to the various African leaders are the core of these relationships. He was the incarnation of the father or godfather image: authoritarian but caring and dependable. Sékou Touré's decision to turn down de Gaulle's offer in the 1958 referendum resulted in punishment for him and for the Guinean people. The estrangement was to last for twenty years before the Guinean leader acknowledged an advantage in negotiating better relations with France. Houphouët-Boigny's continuous cooperation with the president, on the other hand, assured the Ivorian leader and his country a privileged position in Africa. When, however, Jean-Bédel Bokassa, leader of CAR, irritated de Gaulle with his continuous requests for favors, de Gaulle did ask him not to call him "mon cher papa" any longer.[3] The concept of role-playing became well established, each side being well aware of its duties and compensations. De Gaulle encouraged the Francophone African leaders to visit the *métropole* frequently, and they were assured red carpet treatment. Official and private visits of Francophone African heads of state to France and reciprocal visits by French presidents were so numerous that researchers on the relationship between France and Francophone Africa, such as Brigitte Nouaille-Degorce and Alfred Gross, compiled tables.[4] De Gaulle, as well as his three successors, firmly believed that the many aspects of policy in relation to Africa were best regulated by close and regular personal contacts on a kind of extended family principle. During de Gaulle's presidency, the immediate entourage of most Francophone African leaders included many Frenchmen in key positions—chiefs of cabinet, private secretaries, and bodyguards. The main members of this group were experienced colonial administrators who had known the countries they administered—and each other—for many years and were aware of all their relative strengths and weaknesses. Even confidential letters dictated by African leaders were often typed by French secretaries. Although the African leaders must have been aware of the fact that copies of these letters would find their way to the office of the secretary-general of African affairs in Paris, this was less objectionable than having sensitive letters taken care of by African personnel and risking indiscreet use of their content within the country. De Gaulle is known to have solved even personal family problems encountered by African leaders. This is the underlying meaning of belonging to the "club of the elite"—"de Gaulle's family." As in most families, occasional petty quarrels have marred relations between France and certain Francophone African leaders; however, France broke relations only with Guinea, and this rupture has now been mended. This kind of relationship provided a sense of security in a period of transition loaded with fear and stress in the face of the unknown.

In order to establish and carry on his personalized and often secretive relationships with the Francophone political leaders in Africa, de Gaulle chose Jacques Foccart as the first secretary-general of the community.[5] Foccart continued to carry out the African policies of France under Georges Pompidou (1969–74) and Valéry Giscard d'Estaing (1974–81). Foccart's genius lay in his ability to carry out de Gaulle's wishes faithfully; he became the embodiment of a special personalized style of Francophone relations. He established an elaborate network throughout Francophone Africa—an all-embracing system that solved even personal family problems encountered by the African elite. His network included informants throughout Francophone black Africa. These people were generally acquaintances from the days when Foccart worked in the import-export business. Facilitated by Foccart's former *Résistance* connections, the network was extended into the regular French police, military, and intelligence establishments.[6] This network distinguished itself by its longevity, continuity, steadfastness, and strict secrecy. It was especially designed for small countries in which a select, tightly knit group held all the strings of power and was willing to cooperate with the government of the *métropole*. Foccart's office controlled visits to France by African dignitaries and visits to Africa by French presidents; it prepared all important decision documents on issues involving Francophone black Africa and coordinated all presidential briefing. Foccart himself guided, or even made, most major decisions affecting Africa.[7] Thanks to his network of official, semiofficial, and unofficial contacts, little went on in Francophone Africa that Foccart was not quickly made aware of. With the exception of de Gaulle himself, no other Frenchman has left a greater imprint on France's relations with Francophone black Africa. According to Francis Terry McNamara, one of the U.S. Department of State's most experienced Africanists, the only near parallel in recent U.S. history to Foccart's dominance over African affairs in the French government was the power wielded by Henry Kissinger and his National Security Council staff during the Nixon administration.[8] Today, Foccart holds the most important place in the history of the postindependence evolution of Franco-African relations.

INSTITUTIONS SERVING FRANCE'S AFRICAN CONNECTIONS

Politically, de Gaulle could never think of the French republic without including the former dependencies in Africa. Therefore, the Fifth Republic's constitution provided for a close-knit community headed by the French president. In order to enable the smooth functioning of the community's governing body, made up of the heads of state of member countries, a secretariat was established. When the community was dissolved in 1960, this secretariat continued its function, probably because of de Gaulle's insistence on preserving presidential primacy in dealing with the former African dependencies. Important matters have often been discussed and also decided at the level of the heads of state. In 1961 the Ministry of Cooperation (*Ministère de la coopération et du développement*) was established to serve as the key link between the *Élysée* and the former African dependencies.[9] *Coopération* is a completely independent ministry that took over the nonpolitical responsibilities of the former Ministry of Overseas France *(Ministère d'outre-mer)*. It also manages the financial aid programs, both military and civilian, under the cooperation accords. Since the mandate of *coopération* has traditionally been limited almost exclusively to Francophone African states, these states have become accustomed to view *coopération* as their own ministry. When Mitterrand became president in May 1981, the independent status of *coopération* was threatened for the first time in its history. The socialist government called for its abolition, because it was viewed as representing all that was "neocolonial" about France's ties with Africa. It was supposed to be replaced with an agency along the lines of the U.S. Agency of International Development; however, Jean-Pierre Cot, minister of *coopération* from May 1981 to December 1982, did not want to go that far. He simply wanted to integrate *coopération* with foreign affairs under Claude Cheysson and extend French aid to other Third World countries, which is made clear in his book, *À l'épreuve du pouvoir,* published after he had left his ministry.[10] With Cot's departure from the ministry, however, the plan was never executed.

The office of the prime minister generally played a minor role in Francophone African affairs. The only exception was the period of *cohabitation* from May 1986 to May 1988, when Jacques Chirac was prime minister. Following legislative elections in March 1986, in which the right overtook the left and won a majority of seats in the National Assembly, France was faced with a situation unprecedented in the history of the Fifth Republic: a left-wing *Parti Socialiste* (PS) head of state, President François Mitterrand, who had reached only the fifth year of his seven-year term of office, and a right-wing head of government, Jacques Chirac, leader of the *Rassemblement pour la République* (RPR).[11] This political setup was called *cohabitation.* Throughout his two years in office, Chirac played a visible and active role in the conduct of relations with African countries; he paid several visits to heads of state in Africa. Breaking with past practice, he accompanied President Mitterrand to the Franco-African summit held in Lomé (Togo), in November 1986. In 1988, with the loss of power of the center-left coalition and the appointment of a center-left government under Prime Minister Michel Rocard, a moderate socialist, presidential dominance over African affairs returned.

The Ministry of Foreign Affairs *(Ministère des affaires étrangères)* has generally kept a low profile in Francophone African affairs, mainly because the former French dependencies have never been treated by the French as foreign countries. The *Quai d'Orsay,* however, has sometimes become involved peripherally in Francophone African questions, because of its leadership role in French relations with the rest of Africa.[12] The Ministry of Finance *(Ministère des finances)* becomes important in African affairs in time of economic difficulties. Levels and distributions of economic assistance, as well as the control of the vital monetary arrangements with African countries, are the responsibility of this ministry. It may impose economic reforms on certain African countries as a condition for the continued receipt of financial assistance and debt relief.

Sometimes it must impose discreet monetary discipline on certain squandering African heads of state without giving the impression of infringement on sovereignty.

The Ministry of Defense *(Ministère de la défense)* has regularly been involved in African affairs. The continued presence of French troops and the substantial additional outlays for military bases in many African countries under the cooperation agreements make this department important in decision-making policies for Francophone Africa. The ministry's budget also pays for the rapid deployment forces stationed in southern France, ready to intervene in Africa.

A few technical ministries are occasionally consulted on issues of African policy; however, they have no decision-making power but are consulted only on questions pertaining to their areas of specialization. Such ministries include education, agriculture, and transportation.

POMPIDOU AND GISCARD'S AFRICAN POLICIES

De Gaulle's two immediate successors, Georges Pompidou and Valéry Giscard d'Estaing, brought no structural change in French policy toward African countries. They functioned, to a large extent, within a Gaullist framework, making only minor changes. The foundation that de Gaulle established in his policy toward Francophone Africa has proven useful to his successors in expanding the French sphere of influence in other areas of Africa such as Zaïre, Rwanda, Burundi, and Seychelles.

In April 1969 de Gaulle unexpectedly left the presidency. Alain Poher, president of the Senate, assumed the interim presidency of the republic. Due to political expediency, Foccart was dismissed; however, his influence in the Gaullist party and in African affairs was too well established to be ignored by the new president. In addition, several African heads of state pressed Pompidou to restore Foccart to his former position, and Pompidou had no interest in the day-to-day routines of French relations with the Francophone African countries, so Foccart returned to the *Élysée* for the whole period of Pompidou's presidency. During that time, French activities continued to focus on the more prosperous Francophone African countries. The family circle was enlarged to include the Francophone former Belgian dependencies of Zaïre, Burundi, and Rwanda. Certain charter members of the Francophone family resented and even resisted this increase of their membership on grounds that it reduced the closeness of relationships with France and with each other.

President Valéry Giscard d'Estaing continued the Gaullist tradition of treating the formulation and execution of African policy as a presidential *domaine réservé*. In a televised interview he stated, "I am dealing with African affairs, namely with France's interests in Africa."[13] When Giscard d'Estaing became president in May 1974, Foccart left the *Élysée* and was replaced by his former assistant for African affairs, René Journiac.[14] At the same time the General

Secretariat for African Affairs was suppressed by President Giscard. Foccart's disappearance from the *Élysée* constituted no change in the preeminence of the presidency regarding relations with Francophone black Africa. Indeed, Giscard took a much more personal interest in the conduct of relations with Africa than did his two predecessors; he was also faster to intervene militarily. In May 1978 he quickly initiated the repelling of a rebel invasion of Zaïre's vital Shaba Province (former Katanga) by flying in troops from France ahead of those from Belgium and Morocco. Four months later he sent a unit of paratroopers to Bangui to effect Bokassa's removal from power. These interventions were strongly condemned by Giscard's opposition as interference in the affairs of a foreign country.

Giscard made several official trips to Francophone Africa. On his first one in 1975, he visited President Bokassa of CAR and President Sese Seko Mobutu of Zaïre. The French president thus violated the African tradition of respect for age and seniority; he should have visited Houphouët-Boigny and Senghor first. In Zaïre, Giscard revived an old French interest in the country's mineral riches. Mobutu welcomed the visit as it strengthened the legitimacy of his regime and increased his chances of receiving French assistance.[15] He also welcomed membership in the Franco-African family; as an adopted cousin, he has since participated in all of the group's annual summit meetings. In January 1978 Giscard visited Ivory Coast, taking the opportunity to revive proposals for an Afro-European solidarity pact and a pan-African intervention force. Both were supported by President Houphouët-Boigny. At the sixth Franco-African summit conference in Kigali (Rwanda) in May 1979, Giscard suggested the establishment of a new element in France's African policy, that is, a "trilogue" among Europe, Africa, and the oil-producing Arab countries. This policy envisaged developing Africa's economic resources by matching European technical skills with Arab finance. Giscard's most important African visit was the one he paid to Guinea in December 1978. Guinea's reconciliation with its neighbors had been formally endorsed in May 1978 in Monrovia (Liberia), when President Sékou Touré met the presidents of Ivory Coast, Senegal, Gambia, and Togo at a "unity summit," with Liberia's president acting as host. The official reconciliation between Guinea and Ivory Coast was translated into concrete terms with the establishment of normal diplomatic relations and the signing of a treaty of friendship between the two countries. Giscard's visit to Conakry (capital of Guinea) marked the resumption of cooperation between the two countries after twenty years of estrangement. Sékou Touré was welcomed back to the "family" in a lavish state visit to Paris. Critics pointed out that such a welcome was inappropriate in light of the brutality of the Guinean regime and its long Marxist associations.

In 1973 Georges Pompidou began the series of heads of state meetings, known as Franco-African summits, which take place in May either in France or in an African capital.[16] Other African countries have occasionally joined this unique system and become members of the Francophone family. Particularly notable among them are the former Belgian colonies Zaïre, Rwanda, and Burundi; the former Portuguese colonies Guinea Bissau, Cape Verde, São Tomé, and Mozambique; the former British colonies Sierra Leone, Mauritius, Seychelles, and Somalia; the former Spanish colony Equatorial Guinea. Such expansion involves risks. One, for example, is the challenge such action represents to the OAU; another is the antagonism that might be provoked among would-be African powers, particularly Nigeria and Zaïre, whose leaders and intellectuals sometimes seem to regard their own country as the nucleus for expansion.

As was mentioned earlier, Giscard had visited Zaïre's President Mobutu and CAR's President Bokassa during his first official trip to Africa. This was the beginning of a special friendship among the three statesmen that ultimately contributed to Giscard's defeat in the presidential election in 1981. In October 1979 the French satirical weekly, *Le Canard enchaîné*, revealed that Giscard had accepted presents of diamonds from Bokassa, both as minister of finance and as president. Giscard apparently did not deny receiving such gifts; he only questioned their alleged value. *Le Canard enchaîné* later revealed that two of the president's cousins had also received gifts from Bokassa. Giscard's personal involvement in removing Bokassa from power in 1979 was politically especially damaging. In a French diplomat's words, Giscard was a statesman who, by character and temperament, was very remote from Africa but who yielded to its charms, finding there a kind of counterweight to the intellectualism and analytic spirit that were dominant in his personality.[17]

FRANÇOIS MITTERRAND'S AFRICAN POLICIES

When socialist president François Mitterrand took office in May 1981, the news media announced the possibility of major changes in French attitudes toward Africa. In fact, the election manifesto of the French Socialist party had placed an emphasis on establishing a new and closer rapport with African countries on a more integrated, egalitarian basis, devoid of nationalist and racist distinctions or elements of metropolitan exploitation.

Mitterrand was experienced in Francophone African affairs. His personal relations with many African leaders, particularly those with the senior leaders Houphouët-Boigny and Senghor, went back a long way. It was Mitterrand who persuaded Houphouët in 1951 to break with the Communist party and to join the UDSR in the French National Assembly (see Chapter 3). During several of the short-lived governments of the Fourth Republic, Mitterrand was minister for overseas France.

It was commonly assumed that, once in power, the socialists would try to carry out the preelection threats so frequently expressed by party spokesmen. Indeed, many high French officials were replaced. Jean-Pierre Cot, a strong socialist advocate of human equality and anticolonialism, was appointed as

Mitterrand's first minister for cooperation and development. Cot was a *tiers-mondiste* (Third-Worldist); this term has a special meaning in France, because it implies not only supporting aid to Third World countries but also diminishing aid to Francophone Africa. He called for "moralization" of aid programs by being less conniving with African heads of state. While Cot was determined to change the system of privileged personal relationships between French officials and African heads of state, he was aware that the privileged status of Francophone Africa had to be maintained because France depended on good relations for economic and political reasons.[18] The change in government in the *métropole* caused some mixed feelings in Africa. On one hand, many of the Africans who were in political opposition with their regimes expected the new French government to implement its socialist ideology. They wanted to see an end to a diplomacy dependent upon personal acquaintances, blurring the line between personal and official obligations; loyalty to friends can take precedence over, or become confused with, the impersonal imperatives of foreign policy making. Especially the young educated elite expected political liberalization and acceleration of the retirement of an older political generation perceived as corrupt and highly submissive to France. In the *métropole*, too, certain socialist spokesmen described African leaders like Houphouët, Bongo, and Ahidjo as corrupt and repressive. The young African elite saw Mitterrand's advent to power as spelling the end of Gaullist policies of intervention in Africa and as promising more constructive Franco-African cooperation. On the other hand, solidly established power elites in many former French dependencies were alarmed. They feared that the socialists, once in power, would support radical political change and reduce French aid to traditional recipients in Francophone Africa. They saw an end to the traditional close relations of the African leaders with the *Élysée*. Since preindependence days most of the Francophone African leaders had enjoyed close relations with a variety of French senior political figures. These Frenchmen were conservatives; many of them had business interests in Francophone Africa. Thus, the new political regime in France appeared as a dangerous omen to the traditional members of the family.[19]

As soon as Cot took office, he publicly declared opposition to the personalized relationships with a few traditional political leaders in the Francophone African countries. In addition, French aid would no longer go almost exclusively to the former French dependencies; it would be distributed throughout the Third World. Such a broadening of the number of recipients would drastically reduce the share received by the traditional inner-core members. There was, however, disagreement right from the beginning among the new government's African policymakers. Guy Penne, the president's personal counselor for African affairs, did not share Cot's point of view. He accommodated the African leaders who made it clear to him that France, too, enjoyed substantial advantages from its privileged Francophone African connections; these benefits depended on reciprocity. Soon Penne emerged as the voice of the status quo—the "realistic" view of Africa. As a longtime political associate and old friend, the president trusted him. From the beginning, Penne's profile has been more open than that of his predecessors; he spoke to journalists frequently, something his predecessors, above all Foccart, would seldom do. He had no previous experience in African affairs, which was interpreted as a sign of reduced direct presidential interest in Francophone Africa. Penne was also known as a Freemason, with widespread connections to Freemasonry in France and Africa. Since the presence of Freemasonry was considerable in the inner core of Francophone African countries, Penne's connections may have appeared attractive to Mitterrand as an instrument to facilitate the establishment of his own personalized network in Francophone Africa.[20] In the summer of 1982 Penne took Jean-Christophe Mitterrand, son of the president, on his staff as deputy African adviser. This decision shows clearly how Francophone African affairs are truly family affairs. Among his qualifications for the position was the fact that he had worked as a correspondent for *Agence France Presse* in Africa and thus knew many African leaders personally. Having the president's son at *coopération* was welcomed by most traditional Francophone African heads of state; it facilitated their access to the president. Jean-Christophe's appointment was naturally seen as confirming the president's fidelity to the tradition of informal diplomacy in Franco-African relations.

Cot described his job in quite mundane terms as being concerned with "copinage des présidents et la fin du mois" (keeping presidents happy and getting civil servants paid).[21] His attempt to modify the functional and geographical competence of *coopération* met with resounding failure. His forced resignation in December 1982 was brought about mostly by certain Francophone African heads of state and by a coalition, made up of rival bureaucracies, all of whom had particular reasons for feeling threatened by Cot's proposed reforms. His removal from office was further ascribed to the ascendancy of a more cautious presidency and the declining influence of the Socialist party in policy making with regard to Francophone Africa. In addition, recession hit the French economy especially hard in 1981. Mitterrand soon realized that he could not afford the risk of trading solid privileged economic relations in Francophone Africa for Third World ideals. Cot was replaced at *coopération* by Christian Nucci, a reassuring and close political ally of Mitterrand. Cot can be considered the symbol of the Socialist party's contribution to African policy decisions. He was the architect of an expanded role for *coopération* and a devout advocate of human rights. He ran into conflict, however, with the traditional supremacy of the *Élysée* in the formulation of African policies. He also encountered difficulties in his cooperation with Penne. For instance, in 1982 he objected to the presence of Penne in Gabon when Gabonese dissidents were on trial. With Cot's departure, the team of progressive young people he had hired at *coopération* soon disappeared.[22] When Nucci took office, he stated that the president would make all major decisions involving Africa and that Penne would take care of most policy-level contacts with the Francophone African heads of state. Nucci is now best remembered for the *carrefour du développement* scandal, which broke out after he left office in 1986. This scandal concerned funds that were missing in connection with the Franco-African summit in Burundi in 1984. The affair dragged on in the French courts for several years.[23] This damages not only Nucci's reputation but also the one of *coopération* and of the Franco-African summit, the apex of the Franco-African family relationship. It also proves that the members of the socialist government are not immune from the kind of obscure dealings in Francophone Africa that were denounced during their election campaign. Furthermore, the scandal drew attention to the fact that by hosting these summits, the African countries were able to renovate and redecorate the public buildings of their capital at the expense of the French taxpayer. Critics pointed out that this was part of the traditional practice of *dosage,* whereby a certain percentage of aid money goes directly to African heads of state to make sure that they cooperate with France.[24]

With the consolidation of *Élysée's* leading role in the formulation of African policy decisions, Mitterrand has, in his own way, adopted the Gaullist philosophy of close personal links with Francophone African leaders. He was able to mend much of the damage done to traditional African relationships during Cot's tenure. Mitterrand upheld the tradition of close relations with friends in Ivory Coast, Senegal, Niger, Mauritania, Rwanda, Burundi, Zaïre, and Congo. He visited all these countries in two extensive trips in May and October 1982, a few months after he took office. In January 1983 he visited Benin; this was the first visit by a French president since the country achieved independence in 1960.

From mid-1982 until the formation of Chirac's government in 1986, Mitterrand's personal decision-making process in Francophone African relations continued. During a state visit to Gabon in January 1983, Mitterrand stated: "It is I who determines France's foreign policy, not my ministers. . . . The ministers are permitted to think or to have an opinion. . . . It is inconceivable that a policy could be implemented without my consent, more exactly, without my impetus."[25] Some of Mitterrand's initiatives, especially those concerning the Chadian crises in 1982 and 1983–84, have inevitably caused criticism in socialist ranks. The fundamental contradiction faced by Mitterrand is that as leader of a socialist government, he is inextricably tied to a capitalist international economic environment. He was most severely criticized by his own party, however, for maintaining the personal, manipulative relations with Francophone Africa practiced under his three predecessors. In his book, *Réflexions sur la politique extérieure de la France,* published at the beginning of 1986, Mitterrand expressed his ideas of national independence, the creation of a strong Europe, and the continuation of close ties with the Francophone African countries in a purely Gaullist tradition.[26] Like his predecessors, he perceived France's former dependencies in Africa as *le pré carré francophone,* meaning a French-speaking territory that must be maintained as such and as a natural preserve of France, off-limits to other foreign powers.

With the election of a center-right majority to the National Assembly and the appointment of Jacques Chirac as the new prime minister in March 1986,

President Mitterrand's tightly organized control of Francophone African policy making was interrupted. To avoid the risk of a mutually embarrassing break-down in the conduct of Francophone African affairs, the president took the views of the neo-Gaullist prime minister into consideration. In April 1986, to the astonishment of many in France and Africa, Jacques Foccart was appointed by Chirac as his adviser on African affairs. This was another strong indication that Chirac intended to play an active role in an area previously reserved to the president. As head of *coopération,* Penne was replaced by an independent-minded Gaullist, Michel Aurillac. Under Aurillac's guidance and direction, Michel Guillou wrote a new African policy guide that reflects the continuation of a Gaullist approach to Africa.[27] According to this guide, Francophone Africa, particularly its traditional core countries of Ivory Coast, Senegal, Gabon, Cameroon, and Togo, was again to become the principal beneficiary of French aid. Because of France's difficult economic situation, alternative sources for development financing were encouraged. The World Bank, the International Monetary Fund (IMF), and private parties were appealed to for assistance in coping with the severe economic crises in several of the Francophone black African countries. In spite of Chirac's own ambitions to become president of the republic, there were quiet cooperation and little dissent on African policies throughout the period of *cohabitation.* There were, however, a certain immobility and incoherence in African affairs that developed as a result of *cohabitation,* but Francophone African leaders continued to enjoy support in the *métropole,* reaching across party lines. Their main complaint was that *cohabitation* meant too many contact persons at *coopération* and greater difficulty in knowing who really wielded influence in Paris.

With the reelection of Mitterrand as president of the republic and Chirac's loss of the prime ministry in June 1988, *cohabitation* came to an end; presidential predominance over French relations with Francophone Africa returned. With Chirac's exit, Jacques Foccart's days of power and glory ended. Under the government of moderate socialist prime minister Michel Rocard, the more open attitude of Chirac's African policy continued. Jacques Pelletier, a nonsocialist and longtime adherent of the center in French politics and with personal ties to the president, was appointed minister of *coopération,* possibly in response to demands by the large group of politicians who advocated the continuation of the moderate African policy that prevailed under Chirac. Lacking experience in African affairs, Pelletier came to the post without prejudices. Recognizing that France's budgetary constraints made it impossible for it to deal with Francophone Africa's economic development alone, he was willing to involve bilateral, multilateral, and private resources.[28] The concept of *le pré carré francophone* was thus put in jeopardy as foreign powers were undoubtedly not willing to provide aid without having a decision-making voice. During a press conference in July 1988, Pelletier outlined a course of action for his staff. The main preoccupation of *coopération* was to be the affirmation of human rights and the promotion of democracy in the Francophone African countries. He denounced intolerance, segregation, and all forms of dictatorship and was critical of those industrialized countries that consider Africa as a trash can for their toxic waste products.[29]

At the Franco-African summit in La Baule in June 1990, Mitterrand declared that France alone was no longer in a position to stop the current economic decline in Francophone Africa; a worldwide effort was needed to bail out the poor nations on the continent. He called for the establishment of a special international fund to help the African countries.[30] To exemplify France's concern, he announced that the French government would in the future donate, rather than lend, money to the world's thirty-five poorest countries, including twenty-two in Subsaharan Africa; it would introduce new debt-forgiveness programs for countries that had shown progress toward democracy; it would also reduce the interest rate paid on French loans by four African countries from 10 to 5 percent. (Mitterrand did not mention these four countries by name; according to the *Journal Officiel,* they are Cameroon, Congo, Gabon, and Ivory Coast.[31]) In the future French aid would flow more readily to those countries that take steps toward democracy.[32] This indicates a new stance regarding economic, political, and military support to its former dependencies.[33] Mitterrand recognizes the difficulties of establishing democratic governments in destitute African countries that are so different in social structure, civilization, tradition, and habits, but his concept of democracy includes free elections, multiparty systems, freedom of the press, and an independent judiciary. He praised those African heads of state who had announced plans to create multiparty states, among them Omar Bongo (Gabon), Nicéphore Soglo (Benin), Félix Houphouët-Boigny (Ivory Coast), and General Denis Sassou-Nguesso (Congo). The president also stated that French troops would continue to help countries facing external threats; however, he emphasized that France would not intervene in internal conflicts.

Mitterrand's address fell short of satisfying domestic critics who had called on the socialist government to elicit commitment for adoption of democratic principles and human rights in the Francophone African countries still governed by dictators of single political parties. These critics accused Mitterrand of showing no interest in changing African policies that were established by de Gaulle over three decades ago. Some African political exiles asserted that France was still sustaining a number of African dictators with financial and political support and at times through military interventions and that the French government was ignoring large-scale embezzlements by African heads of state of development sources paid for by French taxpayers.

During her 323 days as France's first female prime minister, Édith Cresson kept a low profile on the government's African policies. Because of the Socialist party's precipitous drop in popularity during the regional elections of March 22, 1992, President Mitterrand demanded her resignation and replaced her with Pierre Bérégovoy. After the April 1993 elections, Bérégovoy was replaced by Édouard Balladur, former *chef d'État* under the Jacques Chirac government.[34] During his inaugural address held before the National Assembly on April 8,

1993, Balladur outlined the general course of his policy, expressing "solidarity" with the African nations.[35] Under the present *cohabitation,* Francophone black Africa will probably continue to be the most important geographic focus of French assistance and cooperation programs.

The collapse of communism in Eastern Europe has given a certain impetus to demands for freedom and democracy in African countries. The crucial questions are whether democracy can really take root in Africa and what the Africans mean by freedom.[36] The obvious first step in the direction of democracy is the transition from a partyless or single-party to a multiparty political system.[37] This is difficult to achieve since many heads of state have no experience with pluralism; the notion of fair opposition is alien to them. Opponents are perceived as enemies, not rivals. Furthermore, since the tribe is often their only basis of allegiance, they have difficulty accepting a multiplicity of political opinions. The problem is intensified by the often volatile ethnic mix of African states. Ethnic rivalry anywhere can lead to chaos.[38] As we have seen in previous chapters, colonial powers imposed a political map on Africa that made little sense to the people who live there. A typical example is Benin, a nation of 4.6 million that contains about thirty different ethnic groups, speaking their own dialect or language, superimposed by Moslem, Christian, and traditional animistic beliefs. Under these conditions democracy has a hard time to take root. Indeed, nothing was going right in Benin at the outset of 1990. The government could no longer pay its civil servants; workers and teachers were regularly on strike. Schools had been closed for most of the year. All three national banks had collapsed. In February 1990, in a commendable democratic move, President Mathieu Kérékou, who had seized power in 1972 and two years later declared Benin a Marxist-Leninist state, assembled the nation's top professional and academic people and asked them to find a way out of the desperate situation. The conferees responded with what amounted to a civilian coup d'état.[39] They persuaded Kérékou to relinquish most of his powers and to allow Nicéphore Soglo, a former World Bank executive director, to head a transitional government as prime minister. In March 1991 Soglo defeated Kérékou in a race for the presidency. Thus Benin became the first mainland African country in the postcolonial era to oust a discredited ruler in free elections.[40] Shortly after these events, national leadership conferences modeled on the one of Benin were held in Lomé (Togo), Brazzaville (Congo), and Niamey (Niger). The scenario of political events in these three countries has been the same: (1) organization of a national leadership conference; (2) revision of the constitution with establishment of a multiparty system; (3) multiparty elections; (4) nomination by the president of a prime minister with a moderate political record.[41] In March 1991 President Moussa Traoré of Mali was arrested by a group of military officers. This group called for a *Conseil de réconciliation national,* a national leadership conference also modeled on the one of Benin.[42] Thus tiny Benin has become something of a showcase for democratic change in Africa. In Senegal, Ivory Coast, and Cameroon, the government has adopted a multiparty system, yet opposition candidates have never captured power from the leaders of entrenched ruling parties. These states have a de jure multiparty system but a de facto single-party system.[43] In Mauritania, during his inauguration speech, President Maaouya Ould Sidi Ahmed Taya announced that his country would soon form a real Islamic democratic regime. Since then an opposition party, the *Union des Forces Démocratiques* (UFD), has been allowed to form and take an active part in the political process.[44]

For democracy to work in Africa, it is, first of all, necessary that the industrialized countries acknowledge contribution to the present desperate situation in Africa and express their willingness to help. The most obvious place to start is to reduce or eliminate the continent's crippling debt. By 1990 the Subsaharan African countries owed U.S. $161 billion—112 percent of the entire region's annual economic output. While this debt gives Western countries leverage to spur political and economic liberalization, it could also doom Africa's democratic experiment to failure if the burden is not lifted. Mitterrand has taken some positive steps in this direction, but much more needs to be done. Democratization in Africa is a long process that may take decades and a lot of patience.[45] Africa's leaders are aware that there may be occasional setbacks in this process. The price to be paid may in some cases be short-term turmoil, but the alternative, keeping the single-party elite in power—de facto or de jure—will inevitably lead to revolution.[46]

NOTES

1. Quoted in Edward A. Kolodziej, *French International Policy Under de Gaulle and Pompidou: The Politics of Grandeur* (New York: Cornell University Press, 1974), 37.

2. Considering the present relations of other European powers with their former African dependencies, only the economic element has been maintained. This also holds for the United Kingdom, which might have been expected to have views similar to France's.

3. Jean-Bédel Bokassa, a soldier during World War II in the French army and later promoted to colonel, became president of CAR in 1966, when he overthrew his cousin David Dacko. Bokassa's regime was increasingly repressive. In 1976 he dissolved the country's government and declared a parliamentary monarchy. The following year he crowned himself Emperor Bokassa I. His rule ended in 1979 in a coup that reestablished the republic and reinstated David Dacko as its president.

4. Brigitte Nouaille-Degorce, *La Politique française de coopération avec les états africain et malgache au sud du Sahara, 1958–1978* (Bordeaux: Centre d'étude d'Afrique noire, Institut d'études politiques, 1982), 463-65; Alfred Grosser, *Affaires extérieures: la politique de la France, 1944–1984* (Paris: Flammarion, 1984), 176.

5. Jacques Foccart entered the import-export business at the age of twenty-two. During the German occupation he joined the *Résistance* and began training for missions behind enemy lines. After the war he briefly continued his work in the

import-export business. Due to his deep attachment to General de Gaulle, coupled with an excellent war record, he was appointed to organize what later became the Gaullist party, the *Rassemblement du Peuple Français* (RPF). From here on he became a leading figure in the organization of Gaullist policies. In 1953 he was chosen treasurer-general of the RPF. In this position he began his lifelong preoccupation with Francophone Africa. After de Gaulle returned to power in 1958, Foccart was named secretary-general of the French Community in 1960. During the Algerian war he organized a network of secret army groups *(les barbouzes)* to fight the outlawed *Organisation de l'Armée Secrète* (OAS).

6. On Foccart's role, see Samy Cohen, *Les Conseilleurs du président: de Charles de Gaulle à Valéry Giscard d'Estaing* (Paris: PUF, 1980), 146–69.

7. Pierre Biarnes, *Les Français en Afrique noire de Richelieu à Mitterrand* (Paris: Colin, 1987), 361–64.

8. Francis Terry McNamara, *France in Black Africa* (Washington, DC: National Defense University, 1989), 189.

9. *L'Élysée* is the official residence of the president of the republic.

10. Jean-Pierre Cot, *À l'épreuve du pouvoir: le tiers-mondisme, pour quoi faire?* (Paris: Seuil, 1984), 203. Cheysson had been pivotal in drafting the EEC's Lomé Convention and was seen as sympathetic to the need for a new line in Franco-African policy, particularly in view of ongoing criticism of Giscard's policy in Subsaharan Africa.

11. Jacques René Chirac, in the early 1960s, was the protégé of the Gaullist prime minister (later president) Georges Pompidou. He was first elected to the National Assembly in 1967, and from here on he advanced quickly. When Pompidou died in 1974, Chirac took advantage of a new opportunity to further his career by supporting Valéry Giscard d'Estaing's candidacy for the presidency. Chirac was rewarded by the successful Giscard with the appointment of prime minister in 1974. He resigned that position in 1976 and formed the RPR, which replaced the *Union des Démocrates pour la République* (UDR). In 1977 he was elected mayor of Paris. When the 1988 elections renewed the mandate for socialist president François Mitterrand for a second seven-year term, *cohabitation* came to an end. Chirac resigned his position in May 1988.

12. The *Quai d'Orsay* is the headquarters of the *Ministère des affaires étrangères*.

13. Jacques Amalric, "L'Entretien télévisé du chef d'État: j'exclus le retour à l'OTAN et le retour au colonialisme," *Le Monde,* Jan. 29, 1981, 17 (author's translation).

14. René Journiac was a member of the *Résistance* during World War II. After the war he served as a magistrate in Cameroon before joining the staff of future president Georges Pompidou. In 1967 he was appointed to the General Secretariat for African Affairs under the direction of Foccart. Journiac was actively involved in negotiations over France's involvement in Chad and in arranging the deposition of Emperor Bokassa I of the Central African Empire in 1979.

15. Sese Seko Mobutu began his career in 1949 in the Belgian Congolese army *(Force publique)* as a clerk in its finance department. After his discharge in 1956 he became a reporter and met Congolese nationalist leader Patrice Lumumba through his press contacts and joined Lumumba's party, the *Mouvement National Congolais* (MNC). At Congo's independence in June 1960, the coalition government of President Joseph Kasavubu and Premier Lumumba appointed Mobutu chief of staff of

the *Force publique*. In 1965 Mobutu ousted Kasavubu in a coup and assumed the presidency. He re-established the authority of the central government and succeeded in restoring the Congolese economy to preindependence levels of production. He holds ultimate legislative, executive, and military power in the nation. In 1971 he moved to Africanize names in the nation; the name of the country was changed in October 1971 from Democratic Republic of the Congo to Republic of Zaïre.

16. Jean-Luc Dagut, "Les Sommets franco-africains: un instrument de la présence française en Afrique," in *Année africaine 1980* (Bordeaux: Centre d'étude d'Afrique noire, 1981), 304–25.

17. Jean-Luc Dagut, "L'Afrique, la France et le monde dans le discours giscardien," *Politique africaine* (Paris), 2 (5) (Feb. 1982), 19–27.

18. Cot, 121–27.

19. Pierre Favier and Michel Martin-Roland, *La Décennie Mitterrand: les ruptures,* Vol. 1 (Paris: Seuil, 1990), 321–61.

20. "Freemasonry: The French Connection," *Africa Confidential* (London), 28 (2) (May 27, 1987), 1–2.

21. Kaye Whiteman, "President Mitterrand and Africa," *African Affairs* (Oxford, England), 82 (1983), 336.

22. Jean-Pierre Cot was offered a sidetrack position as ambassador in Madrid by Prime Minister Pierre Mauroy; however, he refused the offer and returned to his professorship at the Law School of the University of Paris.

23. Maurice Peyrot, "L'Affaire 'carrefour du développement' devant la cour d'assises de Paris: M. Christian Nucci au banc des victimes," *Le Monde,* Mar. 25, 1992, 18e.

24. For a typical radical critique of Franco-African policy, see Guy Martin, "Les Fondements historiques, économiques et politiques de la politique africaine de la France: du colonialisme au néo-colonialisme," *Genève-Afrique,* 21 (2) (1983), 39–68.

25. Jean-François Bayart, *La Politique africaine de François Mitterrand* (Paris: Karthala, 1984), 48 (author's translation).

26. François Mitterrand, *Réflexions sur la politique extérieure de la France: introduction à vingt-cinq discours (1981–1985)* (Paris: Fayard, 1986).

27. Michel Guillou, *Une Politique africaine pour la France* (Paris: Albatros, 1985).

28. Eric Fottorino, "Le Gouvernement encourage les sociétés françaises à investir en Afrique," *Le Monde,* Feb. 23, 1990, 30a.

29. "Politique africaine de la France: les orientations de M. Pelletier, nouveau ministre de la coopération," *Le Monde,* July 9, 1988, 4a.

30. At the meeting of European Community leaders in July 1990 and at the economic summit of the world's seven leading industrialized powers in August 1990, Mitterrand reiterated his request for a special international fund for Africa.

31. "Coopération française en direction de l'Afrique, ses différentes formes, recherches de complémentarités," Étude présentée par la Section des relations extérieures, Avis et rapports du Conseil économique et social, *Journal Officiel de la République française* (Paris), 4 (Mar. 8, 1991), 43–44.

32. Jacques de Barrin, "Le Sommet franco-africain de La Baule: M. Mitterrand lie l'octroi de l'aide française aux efforts de démocratisation," *Le Monde,* June 22, 1990, 3a; "Fronde africaine," *Le Monde,* June 23, 1990, 1a.

33. As leader of the socialist bloc in the European Parliament, Jean-Pierre Cot, former minister of *coopération*, stated that the French government should at least set conditions for all its aid to African countries.

34. Édouard Balladur is the seventh prime minister of François Mitterrand's presidency.

35. Jean-Louis Saux, "M. Balladur a appelé les Français à un grand effort de redressement, de rassemblement et de tolérance," *Le Monde,* sélection hebdomadaire, Apr. 15, 1993, 6.

36. Jean-Pierre Langellier and Catherine Simon, "La France n'entend pas 'donner des leçons' à l'Afrique," *Le Monde,* Mar. 22, 1992, 1b, 5.

37. *Rapport Annuel Mondial sur le Système Économique et les Stratégies (RAMSES) 1992,* Institut français de relations internationales, Thierry de Montbrial, ed. (Paris: Dunod, 1991), 37–38.

38. Catherine Simon, "Afrique: la démocratie à tâtons; des élections libres auront lieu cette année dans une vingtaine de pays mais les régimes en place s'accrochent au pouvoir," *Le Monde,* Apr. 25, 1992, 1a, 6.

39. "Démocratie et développement au Sud," *Problèmes économiques* (Paris: la Documentation française), 2.266 (Mar. 11, 1992), 1.

40. Catherine Simon, "Les Balbutiements du multipartisme en Afrique," *Le Monde,* Mar. 13, 1991, 1b, 6.

41. Catherine Simon, "Un Nouvel Acteur: le premier ministre . . . ," *Le Monde,* June 8, 1991, 4c.

42. "Après quatre jours d'émeutes violemment réprimées, l'armée a pris le pouvoir au Mali et arrêté le président Traoré," *Le Monde,* Mar. 27, 1991, 1a, 2.

43. Eric Fottorino, "Les Syndicats africains ont du mal à rompre leurs liens avec le pouvoir," *Le Monde,* Aug. 7, 1991, 13b.

44. Jacques de Barrin, "Passage d'un régime militaire à une démocratie 'islamique': les intégristes en terre de mission," *Le Monde,* Apr. 18, 1992, 6a.

45. Marie-Pierre Subtil, "Les Déçus de la démocratie au Mali: un an après le renversement du président Moussa Traoré, tous les problèmes—chômage, rébellion touareg, etc.—demeurent sans solution, *Le Monde,* Mar. 25, 1992, 6a.

46. Jean-François Bayart, Directeur du Centre d'Études et de Recherches Internationales (Fondation Nationale des Sciences Politiques), "L'Afrique entre guerre et démocratie," conférence-débat, Avignon (France), June 15, 1992.

8

Cultural Considerations

The publications regarding postliberation French African policy deal almost exclusively with neocolonialism, economics, politics, and military matters. To the cultural component they give only minor importance; many works do not even mention it. The strong cultural ties between Francophone African countries and France, made even more conspicuous by the use of French as the official language, actually form the basis on which all other components of French presence in Africa are based.[1] There is no doubt that culture represents an essential and integral part of any country's diplomacy. In a study commissioned by the *Ministère des affaires étrangères,* Jacques Rigaud expressed this idea as follows: "Along with politics and economics, culture—in the broadest sense of the term—is one of the components of international relations."[2] The Cultural Affairs Division of the Ministry of Foreign Affairs is even more explicit in emphasizing the importance of culture in international relations: "Culture is intimately linked to economics and politics . . . . It contributes directly to the power of our country on the international level."[3] Jean-Pierre Cot, former minister of *coopération,* shares this opinion: "There is no sector to which French cooperation is more attached than that of culture. The promotion and the dissemination of our language, the propagation of our ideas, of our art and, more recently, of our technical knowledge, have always been our most important preoccupation."[4] This emphasis given to French language and culture reflects an authentic, long-standing commitment of the French people to a *mission civilisatrice.* French pride in their culture, coupled with an accompanying assumption of cultural superiority, explains to a large extent the French colonialist policy of assimilation that was aimed at Frenchifying their subjects. In his report for the Commission on Studies of Cooperation with Underdeveloped Countries of 1963, Jean-Marcel Jeanneney stated that more than any other nation, France has a need to diffuse its language and culture as far as possible. This need has a strong impact on peoples whose native language does not adapt itself too well to express modern technological ideas or whose language is simply not used in international relations.[5] No other modern colonial power has made such an effort to assimilate its colonial subjects as the French have. Indeed, the French colonizers felt a keen national obligation to share their culture with "uncivilized" peoples. Although the policy of assimilation hardly succeeded in attaining its major objective, that of replacing African cultures, the French have been successful in creating a Francophone elite in each of their former dependencies in Africa. The efforts that the French government has put forth to reinforce and diffuse their culture is probably the best long-term investment it has made in respect to upholding close ties with the Francophone black African countries.

THE STATUS OF THE FRENCH LANGUAGE AND THE EDUCATIONAL SYSTEM

As a result of the big efforts made by French intellectuals, especially by the *philosophes* in the eighteenth century, to spread their language and culture, French became the most popular language in Europe, especially among the aristocracy. This privileged position of the French language lasted until World War I. From 1715 to 1918, it was generally the language in which treaties and diplomatic communiqués were written. Today, French is the mother tongue, the official language, and language of instruction for people living in about thirty countries all over the world.

Foreigners generally assume that the most important aspects of France's presence in Africa are political and economic. This point of view is not necessarily shared by the French. At the first Francophone summit in Versailles in February 1986, President Mitterrand stated that the greatest asset of all countries represented at the conference was a cultural identity based on a language that embodied one of the greatest civilizations known to history. Mitterrand also referred to an encouraging prediction for Romanists: the Romance languages would claim more speakers worldwide than English at the turn of the century.[6] The meeting was an impressive example of unity and diversity within the Francophone world. African presidents, European ministers, and representatives from the Pacific, the Caribbean, Southeast Asia, South America and even from the U.S. state of Louisiana sat under one roof to discuss methods of cooperation. The problem of Canadian representation was solved when Brian Mulroney, the French-speaking former prime minister of Canada, agreed that Robert Bourassa, premier of Quebec, and Richard Hatfield, premier of New Brunswick, should also attend in their own right. The summit approved twenty-eight measures designed to strengthen the French-speaking world, including the establishment of a new agency to produce television programs in French, a graduation examination valid throughout the French-speaking world, and steps to encourage the publishing and distribution of books in French. This attests to the fact that France is located at the center of a linguistic bloc of countries; this position gives France the appearance of a great power in the family of nations.

During colonial days, French was imposed by the colonizing power, but since independence, Francophone African countries have, of their own free will, decided to uphold the ascendancy of the French language. Indeed, the multilingual situation of most African countries, each comprising a variety of different tribes and ethnic groups, makes French a virtually indispensable instrument of national unity. French has also become an instrument of social stratification.[7] Unlike the British, the French colonial system did not favor the traditional African hierarchy. Instead, the French colonizers passed political power in their colonies to an elite group they had created based on their own culture. After independence, a conscious effort was launched to propagate this elite, whose language, modes of thought, professional orientation, and tastes were typically French. The members of the elite have seen their interests and those of France as identical for so long that they have often been the ones to hold on to arrangements France is now prepared to let go. Today, the children and grandchildren of an earlier French-trained elite grow up in cultivated, virtually French home environments. This small, well-educated elite, growing up isolated from the rest of the population, speaks a refined French, sometimes with a Parisian accent. The rest of the population in Francophone African countries generally speaks a rather mediocre French, sometimes even *créole*. The French spoken by the common people, however, may be a more viable means for French influence than the subtle French of the small elite. According to a report by the *Conseil économique et social,* only 10 percent of the local population in the Francophone African countries speaks French like a *francophone réel*, that is, like a native or near-native speaker (see Table 4). Also Jean-Pierre Cot stated that in rural areas and the *quartiers populaires* in cities, the proportion of the population who more or less understands and speaks French does not surpass 10 to 20 percent. He also noted a decline in the quality of French spoken by African students.[8]

There can be no doubt that the Francophone African leaders owe much of their political and economic power, as well as their social standing, to their skill in the French language.[9] When France gave up official control over its African colonies, it was mostly proficiency in French that gave the members of the African elite access to important positions. A few of them had acquired an education in French or African universities because of family influence in traditional African society. The political careers of Sédar Senghor, Félix Houphouët-Boigny, and Sékou Touré are typical examples. Most of the African elite, however, lacked the social position or economic base that would have ensured them ascendancy outside the colonial structure. The French language seems to be the main instrument of power in the hands of the governing oligarchies in all Francophone African countries.[10] Unfortunately, the cultural hegemony of the French language has too often served to justify the right to rule by these

TABLE 4

Native or Near-Native Speakers of French in Francophone Black Africa

Country	Total population in 1992 UN estimated figures (million)	Estimated number of *francophones réels* (adjusted to 1992 UN population figures)	Percentage of local population*
Benin	4.928	492,800	10
Burkina Faso	9.515	666,050	7
Cameroon	12.662	2,279,160	18
CAR	2.930	146,500	5
Chad	5.961	178,830	3
Congo	2.692	942,200	35
Gabon	1.253	375,900	30
Guinea	7.232	361,600	5
Ivory Coast	12.951	3,885,300	30
Mali	8.464	846,400	10
Mauritania	2.108	126,480	6
Niger	8.281	579,670	7
Senegal	7.691	769,100	10
Togo	3.701	740,200	20

Surprisingly, Congo has the highest percentage of *francophones réels,* not one of the traditional core states (Ivory Coast, Senegal, Cameroon, Gabon). Chad's lowest percentage is a result of the Moslem nomads in the northern part of the country, who have traditionally turned their back to French language and culture.

*"Coopération française . . . ," *Journal Officiel de la République française,* no. 4 (Mar. 8, 1991), 31.

oligarchies.[11] Some of the members of the elite have shown a keen enthusiasm for the study of French language and literature. It surprised no one when Senghor was elected in 1983 to become an *immortel,* a member of France's most prestigious intellectual institution, the *Académie française.* Therefore, the Francophone African elite has a vested interest in the continued ascendancy of the French language. This accounts for their lack of interest in the selection of an indigenous language as the official language for their respective countries. The dislodgment of French from its dominant position would erode their power base and social prestige. Furthermore, to change the linguistic status quo in the Francophone African countries would be a politically most sensitive issue, accompanied by the risk of civil dissension. The imposition of an indigenous language as the official language in any of the multilingual countries would lead to disruptive confrontations among antagonistic or rival ethnic groups. Even in countries like Senegal with a linguistically homogeneous society (90 percent of the population speaks Wolof) and where the recognition of Wolof as an official language would be the most logical course of action, political leaders have refrained from a proposal to change the status quo. Indeed, even the most ardent Francophobe, like Sékou Touré at the time of independence, has never sought to displace French as the official language in a former French dependency.

A further factor for the perpetuation of the French language and consequent implication of French cultural influences is the educational system that African countries inherited from the French colonial administration. Not only is French the language of instruction in these countries, but the educational system itself is patterned on that of the *métropole*. The cooperation accords signed with each country (except Guinea) have ensured French support in the vital area of formal education. After independence and in response to the strong desire of their populations, African governments set up vast programs of educational expansion. The resulting increase in school enrollment led to a corresponding shortage of teachers in primary and secondary schools. Since African countries lacked qualified indigenous teaching staff in sufficient numbers to run the expanded systems, they appealed for assistance under the cooperation agreements. In response to the request, the French government sent thousands of its trained nationals to the Francophone African countries to carry out various types of teaching, training, and supervisory assignments. In order to cope with the growing demand for teachers, the French government modified its compulsory military service rules in 1963 to allow draftees to fulfill their obligation by serving under the cooperation agreement system. The modification was also aimed at reducing the ever-increasing costs for training teachers. The majority of these national service volunteers who substitute civilian overseas service for compulsory military service have been teachers. Many of these draftees have developed such an enthusiasm and dedication for their assignment that they opted to stay at their position after their obligatory service period. About 75 percent of French technical assistance personnel continues to be teachers despite a decline in overall numbers in the program since the early 1980s, an indication of the priority that formal education enjoys in the overall assistance program.[12] Budgetary constraints in both France and the receiving African countries have required a reduction in the numbers of French teachers. These reductions were taken mainly in the secondary schools, where departing French teachers could be replaced by qualified, indigenous university graduates.

Traditionally, the French government has been responsible for recruiting the teachers, giving them special overseas training and paying their annual trips to and from Africa, their salaries, and special overseas allowances, while the African countries provided accommodations. Generally, inexperienced French teachers have been delegated mainly for teaching duties to primary and secondary schools while the experienced candidates for overseas duties have been assigned to technical schools and colleges for teacher training. Student supervisory and administrative responsibilities have been mostly in the hands of African nationals. The most outstanding French educators have been recruited to serve in the Ministry of Education of a specific country, where they advise on policies and curricula.

To gratify each Francophone country's wish for prestigious postsecondary educational facilities, the French government agreed to establish institutions of higher learning. Before independence, the University of Dakar was the only postsecondary facility in French colonies south of the Sahara. It was established, administered, funded, and staffed by the French government. Indeed, it was an extension of the French university system, offering the same curriculum as the universities in the *métropole*. After independence, in conjunction with African governments, the French government established universities in Abidjan (Ivory Coast) and Yaoundé (Cameroon) and postsecondary institutions in Porto-Novo (Benin), Lomé (Togo), Brazzaville (Congo), Libreville (Gabon), Bangui (CAR), and N'Djamena (Chad). All of these institutions have now expanded into autonomous national universities, controlled and financed by the respective local governments; however, French aid and supervision are still substantial.[13] The cooperation accords signed with each individual country ensure that academic standards are being maintained, allowing for equivalency with French metropolitan degrees and diplomas. A few institutions, mostly the first ones founded, such as the University of Dakar, enjoy favored status through the cooperation agreements.[14] In these universities the French government reserves itself the privilege to staff a number of academic positions with French nationals or qualified Africans who hold double citizenship, that is, of a Francophone African country and of France. Although these positions are not necessarily being staffed by better-qualified candidates than the positions staffed directly by the government of an African country, the salaries for services rendered by the former used to be considerably higher than those of the latter. Steps have been taken in recent years to alleviate this discriminatory practice.

In its determination to make the services of outstanding French scholars available to Francophone African universities, the French government has initiated a program of visiting lectureships/professorships to African universities. Under the program, well-known French scholars who, for whatever reason, do not want to take a prolonged leave of absence from their university in France, can be sponsored for lecture tours to Africa.

French assistance to educational development in Francophone Africa goes far beyond the recruitment of teaching personnel. Entire university and secondary school systems have been supplied, from the physical plant to details of curricula, expensive scientific and laboratory equipment, examination systems, teaching materials, and even personnel regulations. In several countries the French government also financed the establishment of linguistic institutes whose primary aim is to engage in comparative studies of French and the spoken languages in the respective countries. A number of indigenous languages have been analyzed with respect to their phonology, morphology, and syntax in order to adopt improved methods to teach French to Africans. Due to this kind of expansion of the educational system after independence, French educational models have become increasingly more entrenched in Francophone Africa.

African students have readily taken advantage of France's liberal policy of granting virtually unrestricted access to qualified Africans to study in its institutions. In the immediate postindependence period, France and the African states helped promote the vogue by sponsoring an ever-increasing number of Africans for studies and training in France. As a result, when universities were established in several Francophone African countries, many young Africans avoided them because it had become fashionable to sojourn and study in France, especially in Paris. Under these conditions African universities could not function properly. In order to compel African students to study in their home institutions, the number of scholarships for studies abroad had to be drastically reduced. To assist the African governments in this endeavor, France made most of its scholarships awarded to Africans tenable in African universities. Through these measures the flow of African students to France has been reduced somewhat but not their dream of studies in the *métropole*. The mystique of study in France is still strong in Francophone black Africa. For each of the last ten years there have been about 100,000 Francophone African students enrolled in French institutions of higher learning. Only a few of them benefit from study grants funded by the French government or by their respective African government; most are financed through private means. France has kept its liberal policy in allowing Francophone Africans to compete, on the basis of equality with French nationals, for admission to the *Grandes Écoles* (highly rated institutions, most of them devoted to engineering, applied science, or management studies).[15] Similarly, France allows Francophone Africans to take the extremely competitive and prestigious examinations for the senior teaching diplomas with their rigid *numerus clausus*—the elitist *agrégation* and the *Certificat d'Aptitude Professionnelle à l'Enseignement Secondaire* (CAPES). There are now about twenty times more applicants than places.

Next to the university students, other Africans come to France for secondary and primary education; these are usually the offspring of the affluent black elite of the West Coast. Other young Africans attend short, nonuniversity courses or refresher courses or are placed as apprentices with such governmental agencies as the Railroad or Post-Office Training Schools. Regardless of the experience and professional or intellectual achievements of all these young Africans in France, the mere fact that they have experienced France personally enhances their social prestige and even their career prospects once back in their home country. Generally they become influential people in their respective country and have a keen interest to uphold their prestige acquired in France. They thus become unsolicited agents for the propagation of French culture.

OTHER SOURCES OF FRENCH INFLUENCE

Other major sources of French influence in the former colonies are mass media, means of communication, cultural exchange programs, and cultural centers. The role played by French radio and television in disseminating French culture is enormous. Both have a stronger impact on their audience than the written word because all Francophone African countries still have a relatively large group of illiterates among their peoples. Today radio and television reach virtually all segments of the African population.[16] All Francophone African radio/television stations rely heavily on the French National Radio Broadcasting and Television Office *(Office de Radiodiffusion-Télévision Française*, ORTF) for their programs. These stations relay news and news panorama produced by ORTF. Commercials ensure that the Africans buy things "made in France." ORTF also assists the African stations in producing their educational programs for school broadcasting. Starting in 1989, *Canal France International* (CFI) has been sending programs in French language each day for six hours via satellite to Africa. CFI buys up the best Francophone African productions for redistribution in Africa under the title "Africa gets to know Africa."[17]

The French press has a wide audience among the African elite because most Francophone African countries have only major state-owned newspapers with restricted information. As a result of the leadership conferences in several Francophone African states (see Chapter 7), an atmosphere of liberation of the press exists throughout Francophone Africa. A direct consequence is the lifting of state and self-imposed censorship and the proliferation of private newspapers with a small circulation. These newspapers, catering to the common people and often using Creole language, are especially critical of the elite. In order to propagate this spirit of liberalization of the press, the *Union des Journalistes d'Afrique de l'Ouest* organized a conference in January 1991 in Paris to which the managing personnel of all privately owned Francophone African newspapers were invited.[18] The more educated Francophone Africans turn to French newspapers, magazines, journals, and reviews that offer more objective and wider news coverage and analyses. Many of these publications give extensive coverage to all facets of African affairs. It is obvious that this rich source of information on Africa produced in France reflects French interests and ideology.

In most Francophone African countries France controls the international, and in many cases also the internal, means of communication. Since many of these countries are landlocked and have a relatively small population, establishing telephone, telex, radio, and television links is an expensive undertaking, which cannot be funded by each individual state. The French recognized the enormous advantages offered by establishing and maintaining technical control over these lifelines. In providing the initial necessary equipment and installation, they have now secured a means of access to most sensitive and secret information. In fact, in a few former dependencies the French Intelec controls all telex, radio, and telephone operations. In the field of military communications,

French control is even more prominent. The details are known only by certain top military personnel and government officials. But it is a known fact that in certain former French dependencies the entire military communication system is in the hands of French technicians. They are in charge of coding and radio systems of the armed forces, as well as of military intelligence.

The bilateral cooperation accords between France and its former African dependencies also provide for cultural exchange programs. Each year several French artists travel to Africa to exhibit their work. Some hold seminars or organize workshops for the benefit of promising young African artists. The program has also enabled French orchestras, bands, and theater troupes to perform in African towns. In cooperation with the national radio and television network of Francophone African countries, ORTF has organized annual drama competitions for promising African playwrights. The best plays entered for the competition and written in French language are then broadcast by ORTF and relayed by the African radio and television network. Even sport teams are occasionally sponsored to play against African teams. Such activities have contributed a great deal to the propagation of French culture in Africa.

In the larger cities of the Francophone West Coast, visual evidence of the French connection is conspicuous. Movie theaters show almost exclusively French films. In the shops, the sidewalk cafés, the restaurants, and other public gathering places the atmosphere is typically French. In the hinterland of these cities, the French connection is less obvious. The attitude of the local government toward its own indigenous culture or cultures becomes also an important element in the degree the French culture has been adopted. For instance, in the more traditionally oriented Islamic countries in the Sahel, where there has been a time-honored practice not to accept Western ways of life, French presence is more discreet or even absent. On the other hand, the government of Houphouët-Boigny has opted for what amounts to a systematic Frenchification of the Ivorian people. In all relatively affluent commercial centers the French language and French material culture have become synonymous with modernity.

In the larger Francophone African cities the French have established cultural centers that generally are extensions of the cultural section of the French consulate or embassy. These centers, now called *médiathèques,* are usually endowed with a library, a film/videocassette/record library, a reading/study room, an information booth, and sometimes a multipurpose theater *(salle polyvalente).* The libraries have a good selection of titles on French culture, civilization, history, and geography. They subscribe to French dailies and periodicals. Similarly, the film/videocassette/record library keeps material on French classical, modern, and popular music, teaching/learning aids meant for teachers and students of French, and films that deal mostly with France's history, geography, and socioeconomic and political life. Users of the *médiathèque* may borrow any material to be consulted on the premises or at home. Most centers organize weekly programs on a specific topic of French life. The multipurpose theater is used for public lectures, drama productions, film festivals, music shows, and all kinds of exhibitions. Generally the centers have a budget to operate a mobile library to serve the remote villages and to give technical and financial assistance to groups that want to pursue any kind of activity dealing with the propagation of French culture. It is thus evident that France has made an elaborate effort to maintain and consolidate its cultural presence in the Francophone African countries. In part these efforts are in response to the French people's concept of *mission civilisatrice;* however, there is a link between these cultural activities and economics. The well-established French cultural presence makes the Francophone African countries obvious markets for various types of French books, periodicals, musical equipments, videotapes, records, and other French-made creations advertised in the media. The taste for French products and product identification is of long standing. A report commissioned by the *Ministère des affaires étrangères* gives a clear indication that the French government is well aware of this connection and makes a conscious effort to promote it. The report states that teaching the French language and culture abroad is not just a public service activity; it is also a profitable undertaking for French companies. In fact, still according to the report, creative activities are inseparable from economics; they manifest themselves by the offer of articles and services for sale.[19]

There is also a connection between cultural relations and politics. The creation and continuation of a political elite in each former French dependency well confirm this relationship. Originally the French cultural orientation was the policy of assimilation, which sought to Frenchify the Africans. With some very rare exceptions, this policy failed. The French, however, were successful in making the elite French-oriented what has contributed a great deal to the special relationship France enjoys today with its former black African dependencies. Whether this relationship can be passed on to future generations remains to be seen. Much will depend on the continuation of a major French cultural and educational effort in these countries and on the attitudes of future leaders. As explained earlier, French is still the only viable lingua franca and the only official language, as well as the principal medium of modern education, in most of these countries. Given these linguistic and cultural advantages, France should continue to enjoy a special, privileged political and economic position in Francophone black Africa in the foreseeable future.

NOTES

1. All fourteen former French dependencies in Subsaharan Africa have adopted French as the official language. Mauritania accepted Arabic as its second official language (after French) mainly because of the financial support it could then obtain from the Arab world (see "Mauritania," in *Africa Review 1986,* 10th ed. [Saffron Walden: World of Information, 1986], 177). Cameroon has French and English as official languages.

2. Jacques Rigaud, *Les Relations culturelles extérieures* (Paris: la Documentation française, 1980), 11 (author's translation).

3. Suzanne Balous, *L'Action culturelle de la France dans le monde* (Paris: PUF, 1970), 13 (author's translation).

4. Jean-Pierre Cot, *À l'épreuve du pouvoir: le tiers-mondisme, pour quoi faire?* (Paris: Seuil, 1984), 171 (author's translation).

5. Jean-Marcel Jeanneney, *Rapport*, Ministère d'État chargé de la réforme administrative, Commission d'études de la politique de coopération avec les pays en voie de développement, July 1, 1963.

6. Mitterrand failed to mention, however, that according to the same forecast, French would trail behind both Spanish and Portuguese within the Romance family of languages.

7. Gabriel Manessy and Paul Wald, *Le français en Afrique noire: tel qu'on le parle, tel qu'on le dit* (Paris: Harmattan, 1984), 1–115.

8. Cot, 172.

9. Abdou Touré, *La Civilisation quotidienne en Côte-d'Ivoire: procès d'occidentalisation* (Paris: Karthala, 1981), 11–28.

10. Edward M. Carbett, *The French Presence in Black Africa* (Washington, DC: Black Orpheus Press, 1972), 40.

11. Philip G. Altbach and Gail P. Kelly, *Education and Colonialism* (London: Longman, 1978), 35.

12. French Peace Corps volunteers and French military medical personnel assigned to civilian hospitals are the other groups that make up the technical assistance personnel.

13. Jacques Fortier, "Des Étudiants de plus en plus nombreux; contrastes Nord-Sud," *Le Monde,* July 4, 1991, 14c.

14. Laurent Zecchini, "Recentrage de la politique de coopération, MM. Aurillac, Penne, Foccart et la *famille,*" *Le Monde,* Apr. 5, 1986, 2.

15. John Ardagh, *France Today* (New York: Penguin, 1988), 482.

16. André-Jean Tudesq, *La Radio en Afrique noire* (Paris: Pedone, 1983), 87–89.

17. Catherine Humblot, "Canal France International à Yamoussoukro," *Le Monde,* Feb. 25, 1991, (RT) 25.

18. Alpha Oumar Konaré, "Floraison de journaux indépendants en Afrique francophone," *Le Monde,* Feb. 12, 1991, 23d.

19. Rigaud, 76–77.

9

Economic Ties

TRADE, COMMERCE, AND UNDERDEVELOPMENT

France's commercial interest in Francophone Africa has been centered mainly in four countries that are sufficiently developed to offer attractive markets and investment opportunities or that contain valuable energy and mineral reserves. Traditionally, Ivory Coast, Senegal, Gabon, and Cameroon have provided the major share of French imports from former French dependencies in black Africa and, at the same time, these countries absorbed the major share of the French exports to the Francophone African group. They have adhered to investment and trade policies that cater to French business and government interests. Because of its favorable geographic position, profitable agricultural sector, relatively good infrastructure built by the French, and consistently cordial relations with the *métropole,* Ivory Coast has become the center for French commercial activity in West Africa. Abidjan, its capital with a First World look, is now the region's most important city of French trade and finance. Office towers bear such names as Datsun and Shell, and boulevards are named for Charles de Gaulle and François Mitterrand. The Houphouët-Boigny Sports Palace located downtown could compete with any modern sports center in Western European cities. The Hôtel Ivoire features tropical Africa's only ice-skating rink. Yachts cruse the bay between the affluent Plateau area and Cocody, the Beverly Hills of Abidjan. There, wealthy French and Ivorians (including President Houphouët-Boigny) own homes; these affluent people play the Riviera golf courses or retreat to the *Club Méditerranée* or a private resort down the coast.

Houphouët, who turned eighty-nine in October 1993, is the only ruler Ivory Coast has known since independence. He emphasized peasant agriculture and gave a smaller role to the state in the development process. He was more concerned with efficiency and growth than with fair income distribution. After a stagnation at the beginning of the 1980s due to a severe drought, high cost of international debt service, and a sharp drop in the price of tropical products, economic growth resumed at a brisk rate. Ivory Coast became the world's leading producer of cocoa and an important exporter of coffee, timber, and palm oil. Partly due to this economic comeback, Houphouët's government abandoned sound economic policies. While coastal Abidjan symbolizes an emergent modern African city, Yamoussoukro, the new but, in part, still empty inland capital, represents a fantasy world. It rises as a futuristic marble-and-glass apparition out of the tropical rain forest on the edge of a village that happens to be Houphouët's birthplace. In that village Houphouët had a huge Roman Catholic basilica built; Pope John Paul II consecrated it in September 1990. According to the pope, poverty is not a problem faced by Ivorians, but being "consumed with materialism" is. Although a number of African leaders have planned or created capitals away from the old colonial municipal centers, none were built with the soaring imagination that is invested in Yamoussoukro. Government overspending, coupled with the precipitous fall in commodity prices, a decline in the value of the dollar, and a serious liquidity crisis, increased the total external debt from U.S. $9.6 billion in 1985 to U.S. $13.959 billion in 1989, an increase of 45 percent. In July 1989, an eighteen-month financial stabilization plan, worked out jointly by the IMF and the World Bank, was introduced. Progress toward achieving the objectives of this plan, however, is slow as deteriorating trade agreements continue to cast a shadow over the entire economy.

Senegal's strategic position and tradition play a larger part than commercial considerations in determining French attitudes. With its former *quatre communes* of Saint-Louis, Gorée, Dakar, and Rufisque, Senegal was the first territory in Subsaharan Africa where French presence was established. Today it attracts the largest number of French citizens who establish their place of residence for a prolonged period of time in Subsaharan Francophone Africa (see Table 5). Several years back Abidjan replaced Dakar as West Africa's principal focus of French commerce; however, Dakar remains a point of primary strategic importance in the South Atlantic. Its infrastructure, built by the French over many years, is impressive. In the late 1980s the Gulf states, especially Saudi Arabia, have been the principal financiers of a new conference center at Les Almadies, just outside Dakar.

Due to the problems associated with cash crop production, Senegal has placed emphasis on diversifying agricultural output and on a significant expansion of horticultural production. But despite all efforts at diversification, the peanut is still the most important cash crop; it is estimated that 40 percent of farmland is still taken up by peanut cultivation. Ivory Coast and Senegal are France's favorite recipients of economic assistance. Senegal's total external debt of U.S. $3.6 billion in 1989 is a considerable increase from the 1984 figure of U.S. $2.1 billion. In spite of the fact that it has one of the oldest structural adjustment programs in Africa, its basic structural problems still seem insolu-

TABLE 5

French Living in Francophone Black Africa

Country	Number
Benin	2,865
Burkina Faso	2,795
Cameroon	9,920
CAR	3,209
Chad	1,510
Congo	6,081
Gabon	16,205
Guinea	2,733
Ivory Coast	21,987
Mali	2,889
Mauritania	1,472
Niger	2,793
Senegal	14,807
Togo	3,470

Note: These figures are based exclusively on French citizens registered at their consulates in the various countries; actual figures are higher.

Source: *Quid 1992: tout pour tous,* Dominique Frémy, and Michèle Frémy, eds. (Paris: Laffont, 1991), 590.

ble. Its banking sector has been badly managed and subjected to too much political pressure. Its public service bureaucracy is overwhelming; the adjustment program stipulates that it be cut by one-third in the next few years. The current industrial policy is to reduce state participation and attract new local and foreign investment to boost the agricultural and industrial sectors' sluggish growth rate.

During colonial times Gabon was among the more neglected French territories. In 1990 oil represented some 80 percent of all exports, 65 percent of government revenue, and 50 percent of the gross domestic product (GDP). After Nigeria, it has become Africa's second largest black African oil-producing and exporting country. The oil is largely pumped and sold by Elf Gabon, a French-Gabonese company. In return for this lucrative arrangement, France showers this small nation with aid and attention. Gabon is the world's third largest manganese producer; it is also rich in uranium, with France being its principal customer. France's nuclear-power expansion creates a demand for uranium that can be satisfied exclusively through purchases from the Francophone African countries. Two major parastatals, the *Bureau de recherches géologiques et minières* and the *Compagnie générale de matières nucléaires,* dominate uranium prospecting activities in the producing Subsaharan Francophone countries.[1] In 1989 Gabon had by far the highest per capita income in Subsaharan Africa, U.S. $2,770 (followed by Cameroon, U.S. $1,010). The high salaries paid in industry and construction have led to a particularly dramatic flight from the land; local food production has fallen off so much that it has to be supplemented by large imports. Thus the agricultural sector contributed only 9 percent to the GDP in 1988; it suffers from underinvestment and weak rural infrastructure; less than 1 percent of the total area is under cultivation.

With its modern highrises, its Hypermarché M'Bolo (reputedly the largest supermarket in black Africa), and its affluent people, Libreville has a lot in common with downtown Abidjan. Like Ivory Coast, Gabon depends on a labor force that has to be brought in from surrounding countries. In response to this affluence, the government became increasingly more liberal in its spending practices. For example, Libreville's airport has been undergoing a multimillion-dollar renovation. A sharp fall in oil earnings since 1986 and higher import costs, however, have resulted in a negative trade balance, reversing earlier surpluses. Gabon's total external debt in 1989 was U.S. $2.7 billion, as compared with U.S. $0.9 billion in 1985, an increase of 200 percent. The dramatic reversal in the Gabonese economy is also due to wasteful governmental spending and profiteering by foreign, mainly French, contractors. While the oil companies have visibly prospered, the benefits have not filtered down to the general public. There has been a steady increase in the parallel economy, with the accompanying loss to state coffers, of tax receipts and customs duties. This trend underlines the exclusion of the majority of the Gabonese population from the apparent boom economy. Faced with mass unrest in 1990, the government promised wage increases. In response to the proposed increases of expenditure, the IMF postponed withdrawals on the U.S. $43 million standby credit approved in September 1989 as part of a structural adjustment program.[2]

Cameroon has developed a relatively broad agricultural base. Until oil was exported in the late 1970s, a fairly wide range of cash crops had provided the bulk of Cameroon's export revenue—coffee, cocoa, cotton, and, to a lesser extent, rubber, pineapples, and tea. Most agricultural production is in the hands of smallholders, with the exception of rubber production, which is run under the plantation system. The government of Cameroon has a tradition of treating its farmers well by paying producer prices at relatively high levels. Like Ivory Coast, it is fairly self-sufficient in respect to domestic food requirements and has a liberal investment code. Cameroon was noted for its conservative and pragmatic economic management. Oil, however, provided the money for new government and public sector office buildings, new hospitals, schools, and roads; a new international airport is being built at Nsimalen on the outskirts of Yaoundé. In spite of the oil revenues and massive reserves of bauxite with the installations to refine it into aluminum, Cameroon's total external debt increased

TABLE 6

Median Annual Increase in Percent of GDP per Capita

Country	1960–1970	1970–1980	1980–1988	1960–1988
Benin	2.0	– 0.3	– 0.7	0.7
Burkina Faso	2.7	– 0.3	3.5	1.5
Cameroon	3.4	2.7	2.3	3.6
CAR	– 0.3	0.0	– 0.2	– 0.4
Chad	– 1.6	– 0.2	1.8	– 0.9
Congo	3.7	0.0	1.2	3.2
Gabon	5.5	7.8	– 1.9	4.5
Guinea	– 1.3	2.2	0.6	0.3
Ivory Coast	3.8	2.6	– 2.8	1.9
Mali	– 1.7	1.6	– 0.4	0.4
Mauritania	5.7	– 1.1	– 0.8	0.7
Niger	2.7	– 1.0	– 4.0	– 1.0
Senegal	– 2.0	– 1.3	0.7	– 1.2
Togo	6.3	1.7	– 2.8	1.5

Source: "Coopération française . . . ," *Journal Officiel de la République française,* no. 4 (Mar. 8, 1991), 11.

by 44 percent within the period 1985–88. After the conclusion of a World Bank structural adjustment program in June 1989, the government was encouraged to embark upon a series of sweeping economic reforms, including extensive privatization of many state-owned companies and massive reductions in the public service sector. In the interim, progress is extremely slow, and most sectors of the economy are stagnant. Yaoundé is littered with abandoned construction sites as private contractors for the public sector gave up waiting for their payments and departed.

France has been especially supportive of Cameroon and Ivory Coast because both are relatively powerful and influential in their respective region and have been playing a leading role in Equatorial African and West African affairs.[3] By boosting these states economically, France obtained their political support and the support of their allies.

The backward Francophone countries of the Sahel, like Mauritania, Mali, Burkina Faso, Niger, and Chad, rely heavily on foreign aid to compensate for their deficits. In fact, their dependence is twofold. On one hand, they need economic assistance from France, and, on the other hand, they are dependent

TABLE 7

Basic Demographic Indicator*

Country	Area sq km	Population density per sq km (1992)	Area sq mi	Population density per sq mi (1992)	Population natural increase rate in percent (1992)**
Benin	112,600	43.8	43,450	113.4	3.30
Burkina Faso	274,200	34.7	105,869	89.9	2.99
Cameroon	465,458	27.2	179,714	70.5	3.40
CAR	622,436	4.7	240,324	12.2	2.88
Chad	1,284,000	4.6	495,755	12.0	2.54
Congo	342,000	7.9	132,047	20.4	3.29
Gabon	267,667	4.7	103,347	12.1	2.74
Guinea	245,857	29.4	94,926	76.2	2.60
Ivory Coast	320,763	40.4	123,847	104.6	3.60
Mali	1,240,192	6.8	478,841	17.7	3.00
Mauritania	1,030,700	2.0	398,000	5.3	3.21
Niger	1,186,408	7.0	458,075	18.1	3.26
Senegal	196,722	39.1	75,955	101.3	2.78
Togo	56,785	65.2	21,925	168.8	3.60

*UN figures
**World average: 1.72 percent.

upon the relatively rich coastal states like Ivory Coast, Senegal, Gabon, and Cameroon. For example, a sizable number of migrants from Burkina Faso and Mali are employed in the agrarian sector of Ivory Coast; at the same time Ivory Coast is a major market for these two countries. A similar situation exists in Gabon with respect to its neighbors, Congo and CAR. Due to their underdevelopment and geographic position, the landlocked countries have been effectively barred from coastal commercial centers. Large masses of their peoples live on a subsistence level. The overall picture is even more depressing when compared with the performance of other regions of the Third World. Social and economic indicators of development, such as output growth, health, and literacy, have shown persistently weak performance in black Africa (see Tables 6, 7, and 8). It is probably fair to say that today most peoples in Subsaharan Africa are worse off than they were at independence. The economic deterioration has been so

TABLE 8

Basic Indicator for Health and Education*

Country	Health				Education
	Physicians: 1 physician per x persons (1989)	Infant mortality rate per 1,000 live births (1992)	Life expectancy at birth (years) (1992)		Literacy: total population age 15 and over literate (1991)
			male	female	
Benin	16,025	119.0	49.0	52.0	23.4
Burkina Faso	29,914	127.0	47.6	50.9	18.2
Cameroon	12,540	86.0	53.5	56.5	54.1
CAR	17,292	95.0	48.0	53.0	37.7
Chad	47,640	122.0	45.9	49.1	29.8
Congo	3,873	65.0	52.1	57.3	56.6
Gabon	2,000	94.0	51.9	55.2	60.7
Guinea	9,732	134.0	44.0	45.0	24.0
Ivory Coast	17,847	97.0	52.0	56.0	53.8
Mali	20,602	114.0	45.0	47.0	32.0
Mauritania	10,128	94.0	44.0	50.0	34.0
Niger	38,500	124.0	44.9	48.1	10.8
Senegal	17,072	80.0	48.3	50.3	28.6
Togo	12,992	110.0	54.0	58.0	39.1

*UN figures

severe that this region now has the dubious distinction of being home to twenty-four of the world's thirty-six poorest nations.[4] Total black African foreign debt has risen nineteen times since 1970 to a staggering U.S. $230 billion, equal to its gross national product (GNP), making the region the most heavily indebted in the world. Debt service obligations amounted to 47 percent of export revenue in 1988, but only half was actually paid. The arrears are constantly being rescheduled. With decreasing foreign exchange and more of the revenue needed to service debt obligations, less is available for imports of desperately needed supplies such as spare parts, textbooks, and medicines. The devastation has many sources: prolonged drought accompanied by desertification, lack of skills and of a solid infrastructure, prolonged recession in the industrial countries and

TABLE 9

Basic Economic Indicator

Country	GNP in million U.S. $ (1990)*	GNP per capita in U.S. $ (1990)*	GNP per capita annual increase in percent (1988)**	Public debt, external, outstanding, in million U.S. $ (1990)*
Benin	1,716	360	0.1	1,262.0
Burkina Faso	2,955	330	1.2	750.0
Cameroon	11,223	940	3.7	4,784.0
CAR	1,194	390	–0.5	815.0
Chad	1,074	190	–2.0	430.4
Congo	2,296	1,010	3.5	4,380.0
Gabon	3,654	3,220	0.9	2,945.0
Guinea	2,756	480	–	2,230.0
Ivory Coast	8,920	730	0.9	10,050.0
Mali	2,292	270	1.6	2,306.0
Mauritania	987	500	–0.4	1,898.0
Niger	2,365	310	–2.3	1,326.0
Senegal	5,260	710	–0.8	2,953.0
Togo	1,474	410	0.0	1,096.0

*UN figures

**"Coopération française . . . ," *Journal Officiel de la République française,* no. 4 (Mar. 8, 1991), 13.

the subsequent deteriorating terms of trade, and inappropriate policies pursued by the governments.[5] In a rare moment of courage and forthrightness, some African leaders admirably admitted before the 1986 UN Special Session that defective policies and economic mismanagement were also significant in precipitating the crisis. Tables 7, 8, and 9 illustrate the generally sparse population and poverty of the Sahel region, with most of its economies falling within the World Bank's category of least developed countries.[6] In the near future, these countries will continue to be preoccupied with providing basic goods and services in order to maintain present living standards and will continue to depend on substantial inflows of aid.

THE FRANC ZONE

The Franc Zone, a monetary cooperation arrangement, embraces all those countries and groups of countries whose currencies are linked with the French franc at a fixed rate of exchange. These countries agreed to hold their reserves mainly in the form of French francs and to execute their exchange on the Paris market. Each member state has its own central issuing bank, and its currency is freely convertible into French francs. This monetary union is based on agreements concluded between France and each country or group of countries. It is essentially a relationship between unequal partners. While France is a technically advanced industrial nation, the African members of the Franc Zone are still in the process of launching their programs of development. This special relationship needs to be understood in a broader perspective with the formation of the EEC.

Before independence, all French African territories had the franc of the *Colonies Françaises d'Afrique* (CFA). After independence the abbreviation CFA persisted, but it now stands for *Communauté Financière Africaine*. Before World War I, the CFA franc was equal to 1 metropolitan franc; from then on its value became a multiple of the *franc métropolitain:* between the two world wars, the value was 1 to 1.70, and after 1945 it was 1 to 2.[7] The rate is now fixed at 50 CFA francs to 1 French franc. This fixed rate can be altered only with the unanimous agreement of all parties to the monetary accords. As a result of this fixed parity, the French franc played and is still playing a key role within the Franc Zone; it became a "hard currency" or even a substitute for gold. The performance of the French franc within the European Monetary System (EMS) has therefore an effect on all African countries in the Franc Zone. If the French franc varies within the parameter of its agreed parity with the European Currency Unit (ECU) in the EMS, so does the CFA franc's purchasing power of all member states of the Franc Zone. Thus, any modification in the value of the French franc, with respect to other foreign currencies, fully affects the currencies of member states. On December 10, 1992, former Prime Minister Pierre Bérégovoy announced in Maastricht that the CFA franc would be "linked" to the future single European currency.[8]

Apart from Guinea, all of the territories that formerly constituted AOF and AEF joined the reformed monetary arrangements offered by the Franc Zone and as stipulated in the cooperation agreements. Mali withdrew from the Franc Zone in 1962, establishing its own central and commercial banks, foreign exchange control, and currency, the Mali franc (on July 1, 1992, 1 Mali franc = 0.01 French franc).[9] When a monetary crisis developed in 1967, an agreement was reached on the establishment of a central issuing bank, jointly administered by Mali and France. In 1983 Mali gave up its own currency (1 Mali franc = 2 CFA francs) and rejoined the Franc Zone as a full member. Mauritania left the monetary organization in 1974 to establish its own central bank and currency, the Ouguiya. (On July 1, 1992, 100 Ouguiya = 6.87 French francs.) In 1985

Equatorial Guinea applied for membership in the Franc Zone and was admitted the same year as the first non-Francophone country to become a member.

The former AOF and AEF are still grouped within the currency areas that existed before independence, each group having its own currency issued by a central bank. During colonial times, two *Instituts d'émission* were established to issue and control the money, one for AOF and the other for AEF. The French treasury and the Bank of France had absolute control over the two *Instituts*. Operations accounts were opened at the French treasury for each monetary region. The existence of these accounts guaranteed the CFA franc currency; these accounts are still today the central mechanism for each monetary region; all currency exchange transactions go through them. Thus, the French colonial monetary institutions did not go through the same process of balkanization between 1958 and 1960 as the colonial political institutions. As a result of the change in political status of the overseas territories at the time of independence, the two *Instituts* became regional banks, the *Banque Centrale des États de l'Afrique de l'Ouest* (BCEAO) and the *Banque Centrale des États de l'Afrique Équatoriale et du Cameroun* (BCAEC), both with headquarters in Paris and a branch in the capital city of each respective member state. Negotiations for membership in the two monetary unions were conducted in two stages. In the cooperation agreements economic, commercial, and monetary matters were signed with each state. Then, a detailed multilateral agreement on monetary cooperation was negotiated with the members of both monetary unions. In May 1962 the *Union Monétaire Ouest-Africaine* (UMOA)—West African Monetary Union—was founded by the six states of Dahomey, Ivory Coast, Mauritania, Niger, Senegal, and Upper Volta to provide common external reserves by their central bank, the BCEAO. At the same time, Cameroon, CAR, Congo, Gabon, and Chad formed the *Union Douanière et Économique de l'Afrique Centrale* (UDEAC)—Central African Customs and Economic Union—with their joint central issuing bank, the BCAEC. The mechanics for the two monetary unions' operations were designed with considerable ingenuity and remain essentially intact. Togo became a member of UMOA after the coup d'état and assassination of President Sylvanus Olympio in July 1963.

The structure and status of both central banks remained unchanged for over a decade after independence. The BCEAO was managed by a board of directors composed of two representatives from each member state except France, which maintained seven directors or a third of the membership of the board. Decisions were adopted by a simple majority vote of two-thirds of the members. Reflecting Central Africa's lower level of economic development as compared with West Africa, the African members of the BCAEC had equal representation with the French on the board of directors. This made it easier for the French to block votes on matters they considered of sufficient importance, thus safeguarding the soundness of the system and protecting French reserves. The BCEAO was entitled to lend money to member governments; limits on such lending were carefully set. The BCAEC could not grant credit directly to governments;

French fear of inflation precluded such practice in Central Africa. The tight controls exercised by the joint central banks prevented the zone as a whole from overrunning its own foreign reserves. These restrictions were so efficient that the zone has been in a surplus position with its operations accounts at the French treasury up to 1980. Only since 1981, when world economic recession and lower commodity prices hit even the most stable economies of states such as Ivory Coast and Gabon, has the Franc Zone started to go into a deficit position with the French treasury. These shortfalls reflect chronic balance-of-payments problems of all member states. The problems caused by domestic economic weakness in France have further exacerbated the strains on the Franco-African monetary system.

Both central banks acted as bankers for the commercial banks, which were controlled mostly by foreign interests, though local authorities did participate in ownership. The governing boards of these banks included Africans and representatives of French public and private interests. The two central banks were empowered to issue currency, to regulate the amount of cash a commercial bank had to retain as a proportion of total loans granted (cash ratio), and to rediscount commercial bills for the private sector.

The guarantee extended by the French government to the member states of both monetary unions through the functioning of the operations accounts was the main foundation of the Franc Zone. This system stabilized the currencies throughout the Franc Zone and greatly facilitated exports and imports with France and other member states. Thanks to this system the Franc Zone countries were able to avoid currency black marketing, parallel economies, and overvalued currencies that have damaged the economies in many African countries outside the Franc Zone. France became the major trading partner with all its former colonies in black Africa, and French investments in these nations also outstripped all competitors.[10] On the other hand, the member states had to accept certain strict monetary and financial regulations. Through this arrangement they became less vulnerable to economic crises in their cash crop production. The member states pooled foreign exchange reserves in each of the two joint central banks operations accounts. In normal times, these accounts ensured free transfer of funds among member states; they provided monetary stability and lessened the risks of inflationary pressures. The system enabled countries with severe balance of payments problems to utilize foreign exchange reserves previously accumulated by members in a surplus position. The interest rates on overdrafts varied according to the amounts involved and the nature of the overdraft. At the same time, credit balances earned interest equivalent to the going money market rate at the Bank of France. The balance of pooled reserves was generally placed in short-term accounts with international institutions such as the International Bank for Reconstruction and Development (IBRD), with which all Franc Zone members are affiliated. The member states have also received expert assistance from the *métropole* in managing their monetary affairs. As an incentive, monetary unions provided security for foreign investments that were attracted by the free transfer of profits and resources within the Franc Zone. Coupled with the potential or actual wealth in hydrocarbon resources, the monetary system has attracted multinational companies and banks to countries such as Gabon, Ivory Coast, Cameroon, and Congo. France benefited from the operations accounts when a Franc Zone member's trade balance of payment with a foreign country of a different monetary zone was positive, thus bringing valued foreign currency to the French treasury. If the balance of a Franc Zone's member was negative, all the members of the system were subject to either drawing on IMF reserves or increasing the money supply.[11] The negative effects for the latter solution were possible inflationary pressures, unless exports were expanded.[12]

The establishment of the Franc Zone also had its negative effects. Through their acceptance of the strict membership rules of the Franc Zone, the member governments have actually entrusted all their monetary and financial responsibilities to the *métropole*. With the four devaluations of the French currency that have taken place since 1981, the currencies of the member countries were automatically devalued.[13] A few days before his appointment as prime minister on April 4, 1992, Pierre Bérégovoy stated that he would never become "the minister of devaluation" and that nobody and no event could ever change his stand on this issue.[14] He also remarked that "a devaluation of the French franc is not the answer. In the past, such stopgaps have proved to be air bubbles in the economy, resulting in inflation and loss of competitiveness on the international scene."[15] In his inaugural speech given to the National Assembly on April 8, 1993, Prime Minister Édouard Balladur did not address the issue of devaluation of the French franc.[16]

Inflationary pressures in France were automatically passed on to the states of the Franc Zone. As the French franc fell in value relative to other hard currencies, member states' purchases from other industrialized countries became more expensive. Any economic crisis suffered by the *métropole* affected the member states directly.[17] Due to the fact that these states traded almost exclusively with each other and with France—at least during the first two decades after decolonization—the system has prevented diversification of their products and markets. It has also impeded stimulation of the member states to coordinate their programs of economic development and customs unions; it has not provided any incentive for an eventual integration. The structure of both UMOA and UDEAC has prevented the establishment of a common market; the idea of a permanent secretariat or a customs office was never realized. Thus, some kind of balkanization did occur in the field of economics through the establishment of the Franc Zone.

In 1972 Mauritania claimed that, being one of the poorest members of UMOA, it benefited the least from the existing monetary arrangements while France benefited the most. Thus Mauritania withdrew from UMOA. To prevent any further withdrawals, France took precautionary measures by agreeing to renegotiate the monetary accords. The statutes governing both unions were revised in 1974–75 in line with the new treaty provisions. The tension that existed between the need to respond to changing circumstances and retaining the advantages of the postcolonial system was evident on the African side as well as on the French side. French influence was slightly diminished. UMOA members decided to relocate BCEAO headquarters from Paris to Dakar (Senegal). The name of the union was changed to *Communauté Économique de l'Afrique de l'Ouest* (CEAO)—West African Economic Community. The new provisions brought the institution under the authority of UMOA's heads of state. The Council of Ministers was retained; France's representation on this board was reduced to two directors in a body of fourteen. From now on a simple majority vote settled most issues; BCEAO's money became governed by a Council of Ministers and managed by the central bank, placed under the control of a governor with broad powers. National credit committees were constituted to decide how credit should actually be used in the various countries. There was no French representation on these state committees.

In response to growing pressures from the members of UDEAC, the statutes governing this union were also revised. The central bank's headquarters were shifted from Paris to Yaoundé (Cameroon), and its name was changed to *Banque des États de l'Afrique Centrale* (BEAC). The board of directors was reduced from sixteen to twelve members; France's representation was reduced from eight to three directors. The board was authorized to appoint a governor as the bank's chief executive officer for a five-year renewable term. Like in UMOA member states, credit targets were set by credit committees rather than by the central bank. As a guarantee against abuse and to maintain coherence of policy, however, the governor and two auditors (one of whom is French), constituting the *Collège des censeurs*, were empowered to attend the meetings of the national credit committees in the various member states of UDEAC. (There are no auditing provisions for CEAO member states.)

The statutory revisions in both monetary areas guaranteed a greater degree of national decision making. A new provision stipulated that members of the Franc Zone were allowed to use 35 percent of their external holdings for trade with countries other than France. Both central banks received the power to set reserve requirements and to regulate interest rates within their regions. The CFA franc remained linked to the French franc by a fixed parity; it would continue to follow the float of the French franc. At a meeting in January 1974 the finance ministers of the Franc Zone discussed the consequences of the French franc's floating on the economies of their countries. They decided not to propose any change of the parity between the CFA franc and the French franc. They also recognized that the revision of the statutes governing the two monetary areas did not change existing relations with France. Today, however, the African countries resent the fact that France does not consult them before major decisions are made for the whole of the Franc Zone. Recession in France and heavy debt-servicing charges experienced by the African countries impose a great strain on the Franc Zone. For example, in 1987 relatively prosperous Ivory Coast had to suspend debt repayments, an indication of the seriousness of the problem. The severe liquidity crunch of that country is largely the result of the commercial loans it acquired in the late 1970s and early 1980s. Inadequate financial policies led to ever-deeper budget and external accounts deficits which were financed by external borrowing. Ivory Coast's total external debt in 1979 was U.S. $2.429 billion; in 1989 it was U.S. $13.959 billion, up by 574 percent from the 1979 level. The 1989 ratio to service this debt was 39.9 percent. As mentioned before, the *métropole* has urged all member states to adopt IMF-prescribed austerity plans in order to readjust their operations accounts. In the meantime France is forced to absorb these deficits and is seeking assistance from all possible sources. If the monetary problem becomes more acute (many experts predict another devaluation of the French franc), the benefits of the relationship will look increasingly fragile. It will increase the pressure on member states to look for trading partners outside the Franc Zone.

ASSOCIATION WITH THE EEC

Before France joined the EEC, markets in the Franc Zone were protected by a network of tariffs, quotas, and exchange controls. France had a virtual trade monopoly with its African dependencies. Access to French metropolitan markets for African products was guaranteed. In return the *métropole* extracted prices higher than those in the world market for its manufactured and processed goods. The consumer of these goods paid a *surprix*. Theresa Hayter has shown that the *surprix* paid by the French consumers has been considerably lower than the one paid by the consumers of France's dependencies.[18] Thus trade balances have favored France. With France's membership in the EEC, this exclusivity and closed economic circuit have now ended, although France remains the single most important trading partner for most of Francophone Africa.

Economic relations between the EEC and the developing countries of Africa were initially outlined in the Convention of Association, which was drawn up under the Treaty of Rome in March 1957, when the EEC was established. At that time France was exporting 30 percent of its finished goods to the territories belonging to the French Union. In turn about 70 percent of the goods produced in the French colonies were absorbed in the French market.[19] When France joined the EEC, it became impractical for the country to function in two economic communities, that is, the EEC and the French Union, and bear the respective responsibilities. An association of its dependencies with the EEC would allow France to continue its economic function in the French Union. Therefore, largely on French and Belgium insistence (Belgium at that time was also a colonial power), special provisions were proposed for all African territories south of the Sahara that were controlled, as colonies or protectorates or as trust territories of the UN, by any of the European powers now members of the EEC.[20] An accord was reached on the basis of a Franco-Belgian memorandum that associated the above-mentioned African states with the EEC. This agreement was the first multinational institutionalization with Europe; it gave a broad base to the Eurafrican movement.[21] Its main stipulation was to remove tariffs between EEC partners, a policy that was extended to the African associates; however, the latter could retain or introduce tariffs on their own imports from the EEC in order to protect their own economies. The associated African territories were encouraged to apply the same rules as applied in respect to the EEC members to commercial exchanges between themselves. The quotas for imports into the African-associated countries from the six EEC members were increased. The EEC established a fund to provide grants to the associated territories in the period 1958–63; later called the European Development Fund (EDF), it was created to finance the development of the infrastructure and facilitate trade relations with the EEC. Out of the total U.S. $581.25 million fund, the French colonies received U.S. $311.25 million as assistance in the form of nonrepayable grants. In addition, the associated states received U.S. $325 million from France in price support. The association was continued after 1963 with slight changes. With the exception of Guinea, which chose to withdraw, eighteen associated states signed a new convention in Yaoundé (Cameroon) in July 1963 for another five-year period. Due to the transformation of African states from colonies to independent states, the Treaty of Rome underwent necessary modifications. The associated African states were given representation in the Association Council for allocating EDF. The council's primary task was to decide the orientation of financial and technical cooperation between the six EEC partners and the eighteen African associates. An EEC development fund of U.S. $730 million was established for this period.[22]

All eighteen African countries renewed the Yaoundé Convention for another five-year term, thus called Yaoundé II. For this period an EEC development fund of U.S. $918 million was set up. When the agreements expired in 1975, forty-six African, Caribbean, and Pacific states (ACP) reached new agreements on trade, aid, and cooperation with the EEC (at that time, nine members). These agreements were signed in February 1975 in Lomé (Togo) and are known as the Lomé Convention or Lomé I. The new agreements provided the ACP countries with:

1. Relatively freer access to the EEC market for all ACP exports without reciprocity to the European markets for goods exported from the ACP countries.

2. A stabilization fund to compensate the ACP countries for any fall in the market prices of their principal basic commodities for exports.

3. Financial aid amounting to 3.39 billion European Units of Account (about U.S. $4 billion) from the ECC countries to the ACP countries.

4. Industrial and technical cooperation to promote a better international distribution of labor in favor of the ACP countries.

5. Joint EEC-APC institutions (ministerial council, ambassador's committee, parliamentarian, trade-unionist, and industrialist conferences) to supervise the observance of the agreements and to promote discussions between EEC and ACP partners.[23]

The agreements reached during Lomé I were renewed with minor changes in 1980 (Lomé II), 1985 (Lomé III), and 1990 (Lomé IV). Whenever development funds were negotiated, the Francophone African countries were considered as beneficiaries. In addition, France persuaded its EEC partners to provide price support to selected African associates for certain primary products. Thus the French were able to shift a significant portion of the burden of subsidizing their dependencies to their EEC partners. While only about 33 percent of EDF came from France, about 70 percent of the lucrative contracts in Francophone Africa were placed with French companies. But France ultimately had to pay a price for having associated its former African dependencies with the EEC. Its effective monopoly in trade and investment in the Francophone African countries came to an end; however, its commercial predominance has persisted in most of these states, although at a gradually declining level.

To some extent EEC membership proves to be disadvantageous to the African states. Being mainly cash crop exporters, these states face the problem of fluctuating commodity prices. On the other hand, the prices of capital goods imported from Europe are continuously increasing. This unequal economic relationship resulted in decreased dependence by the EEC members on the associates while the latter's dependence on the EEC progressively increased. This is the most important reason the gap between rich and poor nations has constantly grown wider. Today the APC countries are dependent on the EEC countries for markets, investment, and most aspects of development assistance. APC countries, however, constitute peripheral markets and investment outlets for the EEC members, except for France.

ECONOMIC ASSISTANCE

Economic assistance is another strong link between France and Africa. Bilateral development assistance, development cooperation, or foreign aid is largely a post–World War II phenomenon—a foreign policy tool supplementing, though never replacing, traditional diplomatic and military methods. The variation in the terminology that is used to describe foreign aid suggests the changes that have occurred in the prevailing views about its purposes and roles. In the 1970s, the terms *development assistance* and *development cooperation* largely replaced *foreign aid* to describe public disbursements designed to foster economic and social development in underdeveloped nations. Historically, bilateral aid has been more important for France than multilateral contributions (see Table 10).

TABLE 10

French Public Development Assistance, 1980–91
(Aide Publique au Développement, APD)
(in millions of French francs and respective percentages; DOM-TOM excluded)

Year	Bilateral aid	Multilateral aid	Total aid
1980	7,035 (70.4)	2,964 (29.6)	9,999 (100)
1981	10,654 (75.6)	3,432 (24.4)	14,086 (100)
1982	12,521 (72.7)	4,705 (27.3)	17,226 (100)
1983	13,953 (73.2)	5,105 (26.8)	19,058 (100)
1984	16,900 (75.8)	5,404 (24.2)	22,304 (100)
1985	18,301 (73.5)	6,585 (26.5)	24,886 (100)
1986	17,790 (73.1)	6,531 (26.9)	24,321 (100)
1987	19,777 (73.3)	7,203 (26.7)	26,980 (100)
1988	20,923 (73.5)	7,532 (26.5)	28,455 (100)
1989	24,398 (74.4)	8,394 (25.6)	32,792 (100)
1990	25,322 (73.1)	9,310 (26.9)	34,632 (100)
1991*	28,486 (74.2)	9,913 (25.8)	38,399 (100)

*Announced at the Franco-African Summit at La Baule (June 1990).

Source: "Aide publique bilatérale de la France en faveur de l'Afrique: orientations et instruments," *Problèmes économiques,* no. 2.217 (Mar. 20, 1991), 2.

Broadly speaking, justifications and explanations of bilateral aid fall into two categories, one emphasizing the benefits of economic assistance to the recipient, the other emphasizing the benefits to the donor. According to Paul Masson, bilateral aid always implies some kind of political or economic manipulation by the donor country.[24] Yet, possibly for political reasons, whenever France compiles a report on aid allocations, it stresses only the benefits for France but neglects to indicate how it is trying to influence the receiving countries with its donations. The Jean-Marcel Jeanneney and Pierre Abelin reports, both attempting a far-reaching analysis of the goals, structures, and achievements of French foreign aid, demonstrate the foregoing case.[25] The latest report on the issue was prepared in 1988 by a former French ambassador, Stéphane Hessel, who was critical of aid policies. The report was published but barely noticed at *Élysée* Palace.[26]

French foreign aid policy as it has developed in the last thirty years is largely an effort to replace colonialism with a sphere of influence designed to serve political, economic, and cultural goals. Over the years, French assistance policies have evolved in order to accommodate changing international and domestic realities. Before World War II the limited funds available for development came from local sources or from surpluses generated by the two African federations, AOF and AEF. These funds were modest because local resources were meager and federal budgetary surpluses had to be used first to cover continuing ordinary budget deficits suffered by the poorer territories. Only after World War II did direct French economic assistance to black African territories begin seriously. The efforts were designed solely for French overseas territories, and they stressed the provision of French metropolitan skills in areas ranging from agricultural production and mining to education and health. To finance the programs, two structures were created in 1946. FIDES was authorized to make investment grants to overseas territories, using funds from the metropolitan budget, the budgets of the various overseas territories, and loans from CCFOM. The second structure, the *Fonds d'Investissement pour les Départements d'Outre-Mer* (FIDOM)—Investment Funds for Overseas Departments—was designed to provide similar funds for Martinique, Guadeloupe, French Guyana, and Réunion. Billions of francs were spent in developing infrastructure, undertaking basic research, and staffing essential services in the territories during this period.

Political independence brought some changes in the realm of economic aid and development; however, they were more apparent than substantive. Some names of French aid organizations were changed, but their methods of development assistance remained the same. FIDES and FIDOM continued after 1960. The *Fonds d'Aide et de Coopération* (FAC) was created to oversee cooperation agreements; the CCFOM became the *Caisse Centrale de Coopération Économique* (CCCE), providing development loans both under the authority of FAC and through its own initiative. The Ministry of Overseas France became the Ministry of Cooperation to handle economic relations and technical assistance, while diplomatic relations were placed under the Ministry of Foreign Affairs. In spite of this reorganization, the same people continued to work on the same development projects. Thus the system and the personnel remained largely unchanged. Within this continuity, there have been periodic attempts either to refocus or to restructure French aid. Like the Jeanneney Report in 1963, the Grose Report in 1971 proposed a series of recommendations for reforming economic assistance policies. The Grose Report, however, was never published, presumably for two reasons. First, the government was sensitive to criticisms regarding the influence of some pressure groups on French policy and second, the report noted the inegalitarian nature of many of France's bilateral relationships institutionalized within its cooperation policy.[27] The government's sensitivity suggested that there were important disagreements within official circles over the direction cooperation policy should take. Probably as a consequence of these disputes, the position of secretary of state for cooperation was abolished in 1974, and General Management for Cultural, Scientific, and Technical Relations (within the Ministry of Foreign Affairs) was given responsi-

TABLE 11

Geographical Distribution of France's Public Development Assistance
(in percentages of total aid, DOM-TOM included)

1970–71		1980–81		1987–88	
Réunion	9.7	Réunion	13.0	Réunion	8.1
Algeria	8.8	Martinique	11.7	Martinique	6.1
Martinique	7.0	New Caledonia	4.2	French Polynesia	4.7
Guadeloupe	5.7	French Polynesia	3.6	New Caledonia	4.2
New Caledonia	2.9	Morocco	3.3	Guadeloupe	3.2
Morocco	2.8	**Senegal**	**2.7**	Morocco	2.8
Ivory Coast	**2.6**	**Ivory Coast**	**2.3**	**Ivory Coast**	**2.8**
Madagascar	2.2	French Guyana	2.2	**Senegal**	**2.6**
Tunisia	2.2	**Cameroon**	**2.1**	French Guyana	2.0
French Guyana	2.1	Algeria	1.8	Madagascar	1.6
Indonesia	2.1	Tunisia	1.6	**Cameroon**	**1.5**
French Polynesia	1.9	**CAR**	**1.6**	Egypt	1.3
Senegal	**1.8**	**Burkina Faso**	**1.5**	China	1.3
India	1.8	Brazil	1.5	**Congo**	**1.3**
Gabon	**1.6**	Guadeloupe	1.5	**Gabon**	**1.2**
Cameroon	**1.5**	**Niger**	**1.3**	**CAR**	**1.1**
Chad	**1.5**	**Mali**	**1.3**	**Chad**	**1.1**
Niger	**1.4**	Madagascar	1.3	**Mali**	**1.0**
Burkina Faso	**1.0**	Egypt	1.2	India	1.0
Djibouti	1.0	Indonesia	1.1	**Niger**	**1.0**
Iran	0.9	**Congo**	**1.1**	Algeria	1.0
Congo	**0.8**	**Gabon**	**0.9**	**Guinea**	**1.0**
Egypt	0.8	Mexico	0.8	Zaïre	0.9
CAR	**0.8**	Zaïre	0.8	**Burkina Faso**	**0.9**
Benin	**0.7**	India	0.7	Tunisia	0.9
Total above	65.5	Total above	64.8	Total above	54.3
Multilateral aid	10.2	Multilateral aid	15.2	Multilateral aid	17.5
Not apportioned	16.9	Not apportioned	6.8	Not apportioned	12.9
Total French aid		Total French aid		Total French aid	
(million U.S. $)	1135	(million U.S. $)	4407	(million U.S. $)	6925

Source: "Aide publique . . ," *Problèmes économiques,* no. 2.217 (Mar. 20, 1991), 3.

TABLE 12

Distribution of Grants and Loans in Bilateral
Assistance Programs
(DOM-TOM excluded)

Year	Grants	Loans
1980	72.9	27.1
1981	67.0	33.0
1982	66.3	33.7
1983	74.1	25.9
1984	68.9	31.1
1985	65.8	34.2
1986	63.5	36.5
1987	59.6	40.4
1988	59.7	40.3
1989	61.3	38.7
1990	62.7	37.3

Source: "Aide publique . . . ," *Problèmes économiques,* no. 2.217 (Mar. 20, 1991), 4.

bility for bilateral cooperation with developing countries. Some African heads of state were unhappy. They regarded the change as a downgrading of the traditional linkage used in influencing French policies in Africa and not just as a "normalization" of relations.[28] A few months later, the Ministry of Cooperation was re-created; France thus indicated its renewed priority given to matters concerning Francophone Africa. Even during the few months of changed policy, foreign aid allocations continued to favor Francophone African states (along with DOMs-TOMs).

The socialist initiatives in the early 1980s were probably the most interesting efforts to restructure French aid. The socialist goal was to further normalize relations between France and its traditional Francophone partners in the context of a "new internationalism" to foster human rights, work for adjustments in the international economic system to the benefit of developing nations, and support "progressive" movements in all states throughout the international system.[29] The proposed means to these ends were structural reforms in the administration of foreign assistance and a geographic redistribution of aid designed to develop French ties in Latin America and the Middle East. By the end of 1981, however, it was clear that the new policy initiatives were losing out to traditional concerns. Although there has been a noticeable increase in official French economic assistance, there has not been a significant geographical reorientation of this aid (see Table 11). In 1991 about 68 percent of all French direct aid went to Africa, most of it in the form of grants since few governments are able to repay their debts (see Table 12). The effort to support "progressive" movements in authoritarian Francophone African states, such as Gabon and Guinea, was undermined by Élysée's insistence to do "business as usual" with the governments in power.[30]

NOTES

1. A. D. Owen, "The World Uranium Industry," *Raw Materials Report* (Stockholm), 2, (4) (1984), 6–23.

2. A UN 1990 report entitled *Africa: One Year Later* showed that twenty-eight African countries had adopted economic policy reforms and structural adjustment measures. Among the measures taken were sharp reductions in social spending and government payrolls, enlargement of the private sector, privatization of state corporations, and reduction of subsidies to state enterprises.

3. Eric Fottorino, "La Côte-d'Ivoire reste le principal bénéficiaire de l'aide français," *Le Monde,* Apr. 11, 1992, 21a.

4. *Journal Officiel de la République française* (Paris), 4 (Mar. 8, 1991), 9–12; Philippe Auverny-Bennetot, "La Dette du Tiers monde: mécanismes et enjeux," *Notes et études documentaires* (Paris), 4940, 14–15.

5. Frédéric Fritscher, "Un Cris d'alarme de la FAO: le continent subit l'une des pires sécheresses du siècle," *Le Monde,* Apr. 16, 1992, 6a.

6. *World Development Report 1989,* Basic Indicators, Table 1 (Washington, DC: World Bank, 1990), 164–65.

7. Marcel Capet, *Traité d'économie tropicale, les économies d'A.O.F.* (Paris: Librairie générale de droit et de jurisprudence, 1958), 264.

8. "Business Briefs, West Africa," *Africa Report,* 37 (1) (Jan.–Feb. 1992), 12.

9. Michel Leduc, *Les Institutions monétaires africaines: pays francophones* (Paris: Pedone, 1965), 251–69.

10. "Afrique: un partenaire indispensable," *Actuel Développement* (Paris), 23 (May–June 1980), 39–40.

11. The IMF was created in 1944 with the aim of stabilizing the international monetary system, a task it pursued by establishing rules and mechanisms for regulating exchange rate fluctuations. A stable monetary system was thought to be essential to the expansion of global trade in the post–World War II era. The IMF's principal stabilizing mechanism was the provision of loans of relative short-term duration to countries experiencing temporary deficits in their balance of payments, thereby permitting these countries to maintain their flow of imports. To obtain these loans, the borrower was obliged to observe certain IMF conditions.

12. Guy Martin, "The Franc Zone, Underdevelopment and Dependency in Francophone Africa," *Third World Quarterly,* 8 (1) (Jan. 1986), 210–14.

13. Bernard Vinay, "La Zone franc d'aujourd'hui," *Marchés Tropicaux et Méditerranéens* (Paris), Nov. 28, 1986, 2981.

14. Philippe Simonnot, "De Bonnes Raisons de dévaluer le franc," *Le Monde*, Mar. 10, 1992, 41a (author's translation).

15. "Pour ou contre le franc fort," *Problèmes économiques*, 2.263 (Feb. 19, 1992), 25.

16. Jean-Louis Saux, "M. Balladur a appelé les Français à un grand effort de redressement, de rassemblement et de tolérance," *Le Monde*, sélection hebdomadaire, Apr. 15, 1993, 6–7.

17. René Dumont, "Impérialisme français et sous-développement africain," in François Maspéro, ed., *Tricontinental: la France contre l'Afrique* (Paris: PCM/Petite Collection Maspéro, 1981), 29–37.

18. Teresa Hayter, *French Aid* (London: Overseas Development Institution, 1966), 72–73.

19. "Association des États africains et malgache à la Communauté Économique Européenne," *Notes et études documentaires* (Paris), Secrétariat général du gouvernement, 3327 (Oct. 15, 1966), 6.

20. P. B. Couste, *L'Association des pays d'outre-mer à la Communauté Économique Européenne* (Paris: Librairie technique, 1959), 124.

21. Arnold Rivkin, *Africa and the Common Market: A Perspective* (Denver: Denver University Press, 1966), 7.

22. "Convention de Yaoundé—analyse et commentaires," *Notes et études documentaires* (Paris), Secrétariat général du gouvernement, 3327 (Oct. 15, 1966), 19–28.

23. "Convention Protocols, Final Act and Agreement," *Lomé Dossier*, reprinted in *Courier*, 31, Special Issue (Mar. 1975), 6–81.

24. Paul Masson, *l'Aide bilatérale: assistance, commerce ou stratégie?* (Paris: PUF, 1967), 7–8.

25. Pierre Abelin, *Rapport sur la politique française de coopération*, Ministre de Coopération (Paris: la Documentation française, 1975).

26. Eric Fottorino, "Plaies d'Afrique," *Le Monde*, May 30, 1990, 4a.

27. Jean Touscoz, "Document: le rapport Gorse sur la coopération de la France avec les pays en voie de développement," *Esprit* (Paris), 418 (Nov. 1972), 682–705.

28. Patrick Cadenat, *La France et le Tiers Monde: vingt ans de coopération bilatérale* (Paris: la Documentation française, 1983), 124.

29. *Projet socialiste pour la France des années 80* (Paris: Club socialiste du livre, 1980), 339–45.

30. Jean-François Bayart, *La Politique africaine de François Mitterrand* (Paris: Karthala, 1984), 34–48, 55–63.

10

Historical Perspectives on How the French View the Africans

The French developed negative attitudes toward Africans long before any contacts were actually established between France and Africa. Ideas were inherited from the classical and medieval world of Africa as a land inhabited by monsters and beastly people.[1] Another source of information available to the French was the travel accounts of other Europeans who had preceded them to the continent, notably the Portuguese. In the fifteenth century, a number of travel accounts by persons accompanying these Portuguese expeditions appeared in French translations. In general, these accounts reflected the writers' frustration arising from the inability to understand the people with whom they had come into contact and even reinforced the classical and medieval images of Africa.

Beginning in the sixteenth century, French traders plied the coast of West Africa, trading for gum arabic, ivory, gold, and slaves. None of these early contacts, however, seem to have led to any particular knowledge about Africa and its people. In fact there was a remarkable lack of interest in the African continent during the Renaissance. The thirst for knowledge about people of different races was lacking during that period.[2] Thus, despite opportunities for developing some knowledge about Africa, the classical and medieval lore was allowed to stand.

Increased contacts with Africans in the seventeenth century led the French people to reflect on the nature of blacks. Merchants, travelers, officials, and others visiting Africa tried to understand the strange new world with which they had come into contact. Those early observers were struck by the Africans' physique, manners, and customs. Their accounts often lacked originality and too often fell back on classical and medieval lore about the black continent. The skin color of the Africans surprised the early French explorers, and they tried to explain how they might have become black. They ascribed the Africans' color to the heat of the sun; the sun's ability to darken skin was seen as immediate. Therefore, one reason seamen purportedly were hard to recruit for voyages southward toward the equator was fear that they might turn suddenly black under the sun's rays. Differences in skin colors were attributed to differences in climate. In France, as in the rest of Europe, the color black denoted evil and depravity, and, in an age that believed in symbols, a negative meaning was attached to the fact that some humans were black.[3] Therefore, many French saw the blackness of Africans as symbolic of some inner depravity. Many theories were developed that tried to explain the differences of the black race. All these theories shared the assumption that there was something special in the creation of Africans that set them apart from white people. This special, separate creation denoted some form of disadvantage for Africans, a trait of inferiority. During that period the French, like all other Europeans, were never concerned about their own skin color, which they presumably accepted as the norm.[4] All this interest in the cause of the blacks' physique reveals a strong ethnocentric conviction that blackness indicated an anomaly of man, nature, or even God. These images of blacks created in the sixteenth and seventeenth centuries became deeply implanted in French culture and exercised a pervasive influence over later generations of the French people. Toward the end of the seventeenth century, slavery became the dominant form of labor and the basis for French wealth in the Caribbean. The institutions, customs, and laws that developed around black slavery in the French West Indies confirmed the inequality between the races that travelers of Africa and writers in France had already proclaimed. The social context of slavery dictated to a large degree how Frenchmen viewed blacks. Slavery was not a moral problem for Frenchmen in the sixteenth and seventeenth centuries. The ancient world had essentially accepted slavery as part of the natural order of things: the result of the inequality of humans. This was regarded as a natural law, whereby stronger and more capable humans controlled those less well endowed. Such an image was nearly inevitable, since slave owners have always assumed that their right to domination was based on physical and moral superiority.[5]

During the eighteenth century, the French expansion overseas took the form of missionizing, trade, exploration, or conquest, sometimes all four occurring simultaneously in one region, as was the case in Canada. The *philosophes* in the eighteenth century, particularly Diderot, Montesquieu, Rousseau, and Voltaire, set out to establish the laws that should govern human society. They believed it was possible to discover universal laws, comparable to the laws of physics, that would apply to all societies. Despite a belief in human equality, these thinkers, in their very eagerness to understand and classify people, developed a concept of human inequality based on climatic, cultural, and racial criteria. Their view of man was basically evolutionary. Thus the Africans were considered to be capable of undergoing evolutionary change through contact with European influences or through change of climate. In general, the French felt fewer inhibitions about changing other people's cultures than did the other colonizing powers. Likewise, the French never officially referred to their territorial possessions as "the empire"; they preferred titles such as "la France d'outre-mer," "l'Union française," or "la Communauté française."

It should be noted that few eighteenth-century French travelers to Africa published descriptions of their experiences, and so the image of the African held during the Enlightenment was essentially based on works published in the seventeenth or in the first quarter of the eighteenth century. Thus Abbé Prévost's *Histoire générale des voyages,* the first important collection of travel literature, published in several volumes from 1746 to 1759, was a compilation of the rather contradictory and mostly negative material from seventeenth- and early eighteenth-century travel accounts. The ideas expressed in this work had considerable influence in shaping the *philosophes'* attitudes toward Africans. The *Encyclopédie* and Count Buffon in his important collection of writings on the non-European world entitled *Histoire naturelle* asserted that Africans had become blacks as a result of the tropical environment. The blackness of Africans was seen as a degeneration caused by what were regarded as unnatural ecological conditions. These climatic theories upheld the theory of a common descendant of all human races, but such a doctrine was by no means egalitarian.

Diderot, in an article contributed to the *Encyclopédie,* the compendium of eighteenth-century learning, described the Africans as follows: "These peoples have, so to speak, only ideas from one day to the next, their laws have no principles . . . no consistency other than that of a lazy and blind habit. They are blamed for ferociousness, cruelty, perfidy, cowardice, laziness."[6] This negative opinion of Africans was very common among thinkers of the Enlightenment. As for the rest of the French people, if the literature that was aimed at them is any indication, they remained mostly ignorant of Africa.

The French Revolution proclaimed the rights of the common man: liberty, equality, and fraternity. From an early date it declared all men equal before the courts. Slavery, therefore, could no longer legitimately continue after these broadly stated principles were set forth in the Declaration of the Rights of Man of August 1789. In February 1794, the National Convention emancipated the slaves in all French colonies and even made them French citizens. But in 1802, Napoleon reimposed slavery, perhaps as a result of his wife Joséphine de Beauharnais's upbringing by a settler family of Martinique. He even forbade blacks and coloreds (persons of mixed white and black ancestry) to enter France. The Restoration in 1815 and the reassertion of aristocratic privileges brought a revival of racial doctrines as the explanation for domestic history.[7] With the proclamation of the Second Republic in 1848, slavery was abolished for good.

While the eighteenth century was monogenist, the nineteenth was polygenist, believing in the separate origin of races and their lack of affinity to each other.[8] The most famous medical doctor in the 1850s, Paul Broca, wrote that if four-legged animals were perceived to be as different from each other as whites were from blacks, they would not be included in the same species. The Anthropological Society of Paris, founded in 1859, adopted this point of view.[9] Broca even claimed that the two races could not cross successfully because fewer births resulted from the mating, and those who were born lived a shorter time and would die out by the fourth generation.[10] For Broca and his disciples, measurable physique became the foundation for all the differences perceived between Africans and Europeans.[11] The size of the skull was believed to indicate the size of the brain and, hence, of the intellect. Skull measurements showed a 12 percent difference in cranial capacity between the skulls of blacks and of whites, in favor of the latter.[12] After dissecting the brain of an African, Broca even found it to be darker than the one of a white. Based on these findings, Broca and his disciples asserted the superiority of the white race. Any deviations from the norm as represented by the white race were regarded as signs of inferiority. Joseph-Arthur de Gobineau, a French diplomat who traveled extensively in Africa, proclaimed that physical inferiority was accompanied by cultural inferiority. According to Gobineau, history proved that all civilizations were created by whites; none could ever develop without the help of the white race. Therefore, Africans could accomplish impressive feats only when they had been uplifted by the infusion of French blood.[13]

During the end of the nineteenth century and the first quarter of the twentieth century, French anthropology of Africa reached new levels with Maurice Delafosse, who spent many years in Africa and was well trained in African cultures. He stated that Africans may well be technologically behind Europeans, but they were in no way socially or intellectually inferior to any other race. There was no reason to assume that Africans might not develop in the same direction as Europeans. In his work, Delafosse showed the capacity of Africans to erect complex states, economies, and systems of philosophy, religions, and aesthetics.[14] His views, however, did not make any significant impact on the general public or on most of the writings about Africa. The French explorers, administrators, and soldiers in Africa retained the centuries-old view of Africans as savage, inferior peoples. Even Delafosse in *Les Nègres* claimed that while blacks did not lack foresight and the ability to plan, they rather lacked will. To accomplish great things, Africans needed a strong will imposed upon them, as was being done by the colonial powers.[15]

Imperialism did not cause any reassessment of blacks but rather helped to preserve the negative images that had existed since the earliest stages of Franco-African contact. In fact, the assertion of black inferiority paralleled claims for the need of white rule and domination over the African continent. Thus, a racial and an imperialist theme developed at the same time. The belief that the Africans would benefit from the tutelage of the French made imperialism most acceptable in France. Once the colonies were conquered, intellectual attitudes helped shape policies and methods of rule in Africa. In the nineteenth century, it was the aim of the French government to *assimilate* the Africans by integrating the African colonies with France, politically as well as culturally. This concept was a form of cultural imperialism. But the rapid expansion of the French empire during the early years of the twentieth century made the policy of assimilation impractical. The fact that the French had to deal with civilizations totally different from that of Europe made them fall back on the racist conviction that blacks, in fact, were not assimilable. Therefore, the French decided to adopt the policy of association, which emphasized the need for variation in colonial practice and evolution of natives along their own lines.[16]

During World War II, African colonies contributed a great deal to the war effort and to the liberation of France. In spite of this, traditional views of black inferiority continued. Before 1945, virtually the only Africans living in France were soldiers from the colonial army and some students. This pattern reversed after 1945. Beginning with the constitutional assemblies in 1945–46, a host of African parliamentarians came to Paris and Versailles, where various French assemblies met to discuss the affairs of the French Union. At the same time, increasing numbers of students and trainees began to arrive in France for periods of short or prolonged study. During the 1950s and 1960s, the number of Africans—mostly from Francophone countries—living in France continued to grow. The strength of the national contingents depended greatly on the state of relations between France and their country of origin. The students from the big cash crop-growing countries of the Sahel (Ivory Coast, Senegal, and Gabon) became relatively numerous while those of the landlocked countries (Soudan (Mali), Niger, Upper Volta (Burkina Faso), Oubangui-Chari (CAR), and Chad) were comparatively few.

During the late 1960s and 1970s, droughts and subsequent harsh economic conditions in the Sahel forced many Africans to leave their homes and to seek employment in France. Most of these immigrants, because of difficulties in finding employment and adequate housing, lived in crowded slum conditions, which created a certain contempt for them. Their situation was made even more difficult by the growing numbers of other foreign workers, especially Arab immigrants. The confrontation of the French people with this relatively large Arab and black labor force and the persistence of the negative image toward them sharpened racial prejudice.[17] In 1972 a bill was passed outlawing racial discrimination in France, updated by the "loi Gayssot" in 1991.[18] In order to reduce racial tensions, the government has even limited black migration into France through agreements with African countries. Repatriation of sizable numbers of resident Africans is unlikely as long as they possess valid resident and work permits.

Racial attitudes have deep cultural roots in France; they are the result of feelings experienced and expressed over three centuries of contact with the Africans. With the increased number of blacks in France since World War II, they are perceived as a threatening foreign element in French society, especially during the present depressed economic condition.[19] Foreign workers in general are accused of taking jobs from the French. Black and colored foreigners, being the most conspicuous and different of the group, bear the brunt of this accusation. Many of these people, if employed, are doing the menial and unpleasant jobs that the French now are reluctant to take on. In spite of this, many French

TABLE 13

Nationals from Francophone Black African Countries Living in France

Country of origin	Number*
Benin	4,259
Burkina Faso	2,112
Cameroon	14,118
CAR	2,592
Chad	1,057
Congo	6,816
Gabon	2,301
Guinea	1,592
Ivory Coast	12,213
Mali	17,924
Mauritania	4,383
Niger	1,033
Senegal	22,833
Togo	5,001

*Computed on the bases of latest census figures (often underestimated) and residence permits for foreigners and their dependents *(Ministère de l'intérieur)*. These figures do not include the sizable numbers of negroes and coloreds who have French citizenship and who are living in France.

Source: *Quid 1992*, 584.

are afraid of the black and colored immigrants, mostly because of their high birthrate and—so it has often been alleged, even publicly by Chirac's hard-line interior minister, Charles Pasqua—because they play a large role in crime, vandalism, and drug trafficking, even in the spread of AIDS. Right-wing advocates of immigration controls in France enjoy attentive audiences, especially among working and lower middle classes.[20] These classes in the early 1980s propelled the rise of the *Front National* under Jean-Marie Le Pen, whose blatantly racist platform was: "Send them back home!" Today there are an estimated 650,000 blacks and coloreds living in France. (No precise figures are readily available, except for registered foreigners; see Table 13.) Many have long been full French citizens and have provided France with a number of distinguished intellectuals and politicians.

NOTES

1. Frank M. Snowden, *Blacks in Antiquity* (Cambridge: Cambridge University Press, 1969).

2. Geoffroy Atkinson, *Les Nouveaux Horizons de la Renaissance française* (Paris: Droz, 1935), 136.

3. Kenneth J. Gergen, "The Significance of Skin Color in Human Relations," in John Hope Franklin, ed., *Color and Race* (Boston: Houghton Mifflin, 1968), 112–28.

4. Léon-François Hoffmann, *Le Nègre romantique: personnage littéraire et obsession collective* (Paris: Payot, 1973), 47.

5. Albert Memmi, *Portrait du colonisé, précédé du portrait du colonisateur* (Paris: Payot, 1973), 155–69.

6. *Encyclopédie,* cited in William B. Cohen, "Literature and Race: 19th Century French Fiction, Blacks and Africa," *Race and Class,* Vol. 16 (Oct. 1974), 184.

7. The *ancien régime* was a highly structured society in which a person's rank at birth usually marked him or her for life. The idea that the aristocracy had a right to rule on the basis of its biological descendence from the German Franks who had conquered the Gallo-Romans was particularly influential before the French Revolution. Therefore, the members of the Third Estate were considered inferior to the nobility as a result of inherited biological traits. This idea developed fully in the seventeenth century and became best known through the pen of Count Henri de Boulainvilliers, who wished to reassert the power of the nobility, that had been diminished by the absolutist reign of Louis XIV. On the very eve of the French Revolution this argument was reversed. Abbé Sieyès wrote an apology for the Third Estate and at the same time an attack on the nobility. He did not deny the idea that the different estates were descended from different racial groups, but he drew the opposite conclusion: the nobles were traitors to the national cause because they were descended from the foreign Franks, whereas the Third Estate was descended from the true native elements of France, the Gallo-Romans. Therefore, the Third Estate should rule in France. Having become accustomed to ascribing social and political differences in France to race, it was only natural that the French would extend this approach to explain the great differences among the peoples of Africa.

8. William B. Cohen, *The French Encounter with Africans: White Response to Blacks, 1530–1880* (Bloomington: Indiana University Press, 1980), 84–86, 232–37.

9. Paul Broca, "Sur le volume et la forme du cerveau suivant les individus et suivant les races," *Bulletin de la Société d'anthropologie de Paris (BSAP),* 2 (1861), 139–207.

10. Paul Broca, "Documents relatifs au croisement des races très différentes," *BSAP,* 1 (May 1860), 255–68.

11. Paul Broca, "Sur les proportions relatifs du bras, de l'avant-bras et de la clavicule chez les nègres et les Européens," *BSAP,* 3 (Apr. 1862), 162–72.

12. Gustave Le Bon, "Recherches anatomiques et mathématiques sur les lois des variations du volume du cerveau et du crâne," *Revue d'anthropologie,* 2d ser., 2 (1879), 103–04.

13. Arthur-Joseph de Gobineau, "Essai sur l'inégalité des races humaines," *Revue des Deux Mondes* (Paris), 2d ser., 8 (Mar. 1, 1857), 159–88.

14. Maurice Delafosse, *Civilisations négro-africaines* (Paris: Librairie Stock, 1925), 277–81.

15. Maurice Delafosse, *Les Nègres* (Paris: Rieder, 1927), 56–57.

16. Raymond F. Betts, *Assimilation and Association in French Colonial Theory, 1890–1914* (New York: Columbia University Press, 1961), vii–ix.

17. Jean Daniel, "Comment on devient raciste," *Le Nouvel Observateur* (Paris), Sept. 16–22, 1983, 20–23.

18. *Lutte contre le racisme et la xénophobie,* Rapport de la Commission nationale consultative des droits de l'Homme, présidée par Paul Bouchet, conseiller d'État (Paris: la Documentation française, 1992), 116.

19. Michel Ekwalanga, "Une Solution à l'immigration," *Le Monde,* Mar. 5, 1992, 2c.

20. Robert Solé, "Lancinante immigration: alors que le sujet préoccupe de plus en plus les Français, le pouvoir n'a pas encore trouvé les mots pour en parler," *Le Monde,* Nov. 5, 1991, 1d.

Conclusion

Since independence in the early 1960s, Franco-African relations have been treated as a private domain reserved to the president of the republic. Special organizations in the *Élysée* and in *Coopération* were created to deal directly with the Francophone black African countries. De Gaulle's ingenious design to preserve the most significant French interests in these countries while satisfying African demands for political independence is at the core of this relationship. The policy toward these countries has remained essentially unchanged for the past thirty-three years, with only a short, tentative break in 1981–82 when Jean-Pierre Cot headed *Coopération et développement*. President Mitterrand, however, quickly reversed these tentative changes and returned to the traditional Gaullist policy. Even under *cohabitation* in 1986–88 with Jacques Chirac as prime minister, significant changes of the traditional relationship were avoided.

France's decision to retain its influence in Africa after independence is mostly due to its desire to continue its status as a world power, albeit inferior to the United States and the former USSR. In addition the French had a keen desire to continue the strong sentimental ties that bound them to their former African empire. France's dominating position at the center of a group of sovereign, but dependent, countries gives it a privileged position among its Western allies, in particular within the EEC. For EEC members, the assumption that French influence continues in an otherwise unstable part of the world is crucial to their own planning. No other non-African power could replace France's presence in Africa without an unfavorable reaction from the Africans themselves. The special French role in black Africa has served both African and EEC interests. France not only made an effort to give continuity to its colonial relations but also successfully associated its former dependencies with larger economic groupings like the EEC.

The main reason for establishing the two federations, AOF and AEF, was France's concern that by acquiring and maintaining the African connection, the

African dependencies might become a burden on the French taxpayer. The administration of these federations redistributed revenues collected in the more affluent territories to the poorer territories with chronic budget deficits. This system gave rise to economies of scale by providing services that the smaller and poorer states could not provide for themselves. The breakup of the two federations, as a result of the *loi-cadre* reforms, resulted in a number of small, more manageable, and ethnically more homogeneous units that could be easily controlled by the *métropole*. These countries may thus have been spared the difficulties experienced in the larger multiethnic political units such as Zaïre and Nigeria. On the other hand, the end of the federal system increased the differences in the standpoint the states took in respect to the relationship with each other. Houphouët-Boigny has always rejected the point of view of Sédar Senghor that African states should form federations, on the premise that a union of poverties will never produce abundance. The dissolution of the federations freed resources for the development of the more affluent coastal states with their more promising economic systems. The key resource-rich states of Senegal, Ivory Coast, Cameroon, and Gabon have generally benefited the most from the French concept of *coopération et développement.*

In the Sahel states, where the peoples are periodically suffering the effect of drought and desertification and are unable to feed themselves, French interest has been marginal, sometimes even bordering on neglect. Unfortunately, the few well-intended initiatives by the French and international organizations to improve living conditions have too often contributed to further deterioration of an already fragile physical environment. The fragmented economies of these countries, with growing external dependence in terms of trade, technology, foreign skills, and finance, are today the most vulnerable. Alternative sources of income are difficult to identify. Neither industrialization nor inter-African trade seems to hold much promise for the near future. At the present state of development, Sahel countries are more likely to be competitors than complementary trading partners.

As a result of the French colonial system and continuous French presence after independence, the traditional social order in the Sahel states has been disrupted, sometimes even destroyed, without having been replaced by a functional alternative. Today, the peoples of these countries are probably worse off than at the time of independence; neocolonialism for the Sahel region has proved worse than colonialism. In addition, the French have not been especially successful in helping provide political stability in the region.

The second important aspect of the special Franco-African relationship is the mutual economic benefit that was assumed. Until 1985 France zealously sought to preserve the largely monopolistic economic interests built up in colonial times and upheld through the Franc Zone. It was virtually impossible for other trading powers to infiltrate Francophone Africa because of the comprehensive bilateral economic, political, military, and cultural accords France had signed with each former dependency, except Guinea. Reciprocal advantage within a preferential system was the central theme of these accords, including quotas, freedom from customs duties, guaranteed commodity prices, and unrestricted movement of goods between France and its African trading partners. These accords achieved a certain success in a few coastal states where France has focused its efforts and resources. Thanks to these core states with leaders who opted to serve their national interests by seeking French cooperation, France was able to hold on and consolidate its position in Subsaharan Africa.

In spite of the protective shield the Franc Zone was supposed to provide, Francophone Africa has not been immune to repeated recessions in the 1980s. In 1985 both West and Central African banks began showing a deficit on the *comptes d'opération*. This has been accompanied by a flight of CFA francs out of the Franc Zone, compounded by the adoption of more realistic exchange rates under IMF pressure in neighboring countries such as Ghana, Nigeria, and Zaïre. Because of the acute fluctuation in commodity prices in recent years, the deficit has drastically increased and led to rumors of a possible change in the parity of the CFA franc in relation to the French franc. As this parity has been constant since 1945, any change would diminish the credibility of the zone. It follows that, in regard to problems of the zone, French newspapers regularly feature articles in which French ministers and African presidents publicly deny plans for a parity change.

The French are concerned about the present economic condition and the dim prospects for early improvement in Francophone black Africa. The costs to France for economic assistance, currency stability, and convertibility are constantly rising. Doubts at the *Élysée* are increasing about the republic's capacity and willingness to meet the ever-increasing demands for assistance and development funds by virtually all former Subsaharan dependencies. Most of the Franc Zone countries have been obliged to seek IMF and World Bank assistance and are implementing closely supervised adjustment programs. The potential financial burden that countries without an adjustment program represent is so great that the international financial organizations are no longer offering them assistance. An indication of the seriousness of the situation is France's appeal to other potential donors, such as members of the EEC, the United States, and international institutions like the IMF and the World Bank, to share its financial burden resulting from its African connections. In the early 1980s, when the two concepts of *la chasse gardée* and *le pré carré francophone* were still popular, the *Élysée* would have never considered such a drastic step. The enduring decline in trade between France and the Franc Zone countries in the late 1980s is an obvious manifestation of the crisis. Especially hard-hit are countries, such as Ivory Coast and Cameroon, that earlier had inspired success stories.

The financial problem is particularly acute for France, beset with serious domestic budgetary constraints coupled with repeated devaluations of the franc. Whereas, in the past, France was able to use surpluses deposited in the French treasury by Franc Zone members to help countries with deficits, the republic can no longer rely on the self-financing mechanism of the zone. Nor can it afford to absorb the balance of trade deficits of its former dependencies. The Franc Zone is now in a global deficit, and the prospects for any improvement are dim. The short-term solution for France is to make less money go farther in Francophone Africa. As long as French national interest dictates the survival of the Franc Zone, it will probably continue, but its beneficiaries in Africa are understandably concerned. France's situation is aggravated by the uncertainty of the coming integrated market for EEC countries and the "New Europe of 1993." If the transition materializes according to plan, it will be accompanied by an increased monetary integration that will have serious implications for the Franc Zone. Rumors about converting the Franc Zone into an ECU Zone exist. Such a change would inevitably and drastically impact the present Franco-African relationship.

As a result of the reunification of the two Germanies, a new case of Europhobia or Germanophobia takes root among certain groups of French society. These groups fear that the new Germany with its 80 million people and superior economic system, coupled with the Germans' keen organizational skills, will increasingly become the dominant member of the EEC. France may try to compensate for this German superiority within the EEC through its traditional, albeit modified, African connections, thus giving a new perspective to its relations with former dependencies in Subsaharan Africa.

France's third reason for maintaining the special relationship is the unparalleled French interest in expanding the role of French language and culture throughout the world—an interest that has given rise to accusations of "cultural imperialism." Paris actively promotes this policy through the annual Franco-African summit meetings and the biannual Francophone summit meetings. The importation of the French educational system by the Francophone black African states necessarily leads to a situation of acute cultural dependency. Within the framework of cooperation and technical assistance, education and culture constitute a priority, thereby reinforcing the economic and political influence of the former colonial power. The fact that many Africans, especially the ruling elite, share a common language and culture with France reflects this influence.

Until the late 1970s there remained a relatively large number of influential African leaders who felt closely identified with the concept of *francophonie*, who enjoyed generous economic aid, and who could depend on the support of French troops in case of trouble. France's closest allies were to be found in the center of the two defunct federations. Senegal and Ivory Coast stand out as two countries that have had leaders whose political careers were intimately involved with French political history throughout the Fourth and Fifth republics. For the past forty years Houphouët-Boigny in particular has played a pivotal role that will be hard to replace. Time and again he has shown that he can influence French policies toward Africa and in return facilitate political positions in the *métropole*. Omar Bongo, president of Gabon, may be the only worthy candidate to replace Houphouët in the role of *doyen*. Most of the African leaders who belong to the first generation under the special Franco-African relationship are now deceased or live in retirement. Sentimental ties are weakening as older generations in France and Africa begin to pass on power to younger people who have not experienced the prolonged close association. It is questionable that the aura around the special relationship will prevail, once the leaders with memories of Africans sitting next to French deputies in the French National Assembly are gone. The new African generation that took over the leadership in recent years—although clearly oriented toward France—lacks the sense of involvement with French politics its ancestors had.

While the trend of democratization that is presently sweeping Francophone Africa is putting pressure for change on the Africans, it is creating fear among the French that the resulting political instability might threaten France's interests—not only its commercial stake and the support generally given to the *métropole* by its former dependencies at the UN but also the security of 200,000 French citizens living in Francophone Africa. The younger, more technocratically oriented French generation is questioning whether the uncertain economic advantage, coupled with an ever-present potential for an undesired military engagement, is really worth the added prestige that the special African connection provides. This generation feels more comfortable cohabiting with member states of an integrated Europe than with a group of unimportant and dependent Third World countries, despite historic and cultural ties. Presumably due to this fact, France's relations with its former independencies are changing, assuming a status no different from that with any other country.

None of the foregoing should be interpreted as an indication that the French are abandoning their advantaged position and retreating from Francophone black Africa. At this writing the French are not facing any either-or decisions and may never have to do so. In general, the French people have become increasingly Eurocentric and are adapting well to the concept of "New Europe 1993." Public opinion polls taken in recent years indicate that more than 70 percent of French company executives are looking forward to an increasingly open and integrated European common market. In Africa, France has diversified its interest outside the traditional Francophone circle; non-Francophone countries have become members of the Franc Zone. It is a fact, however, that the decline of France's superior position in Africa is continuing at an accelerating rate. A more general international presence through the EEC, the World Bank, and the IMF is manifesting itself. Francophone Africa will probably continue to be a major source of raw materials for the EEC; however, African markets are clearly not vital to any European industrial country, including France. Nevertheless, the French are likely to enjoy continued advantage as a result of long-established economic and cultural ties. There are also strong moral and humanitarian reasons France and its EEC partners cannot simply turn their back on a sizable part of Africa's most disadvantaged people.

Appendix 1

Constitution of the Fourth Republic, October 27, 1946

Preamble

On the morrow of the victory gained by the free peoples over the regimes which attempted to enslave and degrade the human person, the French people proclaim anew that every human being, without distinction of race, religion or creed, possesses inalienable and sacred rights. They solemnly reaffirm the rights and liberties of man and the citizen consecrated by the Declaration of Rights of 1789 and the fundamental principles recognized by the laws of the Republic.

They further proclaim as most necessary in our time the following political, economic and social principles:

The law shall guarantee to women rights equal to those of men in all spheres.

Any man persecuted by reason of his activities in the cause of liberty shall have the right of asylum in the territories of the Republic.

It shall be the duty of all to work, and the right of all to obtain employment. None may suffer wrong, in his work or employment, by reason of his origin, opinions or beliefs.

Every man may protect his rights and interests by trade union or professional activity and belong to the organization of his choice.

The right to strike shall be exercised within the framework of the laws which govern it.

Every worker shall participate, through his delegates, in collective bargaining on the conditions of labor as well as in the management of the firm.

Any property, or firm, which possesses or acquires the character of a national public service or of a *de facto* monopoly must come under common ownership.

The Nation shall ensure to the individual and family the conditions necessary to their development.

It shall guarantee to all, especially to the child, the mother and aged workers, the protection of their health, material security, rest and leisure. Every human being who is unable to work on account of his age, his physical or mental condition, or the economic situation, shall be entitled to obtain from the community decent means of support.

The Nation proclaims the solidarity and equality of all Frenchmen with respect to burdens imposed by national disasters.

The Nation shall guarantee the equal access of children and adults to education, professional training and culture. It shall be a duty of the State to organize free and secular public education at all levels.

The French Republic, faithful to its traditions, shall abide by the rules of public international law. It will undertake no war for the object of conquest and will never employ its forces against the liberty of any people.

On condition of reciprocity, France will accept the limitations of sovereignty necessary to the organization and defense of peace.

France together with the overseas peoples shall form a Union founded upon equality of rights and duties, without distinction of race or religion.

The French Union shall consist of nations and peoples who pool or coordinate their resources and their efforts to develop their respective civilizations, increase their well-being and ensure their security.

Faithful to her traditional mission, France proposes to guide the peoples for whom she has taken responsibility into freedom to administer themselves and conduct their own affairs democratically; rejecting any system of colonial rule based upon arbitrary power, she shall guarantee to all equal access to public office and the individual or collective exercise of the rights and liberties proclaimed or confirmed above.

Title VIII: The French Union

Section I: Principles

Art. 60. The French Union shall be composed, on the one hand of the French Republic which comprises metropolitan France, the overseas departments and territories, and on the other hand of the associated territories and States.

Art. 61. The position of the associated States within the French Union shall depend in each case on the act which defines their relationship with France.

Art. 62. The members of the French Union shall pool all their resources in order to guarantee the defense of the whole Union. The Government of the Republic shall undertake the coordination of these resources and the direction of the policy appropriate to prepare and ensure this defense.

Section II: Organization

Art. 63. The central organs of the French Union shall be the Presidency, the High Council and the Assembly.

Art. 64. The President of the French Republic shall be President of the French Union, whose permanent interests he shall represent.

Art. 65. (i) The High Council of the French Union shall consist of the President of the Union as chairman, a delegation of the French Government, and the representatives that each of the associated States shall be entitled to accredit to the President of the Union. (ii) Its function shall be to assist the Government in the general direction of the Union.

Art. 66. (i) The Assembly of the French Union shall consist, half of members representing metropolitan France, and half of members representing the overseas departments and territories and the associated States. (ii) An organic law will decide the conditions under which the different sections of the population may be represented.

Art. 67. The members of the Assembly of the Union shall be elected, for the overseas departments and territories, by the territorial Assemblies; they shall be elected, for metropolitan France, in the proportion of two-thirds by the members of the National Assembly representing metropolitan France and one-third by the members of the Council of the Republic representing metropolitan France.

Art. 68. The associated States may designate delegates to the Assembly of the Union within limits and conditions settled by a law and a domestic act of each State.

Art. 69. (i) The President of the French Union shall convene the Assembly of the French Union and close its sessions. He must convene it at the request of half its members. (ii) The Assembly of the French Union cannot sit during Parliamentary recesses.

Art. 70. The rules of Articles 8, 10, 21, 22 and 23 shall apply to the Assembly of the French Union under the same conditions as to the Council of the Republic.

> Art. 8. Each of the two Houses shall judge the eligibility of its members and the regularity of their election, and alone may accept their resignation.
>
> Art. 10. (i) The sittings of the two Houses shall be public. Verbatim reports of debates and also parliamentary documents shall be published in the *Journal officiel*. (ii) Each of the two Houses may go into committee for a secret session.

Art. 21. No member of Parliament may be prosecuted, sought out, arrested, detained or judged on account of opinions expressed or votes cast by him in the exercise of his functions.

Art. 22. During his term of office, no member of Parliament may be prosecuted or arrested for a crime or misdemeanor without the authorization of the House to which he belongs, except *flagrante delicto*. The detention or prosecution of a member of Parliament shall be suspended if the House to which he belongs so demands.

Art. 23. Members of Parliament shall receive compensation settled in relation to the remuneration of a category of civil servants.

Art. 71. (i) The Assembly of the French Union shall be cognizant of the bills or proposals which are submitted to it for its opinion by the National Assembly or the Government of the French Republic or the Governments of the associated States. (ii) The Assembly shall be entitled to pronounce on motions presented by one of its members, and, if it decides to consider them, to instruct its *bureau* to send them to the National Assembly. It may make proposals to the French Government and to the High Council of the French Union. (iii) To be in order, the motions covered by the preceding paragraph must relate to legislation pertaining to the overseas territories.

Art. 72. (i) In the overseas territories, legislative power shall belong to Parliament in matters of criminal law, the regulation of civil liberties and political and administrative organization. (ii) In all other matters, French laws shall apply in the overseas territories only by express provision or if they have been extended by decree to the overseas territories after an opinion from the Assembly of the Union. (iii) Further, by derogation from Article 13, special provisions for each territory may be enacted by the President of the Republic in Cabinet after a prior opinion from the Assembly of the Union.

Section III: Departments and Overseas Territories

Art. 73. The legislative system of the overseas departments shall be the same as that of the metropolitan departments, unless otherwise determined by law.

Art. 74. (i) The overseas territories shall be granted a special status which takes into account their particular interests within the framework of the general interests of the Republic. (ii) This status and the internal organization of each overseas territory or group of territories shall be settled by law, after an opinion from the Assembly of the French Union and consultation with the Territorial Assemblies.

Art. 75. (i) The individual status of a member of the Republic and of the French Union shall be subject to change. (ii) Alterations of status and transfers from one category to another, within the framework settled by Article 60, may follow only from a law voted by Parliament, after consultation with the Territorial Assemblies and the Assembly of the Union.

Art. 76. (i) The powers of the Republic shall be vested in the representative of the Government in each territory or group of territories. He shall be the head of the territorial administration. (ii) He shall be responsible to the Government for his actions.

Art. 77. An elected Assembly shall be instituted in each territory. The electoral system, composition and competence of this Assembly shall be decided by law.

Art. 78. In the groups of territories, the management of common interests shall be entrusted to an Assembly consisting of members elected by the Territorial Assemblies. (ii) Its composition and powers shall be settled by law.

Art. 79. The overseas territories shall elect representatives to the National Assembly and to the Council of the Republic under the conditions prescribed by law.

Art. 80. All subjects of the overseas territories shall have the status *[qualité]* of citizen, by the same right as French nationals of metropolitan France or of the overseas territories. Special laws will lay down the conditions under which they exercise their rights as citizens.

Art. 81. All French nationals and subjects of the French Union shall have the status of citizen of the French Union which shall ensure for them the enjoyment of the rights and liberties guaranteed by the Preamble to the present Constitution.

Art. 82. (i) Citizens who are not subject to French civil law shall retain their personal status *(subject to indigenous law)* so long as they do not renounce it. (ii) This status *[statut]* may in no circumstance constitute a ground for refusing or restricting the rights and liberties pertaining to the status *[qualité]* of French citizen.

Title X: Territorial Units

Art. 85. (i) The French Republic, one and indivisible, shall recognize the existence of territorial units. (ii) These units shall be the communes and departments, and the overseas territories.

Art. 86. The framework, the extent, the possible regrouping and the organization of the communes and departments, and the overseas territories shall be settled by law.

Art. 87. (i) The territorial units shall administer themselves freely by councils elected by universal suffrage. (ii) Their mayor or president shall be responsible for carrying out the decisions of these councils.

Art. 88. The coordination of the activity of civil servants, the representation of the national interest and the administrative supervision of the territorial units shall be ensured, within the departmental framework, by Government delegates designated in Cabinet.

Art. 89. (i) Organic laws will extend departmental and communal liberties; they may prescribe for certain large cities, rules of operation and structures different from those of small communes, and may include special provisions for certain departments; they will decide the conditions of implementation of Articles 85 to 88 above. (ii) Laws will also decide the conditions under which the local services of the central administration shall operate, in order to bring the administration closer to those with whom it deals.[1]

1. *Source:* Philip M.Williams, *Crisis and Compromise* (Garden City, NY: Anchor Books, 1966), 520–25.

Appendix 2

Constitution of the Fifth Republic, October 4, 1958

Preamble

The French people solemnly proclaim their attachment to the Rights of Man and to the principles of national sovereignty as they were defined by the Declaration of 1789, confirmed and completed by the Preamble of the Constitution of 1946.

By virtue of these principles and that of the free determination of peoples, the Republic offers to the overseas territories which express the wish to adhere to them new institutions based on the common ideal of liberty, equality, and fraternity and conceived with a view towards their democratic development.

Art. 1. The Republic and the peoples of the overseas territories who, by an act of free determination, adopt this Constitution establish a Community.

The Community is based on the equality and the solidarity of the peoples who constitute it.

Title XI. Territorial Units

Art. 72. The territorial units of the Republic are the communes, the departments, and the overseas territories. Other territorial units are created by law.

These units are administered freely by elected councils and under conditions established by law.

In the departments and territories, the delegate of the Government is responsible for national interests, administrative supervision, and respect for the laws.

Art. 73. The legislative system and administrative organization of the overseas departments may be adapted by measures required by their special situation.

Art. 74. The overseas territories of the Republic have a special organization which takes account of their own interests within the overall interests of the Republic. This organization is defined and modified by law after consultation with the territorial assembly concerned.

Art. 75. The citizens of the Republic who do not have ordinary civil status, the only status referred to in Article 34, retain their personal status as long as they have not renounced it.

Art. 76. The overseas territories may retain their status within the Republic.

If they express the desire to do so by a decision of their territorial assembly made within the period specified in the first paragraph of Article 91, they become either overseas departments of the Republic or, in groups or individually, member States of the Community.

Title XII.   The Community

Art. 77. Within the Community established by this Constitution, the States enjoy autonomy; they administer themselves and manage their own affairs democratically and freely.

There is only one citizenship of the Community.

All citizens are equal before the law, whatever their origin, their race, or their religion. They have the same duties.

Art. 78. The Community's jurisdiction includes foreign policy, defense, currency, common economic and financial policy, and policy concerning strategic raw materials.

It also includes, except when there are special agreements, the supervision of justice, higher education, the general organization of external and common transportation, and telecommunications.

Special agreements may create other common jurisdictions or govern any transfer of jurisdiction from the Community to one of its members.

Art. 79. The member States benefit from the provisions of Article 77 as soon as they have exercised the choice referred to in Article 76.

Until the measures necessary for the implementation of this Title go into effect, matters within the common jurisdiction are governed by the Republic.

Art. 80. The President of the Republic presides over and represents the Community.

The institutions of the Community are an Executive Council, a Senate, and a Court of Arbitration.

Art. 81. The member States of the Community participate in the election of the President under the conditions specified in Article 6.

The President of the Republic, in his capacity as President of the Community, is represented in each State of the Community.

Art. 82. The Executive Council of the Community is presided over by the President of the Community. It consists of the Premier of the Republic, the Heads of Government of each of the member States of the Community, and the Ministers responsible for the common affairs of the Community.

The Executive Council organizes the cooperation of the members of the Community on the governmental and administrative levels.

The organization and operation of the Executive Council are specified by an organic law.

Art. 83. The Senate of the Community is composed of delegates chosen by the Parliament of the Republic and the legislative assemblies of the other members of the Community from their own members. The number of delegates from each State depends upon its population and the responsibilities it assumes in the Community.

It holds two sessions each year which are opened and closed by the President of the Community and which may not last longer than one month each.

When called upon by the President of the Community, it deliberates on common economic and financial policy before laws on these matters are voted on by the Parliament of the Republic and, when the case arises, by the legislative assemblies of the other members of the Community.

The Senate of the Community examines the acts and treaties or international agreements referred to in articles 35 and 53 and which commit the Community.

It makes enforceable decisions in the domains in which it has received delegations of power from the legislative assemblies of the members of the Community. These decisions are promulgated in the same form as the law on the territory of each of the States concerned.

An organic law governs its composition and specifies its rules of operation.

Art. 84. A Court of Arbitration of the Community decides litigation among the members of the Community.

Its composition and its jurisdiction are specified by an organic law.

Art. 85. [The paragraphs in italics were added by constitutional law no. 60-525 of June 4, 1960 (*Journal officiel,* June 8, 1960)].

The procedure specified in Article 89 notwithstanding, the provisions of this Title which concern the operation of the common institutions are amended by laws voted in the same terms by the Parliament of the Republic and by the Senate of the Community.

The provisions of this Title may also be amended by agreements concluded among all the States of the Community; the new provisions are put into effect under the conditions required by the Constitution of each State.

Art. 86. A change in the status of a member State of the Community may be requested either by the Republic or by a resolution of the legislative assembly of the State concerned, confirmed by a local referendum, the organization and supervision of which are ensured by the institutions of the Community. The procedures involved in such a change are determined by an agreement approved by the Parliament of the Republic and the legislative assembly concerned.

Under the same conditions, a member State of the Community may become independent. It thereby ceases to belong to the Community.

A member State of the Community may also, by agreement, become independent without thereby ceasing to belong to the Community.

An independent State not a member of the Community may, by agreement, join the Community without ceasing to be independent.

The position of these States within the Community is determined by agreements concluded for this purpose, in particular the agreements mentioned in the preceding paragraphs, as well as, on occasion, the agreements mentioned in the second paragraph of Article 85.

Art. 87. The special agreements concluded for the implementation of this Title are approved by the Parliament of the Republic and the legislative assembly concerned.

Title XIII: Agreements of Association

Art. 88. The Republic or the Community may make agreements with States which want to associate with it in order to develop their civilizations.

Title XIV: Amendment

Art. 89. The initiative for amending the Constitution belongs both to the President of the Republic on the proposal of the Premier and to the Members of Parliament.

The Government or parliamentary bill for amendment must be passed by the two assemblies in identical terms. The amendment is final after having been approved by a referendum.

However, the Government bill for amendment is not submitted to a referendum when the President of the Republic decides to submit it to Parliament convened in Congress; in this case, the Government bill for amendment is approved only if it is adopted by a three-fifths majority of the valid ballots cast. The *bureau* of the Congress is that of the National Assembly.

No amendment process may be undertaken or continued when the integrity of the territory is in jeopardy.

The republican form of government is not subject to amendment.[1]

---

1. *Source:* Roy Pierce, *French Politics and Political Institutions* (New York: Harper & Row, 1973), 313–38.

Appendix 3

Maps

FRENCH POSSESSIONS AT THE TIME OF THE
CONGRESS OF BERLIN, 1884–85

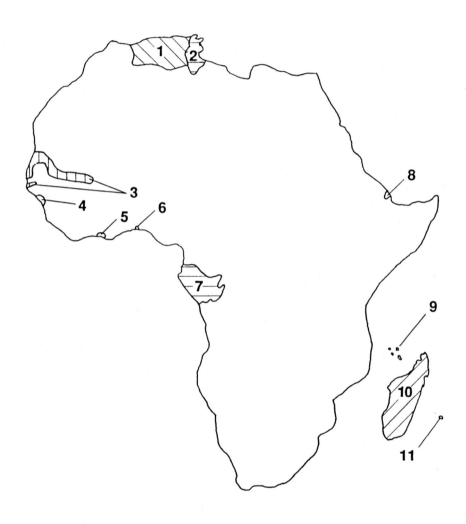

1 Algeria	5 Ivory Coast	9 Comoros
2 Tunisia	6 Dahomey	10 Madagascar
3 Senegal	7 French Congo	11 Réunion
4 Rivières du Sud	8 Obok	

FRENCH POSSESSIONS BEFORE THE
OUTBREAK OF WORLD WAR I

1 Morocco	4 French West Africa	7 Comoros
2 Algeria	5 French Equatorial Africa	8 Madagascar
3 Tunisia	6 French Somaliland	9 Réunion

FRENCH POSSESSIONS AT THE TIME OF THE 1958 REFERENDUM

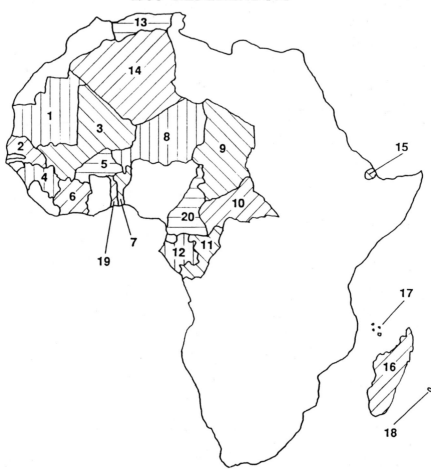

French West Africa:

1 Mauritania	3 Soudan	5 Upper Volta	7 Dahomey
2 Senegal	4 Guinea	6 Ivory Coast	8 Niger

French Equatorial Africa:

9 Chad	10 Oubangui-Chari	11 French Congo	12 Gabon

Other possessions:

13 Algeria	15 French Somaliland	17 Comoros
14 Southern Territories (Algeria)	16 Madagascar	18 Réunion

UN trusteeships:

19 French Togo	20 French Cameroon

FRANCOPHONE AFRICA IN 1993

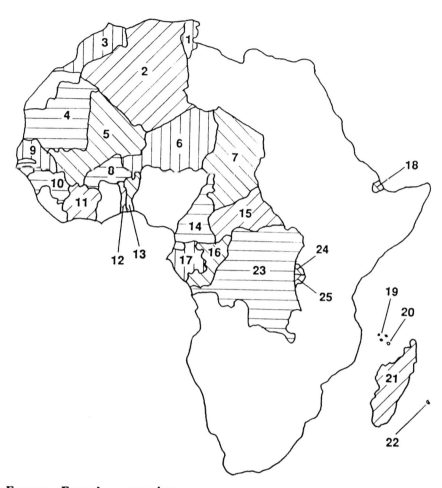

Former French possessions:

1 Tunisia	7 Chad	13 Benin	19 Comoros
2 Algeria	8 Burkina Faso	14 Cameroon	20 Mayotte*
3 Morocco	9 Senegal	15 CAR	21 Malagasy Republ.
4 Mauritania	10 Guinea	16 Congo	22 Réunion*
5 Mali	11 Ivory Coast	17 Gabon	
6 Niger	12 Togo	18 Djibouti	

*In 1993, Mayotte is a French territory; Réunion is an overseas department of the French Republic.

Former Belgian possessions:

23 Zaïre   24 Rwanda   25 Burundi

Appendix 4

Profiles of Individual Countries

Benin

Official name: *République du Bénin* (Republic of Benin) [*République populaire du Bénin*, from November 1975 to February 1990; before that time: *Dahomey*].

Colonial name: *Dahomey*.

Capital: *Porto-Novo* (official, established under the constitution); *Cotonou* (de facto, where the president and most government ministers reside.

Population: Midyear 1992 UN estimate: 4,928,000
most recent census (1992): 4,855,349

Date of current or last constitution: December 2, 1990.

Form of government: Multiparty republic with one legislative house *(Assemblée Nationale)*, sixty-four members, elected for a four-year term.

Head of state and government (1993): President *Nicéphore Soglo*, elected for a five-year term by universal suffrage for a maximum of two terms. The president appoints the members of the council.

Political parties: The former exclusive ruling party, *Parti de la Révolution Populaire du Bénin* (PRPB) was dissolved in May 1990. About fifty groups have registered as political parties for the national conference of February 1990. The main opposition parties are *Union Nationale pour la Démocratie et le Progrès* (UNDP), *Rassemblement Démocratique Dahoméen* (RDD), and *Rassemblement National Démocratique* (RND). These parties attended the national conference under an umbrella grouping, the *Rassemblement des Forces Démocratiques* (RFD), and plan to merge as a single party.

Heads of state since independ.:		Coups d'état:
Hubert Maga	1960–63	
Gen. Christophe Soglo	1963–64	1963 Hubert Maga overthrown
Sourou Migan Apithy	1964–65	
Tahirou Congacou	1965	
Gen. Christophe Soglo	1965–67	1965, Tahirou Congacou overthrown
Lt. Col. Alphonse Allev	1967–68	1967, Christophe Soglo overthrown
Dr. Émile Derlin Zinsou	1968–69	
Lt. Col. Kouandete	1969–70	1969, Émile Derlin Zinsou overthrown
Hubert Maga	1970–72	
Justin Ahomadegbé	1972	
Gen. Mathieu Kérékou	1972–91	1972, Justin Ahomadegbé overthrown
Nicéphore Soglo	1991–	

Ethnic composition (1983): Fon 65.6%; Bariba 9.7%; Yoruba 8.9%; Somba 5.4%; Fulani 4.0%; other 6.4%.

Religious affiliation (1980): Animistic beliefs 61.4%; Christian 23.1% (Roman Catholic 18.5%; Protestant 2.8%); Moslem 15.2%; other 0.3%.

Exports (1987): Cotton 55.6%; energy 27.5%; food products 4.3%; palm kernel oil and palm oil 3.8%; manufactured goods 1.7%. *Major export destinations* (1989): Portugal 15.2%; Italy 9.9%; Thailand 9.6%; Taiwan 9.0%; United States 7.4%; Niger 6.2%; France 6.1%.

Imports (1990): Manufactured goods 38.5%; food products 23.5%; machinery and transport equipment 13.5%; beverages and tobacco 7.6%. *Major import sources* (1989): India 23.4%; France 15.9%; the Netherlands 5.0%; Ivory Coast 4.6%; Thailand 4.6%; United States 3.7%; Italy 3.2%; Taiwan 2.9%; Korea 2.7%.

Burkina Faso

Official name: *Burkina Faso* (Burkina Faso)
[*Haute-Volta* (Upper Volta) before August 1984].

Colonial name: *Haute-Volta* (Upper Volta).

Capital: Ouagadougou.

Population: Midyear 1992 UN estimate: 9,515,000
most recent census (1985):   7,964,705
(data are for de jure population)

Date of current or last constitution: June 11, 1991 (transitional).

Form of government: Democratic and popular republic (a military regime, which abandoned Marxism-Leninism in March 1991). Popular participation has been sought through the nationwide creation of the *Comités Révolutionnaires* (CR) in 1991. The first legislative elections in fourteen years were held on May 24, 1993; President Blaise Compaoré's parties, the *Organisation pour la Démocratie Populaire* (ODP) and the *Mouvement du Travail* (MT), won a landslide victory.

Head of state and government (1993): President Capt. *Blaise Compaoré*, chairman of the *Front Populaire* (FP). Prime minister: *Youssouf Ouedraogo*.

Political parties: Seven parties form the FP, including the *Organisation pour la Démocratie Populaire* (ODP) and the *Mouvement du Travail* (MT).

Heads of state since independ.:		Coups d'état:
Maurice Yameogo	1960–66	
Gen. Sangoulé Lamizana	1966–71	1966, Maurice Yameogo overthrown
Gérald Kango Ouedraogo	1971–74	
Gen. Sangoulé Lamizana	1974–80	1974, Gérald K. Ouedraogo overthrown
Col. Saye Zerbo	1980–82	1980, Sangoulé Lamizana overthrown
Maj. Jean-Baptiste		
Ouedraogo	1982–83	1982, Saye Zerbo overthrown
Capt. Thomas Sankara	1983–87	1983, J.-B. Ouedraogo overthrown
Capt. Blaise Compaoré	1987–	1987, Thomas Sankara killed

Ethnic composition (1983): Mossi 47.9%; Mande 8.8%; Fulani 8.3%; Lobi 6.9%; Bobo 6.8%; Senufo 5.3%; Grosi 5.1%; Gurma 4.8%; Tuareg 3.3%; other 2.8%.

Religious affiliation (1980): Animistic beliefs 44.8%; Moslem 43.0%; Christian 12.2% (Roman Catholic 9.8%; Protestant 2.4%).

Exports (1988): Raw cotton 45.3%; manufactured goods 33.7%; machinery and equipment 6.0%; live animals 4.0%; vegetable food products 2.0%. *Major export destinations* (1990): France 29.5%; Taiwan 12.9%; Portugal 8.2%; Italy 7.6%; Japan 5.7%; Tunisia 5.0%.

Imports (1988): Machinery and transport equipment 28.1%; manufactured goods 26.5%; chemicals 11.8%; cereals 9.2%; crude oil products 7.3%; dairy products 3.9%; raw materials 2.6%; grease and lubricants 1.0%. *Major import sources* (1990): France 30.5%; Ivory Coast 29.9%; Italy 4.7%; Japan 4.0%; Germany 3.3%; the Netherlands 3.1%.

Cameroon

Official name: *République du Cameroun* (Republic of Cameroon).

Colonial name: French Cameroun and British Cameroons.

Capital: Yaoundé.

Population: Midyear 1992 UN estimate: 12,662,000
                    most recent census (1987): 10,493,655

Date of current or last constitution: June 2, 1972, revised several times.

Form of government: Multiparty republic with one legislative house *(Assemblée Nationale)*, 180 members, elected for a five-year term. In practice political power is held by the central committee of the *Rassemblement Démocratique du Peuple Camerounais* (RDPC). The RDPC, headed by President *Paul Biya,* garnered eighty-eight of the 180 seats in the National Assembly in the legislative elections held on March 1, 1992.

Head of state and government (1993): President *Paul Biya,* elected for a five-year term by universal suffrage. The president appoints the members of the cabinet. The first multiparty presidential election, which President Biya won by 4 percentage points, was so filled with irregularities—according to outside observers—as to be completely discredited. Prime minister: *Simon Achidi Achu.*

Political parties: The RDPC replaced the *Union Nationale Camerounaise* (UNC) as the exclusive ruling party in March 1985. In December 1990 a law was passed that allows multiparty politics but regulates the scope of new parties. Approved opposition parties are *Social Democratic Front* (SDF), founded in March 1990; *Mouvement National pour la Démocratie* (MND); *Union des Populations du Cameroun* (UPC), founded in 1948, prohibited in 1960, and restored in 1991. Thirty-two groups had registered as political parties and participated in the legislative elections held on March 1, 1992.

Heads of state since independ.:		Coups d'état:
Ahmadou Ahidjo	1960–82	none
Paul Biya	1982–	

French military interventions: Between 1959 and 1964 the French gave considerable support to government forces fighting the Bamileke-led UPC, which in turn received help from the Soviet Union. Some 300 French officers and senior noncommissioned officers were operating as military assistants to the Cameroon government and managed the *Zone de Pacification du Cameroun* (ZOPAC), which the French government had set up to control the rebellion.

Ethnic composition (1983): Fang 19.6%; Bamilcke and Bamum 18.5%; Duala, Luanda, and Basa 14.7%; Fulani 9.6%; Tikar 7.4%; Mandara 5.7%; Maka 4.9%; Chamba 2.4%; Mbum 1.3%; Hausa 1.2%; French 0.2%; other 14.4%. Cameroon has a highly diversified population comprising some 200 ethnic groups and twenty-four linguistic groups.

Religious affiliation (1980): Christian 53.0% (Roman Catholic 35.0%; Protestant 18.0%); animistic beliefs 25.0%; Moslem 22.0%.

Exports (1990): Crude oil 54.2%; cacao 10.5%; coffee 10.0%; saw wood and logs 7.9%; cotton 5.8%. *Major export destinations* (1990): France 32.7%; United States 14.9%; the Netherlands 14.4%; Italy 7.8%; Germany 4.2%; Spain 4.2%; Korea 3.3%; China 1.9%; Equatorial Guinea 1.9%.

Imports (1987): Machinery and transport equipment 35.6%; motor vehicle tires 5.5%; iron and steel 4.6%; flour products 3.4%; chemical products 3.2%; nonmetallic minerals 2.8%; paper and paper products 2.6%; plastic products 2.5%. *Major import sources* (1990): France 32.9%; Germany 10.6%; Japan 5.7%; Belgium-Luxembourg 5.5%; Italy 5.2%; United States 4.7%; the Netherlands 3.4%; Guinea 3.3%; United Kingdom 3.0%.

Central African Republic (CAR)

Official name: *République Centrafricaine* (Central African Republic).

Colonial name: Oubangui-Chari.

Capital: Bangui.

Population: Midyear 1992 UN estimate: 2,930,000
most recent census (1988): 2,688,426

Date of current or last constitution: November 21, 1986.

Form of government: Single-party republic with part-military, part-civilian government. It has a bicameral Congress that meets as two chambers, an upper *(Conseil économique et régional)* and a lower *(Assemblée Nationale)*. The latter has fifty-two members, elected for a five-year term by universal suffrage; the numbers of seats of the upper chamber are not available.

Head of state and government (1993): President Gen. *André Kolingba*. Prime minister: *Edouard Franck*.

Political parties: The *Rassemblement Démocratique Centrafricain* (RDC) is the exclusive ruling party. On November 30, 1990, President Kolingba announced that a multiparty system could be introduced in the longterm, without setting a date.

Heads of state since independ.:		Coups d'état:
David Dacko	1960–66	
Lt. Col. (later Emperor)		
Jean Bédel Bokassa	1966–79	1966, David Dacko overthrown
David Dacko	1979–81	1979, Emperor Bokassa overthrown
Gen. André Kolingba	1981–	1981, David Dacko overthrown

French military interventions: In January 1979 students and schoolchildren in Bangui demonstrated against a government order to wear uniforms made in a factory owned by Emperor Bokassa. The Imperial Guard intervened, and over 100 schoolchildren were killed. A few days later Amnesty International denounced the massacre. Probably under pressure of Francophone African chiefs of state, French paratroopers launched a coup de force, *opération Barracuda,* to depose Jean Bédel Bokassa, who was in Libya at the time. He was replaced with a less erratic successor, his cousin David Dacko.

Ethnic composition (1983): Banda 28.6%; Baya (Gbaya) 24.5%; Ngbandi 10.6%; Azande 9.8%; Sara 6.9%; Mbaka 4.3%; Mbum 4.1%; Kare 2.4%; French 0.1%; other 8.7%.

Religious affiliation (1980): Christian 68.0% (Protestant 40.0%; Roman Catholic 28.0%); animistic beliefs 24.0%; Moslem 8.0%.

Exports (1990): Diamonds 66.2%; wood 13.4%; coffee 13.0%; cotton 2.6%. *Major export destinations* (1990): Belgium-Luxembourg 65.9%; France 22.8%; Switzerland 5.0%; Germany 1.2%.

Imports (1990): General manufactures 36.2%; food products 24.3%; motor cars 9.2%; pharmaceuticals 7.1%. *Major import sources* (1990): France 46.6%; Cameroon 11.2%; Germany 7.0%; Japan 5.8%; Congo 3.8%.

Chad

Official name: *République du Tchad* (Republic of Chad).

Colonial name: Chad.

Capital: N'Djamena.

Population: Midyear 1992 UN estimate: 5,961,000
                 most recent census (1975):   4,029,917

Date of current or last constitution: December 10, 1989, suspended on December 2, 1990. A new constitution, followed by multiparty elections, is not expected before late 1993.

Form of government: Republic (military regime). Its president has announced plans for a national conference to deal with the country's political problems.

Head of state and government (1993): Supreme political power rests with the *Conseil d'État Provisoire*, formed on February 28, 1990, after the takeover by President Col. *Idriss Déby*. The *Conseil* is the executive committee of the *Mouvement Patriotique du Salut* (MPS, Patriotic Movement for Salvation) and has about thirty members drawn from various factions; it is chaired by the prime minister, *Joseph Yodoyman*, appointed on May 20, 1992, by President Déby.

Political parties: The *Mouvement Patriotique du Salut* is the exclusive ruling party.

Heads of state since independ.:		Coups d'état:
François Ngarta Tombalbaye	1960–75	
Maj. Gen. Félix Malloum	1975–79	1975, François N. Tombalbaye killed
Goukouni Oueddeï	1979–82	1979, Félix Malloum overthrown
El Hadj Hissène Habré	1982–90	1982, Goukouni Oueddeï overthrown
Gen. Idriss Déby	1990–	1990, El Hadj H. Habré overthrown

French military interventions: In 1960 French troops intervened briefly to quell disturbances between opposing political factions.

In 1968 French military forces aided the southern, animist-Christian government, headed by President François Ngarta Tombalbaye, in defense against a challenge mounted by the Moslem nomads in the northern provinces. French intervention in this troubled country has been repeated several times since. The most serious crisis came in 1982, when Libyan forces invaded northern Chad. In response to this incursion, the French sent in troops but limited them to the southern half of the country in order to avoid a direct confrontation with the Libyan forces. This maneuver virtually partitioned the country along the 16th parallel. In 1983, after the strategically important northern town of Laya-Largeau fell to the leader of the opposition party backed by Libyan forces, international involvement (Zaïre and United States) escalated rapidly. Mitterrand accused Libya of having internationalized the conflict and dispatched troops and air support to the north of N'Djamena *(opération Manta),* but there was no significant military action. Throughout 1984 and 1985 the situation remained at an impasse both politically and militarily. Following reports in February 1986 that President Hissène Habré's troops had been attacked by Libyan forces in central Chad, the French stepped up their military support of Habré's government *(opération Épervier).* In 1989 the Libyan troops in Chad were decisively defeated by the French-backed Habré forces. Without the French logistics support, the

Chadians would not have been able to stand their ground against the well-supplied Libyan army. Diplomatic relations between the two countries were restored in October 1989.

In December 1990, when President Habré was overthrown and the government taken over by Gen. Idriss Déby, France was obliged to send reinforcements to eastern Chad to protect French nationals.

Ethnic composition (1983): Sara, Bagirmi, and Kreish 30.5%; Sudanic Arab 26.1%; Teda (Tubu) 7.3%; Mbum 6.5%; Masalit, Maba, and Mimi 6.3%; Tama 6.3%; Mubi 4.2%; Kanuri 2.3%; Hausa 2.3%; Masa 2.3%; Kotoko 2.1%; other 3.8%.

Religious affiliation (1989): Moslem 40.4%; Christian 33.0% (Roman Catholic 21.0%; Protestant 11.6%); animistic beliefs 26.6%.

Exports (1988): Raw cotton 91.1%; live cattle and frozen bovine meat 1.8%; hides and skins 0.4%. *Major export destinations* (1990): Portugal 21.0%; Germany 16.9%; Japan 13.3%; France 9.9%; Spain 8.4%.

Imports (1988): Crude oil products 16.8%; cereal products 16.8%; pharmaceutical products and chemicals 11.5%; machinery and transport equipment 8.5%; electrical equipment 5.7%; textiles 2.9%; raw and refined sugar 2.3%. *Major import sources* (1989): France 36.2%; United States 20.4%; Cameroon 18.4%; Italy 5.6%.

Congo

Official name: *République Populaire du Congo* (People's Republic of the Congo).

Colonial name: Moyen-Congo (Middle Congo).

Capital: Brazzaville.

Population: Midyear 1992 UN estimate: 2,692,000
most recent census (1984):   1,909,248
(data are for de jure population)

Date of current or last constitution: March 15, 1992.

Form of government: People's republic with one legislative body *(Assemblée Nationale Populaire)*, 153 members, elected for a five-year term by universal suffrage from a list approved by the party. The assembly is responsible to the president, who in turn is responsible to the party. A national conference on transition to multiparty democracy was held in March 1991. (Congo was the first African state to adopt a Marxist-Leninist regime.) Multiparty elections were held on May 10, 24, and 31, 1992; presidential elections on June 14 and 28, 1992.

Head of state and government (1993): President *Pascal Lissouba,* chairman of the *Union Panafricaine pour la Démocratie Sociale* (UPADS). Prime minister since the beginning of 1993: *Antoine da Costa.*

Political parties: The *Parti Congolais du Travail* (PCT) was the exclusive ruling party, though PCT's list for legislative elections in 1989 included seventy-four seats for nonparty interest groups and individuals. The end of single-party rule, approved by a PCT Congress, took formal effect on January 1, 1991. There are three official affiliate organizations for PCT trade unionists, women, and youth: the *Confédération Syndicale Congolaise* (CSC), the *Union Révolutionnaire des Femmes Congolaises* (URFC), and the *Union de la Jeunesse Socialiste Congolaise* (UJSC).

Heads of state since independ.:		Coups d'état:
Abbé Fulbert Youlou	1960–63	
Alphonse Massemba-Débat	1963–68	
Maj. Marien Ngouabi	1968–77	1968, Massemba-Débat overthrown
Col. Joachim Yhombi-Opango	1977–79	1977, Marien Ngouabi killed
Gen. Denis Sassou-Nguesso	1979–92	1979, J. Yhombi-Opango overthrown
Pascal Lissouba	1992–	

French military interventions: A small-scale French intervention took place in 1960 to end conflicts between political rival forces.

Ethnic composition (1983): Kongo 51.5%; Teke 17.3%; Mboshi 11.5%; Mbete 4.8%; Punu 3.0%; Sango 2.7%; Maka 1.8%; Pygmy 1.5%; other 5.9%.

Religious affiliation (1980): Christian 78.8% (Roman Catholic 53.9%; Protestant 24.9%); animistic beliefs 19.0%; other 2.2%.

Exports (1989): Crude oil and crude oil products 76.7%; wood and wood products 15.6%; diamonds 2.1%; iron and steel 0.1%. *Major export destinations* (1989): United States 42.9%; France 16.1%; Belgium-Luxembourg 8.3%; Italy 7.8%; the Netherlands 7.2%; Spain 6.2%.

Imports (1988): Machinery and transport equipment 33.2%; food, beverages, and tobacco 21.3%; chemicals and chemical products 12.5%; metal manufactures 7.6%; basic manufactures 3.4%. *Major import sources* (1989): France 48.1%; Cameroon 6.4%; Italy 6.1%; Zaïre 4.1%; the Netherlands 3.9%.

Gabon

Official name: *République Gabonaise* (Gabonese Republic).

Colonial name: Gabon.

Capital: Libreville.

Population: Midyear 1992 UN estimate: 1,253,000
              most recent census (1961):   448,564

Date of current or last constitution: March 26, 1991.

Form of government: Multiparty republic with one legislative house *(Assemblée Nationale)*, 120 members, including nine nonelective members appointed by the head of state. In addition to the Party Congress, which sets policy, there is a twenty-seven-member political bureau and a 253-member central committee. The political bureau can override the council of ministers by issuing decrees. The central committee operates in an advisory capacity.

Head of state and government (1993): President *El Hadji Omar Bongo*, elected for a seven-year term by universal suffrage; he appoints and leads the council of ministers, including a prime minister, since April 27, 1990: *Casimir Oye-Mba.*

Political parties: In 1990 the *Rassemblement Social-Démocratique Gabonais* (RSDG) replaced the exclusive ruling party, the *Parti Démocratique Gabonais* (PDG). Several other parties have recently been created and approved.

Heads of state since independ.:		Coups d'état:
Léon M'Ba	1960–67	none
El Hadji Omar Bongo	1967–	

French military interventions: A small-scale French intervention took place in 1960 to end conflicts between political rival groups.

    None of the French interventions associated with the process of decolonization received as much publicity as the one in Gabon in February 1964 in support of President Léon M'Ba. In accordance with the defense agreement with Gabon, which implicitly provided for the personal protection of the Gabonese president, French forces intervened to put down an uprising led by the leaders of the opposition party, who took President M'Ba prisoner. French paratroops dispatched to Libreville squashed the rebellion and restored M'Ba to power. This intervention came as a surprise. France had not intervened in Togo during the disturbance that followed the assassination of President Olympio in 1963, nor were troops sent to Congo-Brazzaville during the troubles in the same year to support Abbé Fulbert Youlou, who was forced to resign his presidency. Presumably the presence of substantial quantities of oil and a compliant government in Gabon made the difference. The publicity surrounding the Gabon affair led to a review of French African policy. A decision was made to accelerate the withdrawal of troops from African soil and to rely on the deterrent value of the *Force d'intervention*.

In May 1990, following the mysterious death of opposition leader Joseph Rendjambe, riots broke out in Libreville and Port-Gentil. The French government ordered troop reinforcements to these two cities and evacuated hundreds of French citizens. Paris insisted that it was merely protecting French lives and property and was not taking sides in the dispute.

Ethnic composition (1983):   Fang 35.5%;   Mpongwe 15.1%;   Mbete 14.2%; Punu 11.5%; other 23.7%.

Religious affiliation (1980):   Christian 96.2% (Roman Catholic 65.2%; Protestant 18.8%); animistic beliefs 15.0%; Moslem 0.8%; other 0.1%.

Exports (1989): Crude oil and crude oil products 70.8%; manganese ore and concentrate 11.6%; wood 9.4%; uranium ore and concentrate 4.1%. *Major export destinations* (1989): France 36.2%; United States 26.1%; the Netherlands 6.2%; Japan 3.3%; Ivory Coast 2.9%; Italy 2.3%.

Imports (1989): Machinery and mechanical equipment 29.2%; food and agricultural products 14.6%; transport equipment 12.5%; manufactured products 12.1%; metal and metal products 11.2%; chemical products 5.4%; mining products 1.6%. *Major import sources* (1989): France 46.3%; Cameroon 9.7%; the Netherlands 5.5%; United States 5.4%; Japan 4.1%; United Kingdom 2.9%; Italy 2.4%; Belgium-Luxembourg 1.9%.

Guinea

Official name: *République populaire et révolutionnaire de Guinée* (Popular and Revolutionary Republic of Guinea).

Colonial name: French Guinea.

Capital: Conakry.

Population: Midyear 1992 UN estimate: 7,232,000
                   most recent census (1983):   5,781,014

Date of current or last constitution: December 23, 1990 (transitional).

Form of government: Political power rests with the *Comité Militaire pour le Renouveau National* (CMRN). The new constitution provides for a five-year transition to civilian government, conversion of the Military Committee for National Recovery into a *Comité National de Transition* (CNT, eighty members), composed of military and civilian representatives. The CNT will eventually lead to elections for a unicameral parliament, contested by two political parties.

Head of state and government (1993):   President (and chairman of CMRN) General *Lansana Conté*. Future presidents will be elected for a five-year term for a maximum of two terms.

Political parties: None—the exclusive ruling party, the *Parti Démocratique de Guinée* (PDG), was dissolved in 1984. The new constitution provides for a two-party political system.

Heads of state since independ.:		Coups d'état:
Ahmed Sékou Touré	1958–84	
Gen. Lansana Conté	1984–	1984, bloodless military coup led by Lansana Conté after the natural death of Sékou Touré.

Ethnic composition (1983):   Fulani 38.6%;   Malinke 23.2%;   Susu 11.0%; Kissi 6.0%;   Kpelle 4.6%;   other 16.6%.

Religious affiliation (1988):   Moslem 85.0%;   animistic beliefs 5.0%; Christian 1.5%;   other 8.5%.

Exports (1990): Bauxite and alumina 77.6%;   diamonds 8.9%;   gold 5.8%; coffee 4.5%;   fish 1.8%. *Major export destinations* (1990):   United States 23.0%;   France 14.0%;   Germany 14.0%;   Spain 13.0%;   Ireland 9.0%.

Imports (1988):   Intermediate goods 43.9%;   capital goods 17.0%;   crude oil products 13.7%;   food products 12.8%;   consumer goods 12.6%. *Major import sources* (1990):   France 36.0%;   United States 9.0%;   Belgium-Luxembourg 9.0%;   Germany 6.0%;   Italy 5.0%.

Ivory Coast

Official name: *République de Côte-d'Ivoire* (Republic of Côte-d'Ivoire). In 1986 Côte-d'Ivoire has requested that the French version of the country's name be used as the official protocol version in all languages.

Colonial name: Côte-d'Ivoire (Ivory Coast).

Capital: Yamoussoukro was officially named capital in 1983, but the transfer of government functions from Abidjan (de facto capital) remains incomplete.

Population: Midyear 1992 UN estimate: 12,951,000
most recent census (1975):   6,702,866

Date of current or last constitution: October 31, 1960, revised several times.

Form of government: Multiparty republic with one legislative house *(Assemblée Nationale),* 175 members, elected for a five-year term. The president can ask the assembly to reconsider a measure or submit it to referendum.

Head of state and government (1993): The nation's leadership position became vacant on December 7, 1993, with the death of *Félix Houphouët-Boigny,* the Ivory Coast's only ruler since independence from France in 1960. After a short power struggle, the Supreme Court confirmed former diplomat *Henri Konan Bédie* as the new president; former Finance Minister *Duncan Kablan* was appointed prime minister.

Political parties: Until 1990 the *Parti Démocratique de la Côte-d'Ivoire* (PDCI) was the exclusive ruling party. In May 1990 the PDCI requested that the government respect article 7 of the constitution and allow legal formation of political parties. Between May and August 1990, twenty-five opposition parties were officially recognized, including the *Front Populaire Ivorien* (FPI).

Heads of state since independ.:	Coups d'état:
Félix Houphouët-Boigny 1960–93	none
Henri Konan Bédie 1993–	

Ethnic composition (1975): Akan 41.4%; Kru 16.7%; Voltaic 15.7%; Malinke 14.9%; Southern Mande 10.2%; other 1.1%.

Religious affiliation (1989): Animistic beliefs 60.0%; Moslem 20.0%; Christian 20.0% (Catholic 15.0%; Protestant 5.0%).

Exports (1989): Food products 59.7%; energy products 9.6%; cotton and cotton cloth 5.4%. *Major export destinations* (1989): the Netherlands 16.9%; France 15.2%; United States 10.5%; Italy 7.3%.

Imports (1989): Food and food products 21.0%; crude oil 20.3%; machinery and transport equipment 16.4%; chemicals 14.8%. *Major import sources* (1988): France 28.7%; Nigeria 16.0%; Italy 5.3%; the Netherlands 4.7%.

Mali

Official name: *République du Mali* (Republic of Mali).

Colonial name: Soudan.

Capital: Bamako.

Population: Midyear 1992 UN estimate: 8,464,000
                    most recent census (1987):   7,696,348

Date of current or last constitution: February 14, 1992.

Form of government: Multiparty republic with one legislative house *(Assemblée Nationale)*, eighty-two members elected for a four-year term by universal suffrage. In April 1991 a twenty-five-member military/civilian Transitional People's Salvation Committee took over the government functions. The first multiparty legislative elections were held in January 1992.

Head of state and government (1993): In presidential elections held April 12 and 26, 1992, *Alpha Oumar Konaré*, the leader of the Alliance for Democracy in Mali (ADEMA), was elected with a 69 percent majority by a modest 21 percent of eligible voters. Prime minister since April 13, 1993: *Abdoulay Sékou Sow.*

Political parties: The *Union Démocratique du Peuple Malien* (UDPM) was the only legal political party under Gen. Amadou Touré.

Heads of state since independ.:		Coups d'état:
Modibo Keita	1960–68	
Gen. Moussa Traoré	1968–91	1968, Modibo Keita overthrown
Gen. Amadou Toumani		
Touré	1991–92	1991, Moussa Traoré overthrown
Alpha Oumar Konaré	1992–	

Ethnic composition (1983): Bambara 31.9%; Fulani 13.9%; Senufo 12.0%; Soninke 8.8%; Tuareg 7.3%; Songhai 7.2%; Malinke 6.6%; Dogon 4.0%; Dyula 2.9%; Bobo 2.4%; Arab 1.2%; other 1.8%.

Religious affiliation (1983): Moslem 90.0%; animistic beliefs 9.0%; Christian 1.0%.

Exports (1990): Raw cotton and cotton products 44.9%; live animals 24.0%; gold and diamonds 12.5%. *Major export destinations* (1987): France 11.2%; United Kingdom 9.5%; Morocco 7.6%; Belgium-Luxembourg 5.7%; Algeria 5.7%; Portugal 5.6%; Spain 5.0%; the Netherlands 4.4%; Réunion 4.1%; Tunisia 3.1%.

Imports (1990): Machinery, appliances, and transport equipment 29.3%; food products 12.7%; construction materials 9.4%; chemicals 9.2%; crude oil products 9.1%. *Major import sources* (1987): France 24.7%; Ivory Coast 21.8%; Italy 5.0%; Senegal 4.2%; Spain 3.6%; the Netherlands 3.5%; Belgium-Luxembourg 2.7%; United States 2.3%; Hong Kong 2.3%; United Kingdom 2.0%; Japan 1.8%; China 1.3%; Switzerland 0.6%.

Mauritania

Official name: *République Islamique de Mauritanie* (Islamic Republic of Mauritania).

Colonial name: Mauritania.

Capital: Nouakchott.

Population: Midyear 1992 UN estimate: 2,108,000
                 most recent census (1977):   1,419,939

Date of current or last constitution: July 12, 1991.

Form of government: Islamic republic (military regime).

Head of state and government (1993): President Col. *Maaouya Ould Sidi Ahmed Taya,* nominated by the twenty-four-member *Comité Militaire de Salut National* (CMSN, Military Committee for National Salvation). In January 1992 Taya won the first democratic presidential elections after twenty-eight years of one-party rule. Prime minister: *Sidi Mohamed Ould Boubacar.*

Political parties: The exclusive ruling party, the *Parti du Peuple Mauritanien* (PPM), was dissolved in July 1978. In April 1992, an opposition party to the CMSN, the Union des Forces Démocratiques (UDF), was legally formed.

Heads of state since independ.:	Coups d'état:
Moktar Ould Daddah 1960–78	
Lt. Col. Mustapha Ould Muhammed Salek 1978–79	1978, Moktar Ould Daddah overthrown
Lt. Col. Mohamed Mahmoud Ould Louly 1979–80	
Lt. Col. Mohamed Khouna Ould Haidalla 1980–84	1980, M. M. Ould Louly overthrown
Lt. Col. Maaouya Ould Sidi Ahmed Taya 1984–	1984, M. K. Ould Haidalla overthrown

French military interventions: From 1956 to 1963, until the newly formed Mauritanian government was organized and able to assert itself in the vast, empty northern reaches of the country, French troops were stationed in western Sahara .

Ethnic composition (1983): Moor 81.5% (about half Arab-Berber and half African Sudanic); Wolof 6.8%; Tukulor 5.3%; Soninke 2.8%; Fulani 1.1%; other 2.5%.

Official religion: Islam.

Religious affiliation (1980): Moslem 99.4%; Christian 0.4%; other 0.2%.

Exports (1989): Fish 58.6%; iron ore 31.3%. *Major export destinations* (1989): Japan 31.4%; France 11.8%; Belgium 10.2%; Italy 10.1%; Spain 7.0%; Ivory Coast 6.6%; United Kingdom 3.0%; United States 2.0%; Panama 0.3%.

Imports (1988): Machinery and transport equipment 51.0%; food 30.6%; consumer goods 9.0%; crude oil and crude oil products 7.0%. *Major import sources* (1989): France 42.6%; Spain 8.2%; United States 6.0%; the Netherlands 5.5%; Thailand 5.2%; China 4.3%; Algeria 3.9%.

Niger

Official name: *République du Niger* (Republic of Niger).

Colonial name: Niger.

Capital: Niamey.

Population: Midyear 1992 UN estimate: 8,281,000
most recent census (1988): 7,228,552
(data are for de jure population)

Date of current or last constitution: September 24, 1989, suspended by the National Conference on August 9, 1991. An interim legislative body, the Haut conseil de la République, was subsequently delegated to draft a new constitution, which is expected to provide for the creation of a civilian, multiparty political system in late 1993.

Form of government: Multiparty republic with one legislative house *(Assemblée Nationale)*, fifty members, elected for a five-year term, dissolved from 1974 to 1989, reinstated in 1989.

Head of state and government (1993): President Brig. Gen. *Ali Saibou,* assisted by the *Conseil Supérieur d'Orientation Nationale* (CSON, Supreme Council of National Orientation), and a prime minister, *Amadou Cheiffou.*

Political parties: Although the constitution provides for a multiparty political system, the *Mouvement National pour une Société de Développement* (MNSD) is the only party.

Heads of state since independ.: | **Coups d'état:**
Hamani Diori   1960–74 |

Lt. Col. Seyni Kountché   1974–87 | 1974, Hamani Diori overthrown
Col. Ali Saibou   1987–

French military interventions: In 1960 French forces intervened to quell clashes between political rival groups.

Ethnic composition (1988): Hausa 52.8%; Zerma-Songhai 21.0%; Tuareg 10.6%; Fulani 9.8%; Kanuri-Nanga 4.5%; Teda 0.5%; Arab 0.3%; Gurma 0.3%; other 0.2%.

Religious affiliation (1988): Sunni Moslem 80.0%; animistic beliefs 20.0%.

Exports (1989): Uranium 71.5%; live animals 10.5%; cowpeas 5.2%. *Major export destinations* (1989): France 80.1%; Spain 8.4%; Nigeria 7.4%; Portugal 6.3%; Canada 2.6%; Ivory Coast 0.8%.

Imports (1989): Raw materials and machinery 42.5%; consumer goods 36.6%; cereals 12.2%; crude oil products 6.0%. *Major import sources* (1989): France 32.1%; Ivory Coast 10.7%; Japan 4.5%; Italy 4.0%; Nigeria 3.5%; the Netherlands 3.5%.

Senegal

Official name: *République du Sénégal* (Republic of Senegal).

Colonial name: Sénégal.

Capital: Dakar.

Population: Midyear 1992 UN estimate: 7,691,000
                    most recent census (1988):   6,928,405

Date of current or last constitution: March 7, 1963, revised February 22, 1970, and September 21, 1991.

Form of government: Multiparty republic with one legislative house *(Assemblée Nationale)*, 100 members, elected for a five-year term.

Head of state and government (1993): President *Abdou Diouf,* elected for a seven-year term by universal suffrage; he appoints the members of the Council of Ministers headed by the prime minister (PM), *Hanib Thiab* (PM since April 7, 1991). President Diouf easily won a third term in February 1993 but his nearly two to one margin of victory was marred by controversy over the electoral process.

Political parties: The ruling party is the *Parti Socialiste Sénégalais* (PSS). Since September 1991, several groups have registered as political parties.

Heads of state since independ.: | **Coups d'état:**
Léopold Sédar Senghor   1960–80 | none
Abdou Diouf   1980– |

French military interventions: In 1960 radical Soudanese leaders of the short-lived Mali Federation, led By Modibo Keita, tried to take political control of the federation's government in Dakar. Senegalese gendarme units in cooperation with French officers outmaneuvered Keita and his companions and thus prevented the expulsion of Sédar Senghor from power.

Ethnic composition (1988): Wolof 43.7%; Fulani- (Peul-) Tukulor 23.2%; Serer 14.8%; other 18.3%.

Religious affiliation (1988): Sunni Moslem 94.0%; Christian 4.9%; animistic beliefs and other 1.1%.

Exports (1989): Peanut oil 14.2%; crude oil products 13.6%; crustaceans, mollusks, and shellfish 11.9%; phosphates 10.0%; canned fish 7.4%; fresh fish 6.6%. *Major export destinations* (1989): France 35.0%; India 10.1%; Italy 6.7%; Mali 4.6%; Japan 4.1%; Spain 3.9%; the Netherlands 3.2%; Ivory Coast 2.7%; Philippines 2.5%; Cameroon 1.8%; Greece 1.3%.

Imports (1989): Crude oil products 17.1%; agricultural and industrial equipment 13.8%; rice 9.8%; transport equipment and parts 5.9%; pharmaceutical products 3.3%; paper and paper products 3.3%; wheat and wheat products 3.2%; dairy products 3.1%. *Major import sources* (1989): France 31.8%; United States 7.3%; Italy 5.3%; Nigeria 5.0%; Ivory Coast 4.7%; Spain 4.1%; Thailand 3.6%; Gabon 3.6%; the Netherlands 3.2%; Japan 3.1%; Pakistan 3.0%.

Togo

Official name: *République Togolaise* (Republic of Togo).

Colonial name: Togo or Togoland.

Capital: Lomé.

Population: Midyear 1992 UN estimate: 3,701,000
                 most recent census (1981):   2,719,567

Date of current or last constitution: September 27, 1992.

Form of government: Multiparty republic with one legislative house *(Assemblée Nationale)*, seventy-seven members, elected for a five-year term by universal suffrage. Legislative elections were held on June 21 and July 5, 1992.

Head of state and government (1993): President General *Gnassingbé Eyadéma*, elected for a seven-year term by universal suffrage. He appoints and leads the council of ministers. Prime minister since March 22, 1993: *Jean-Lucien Savi de Tové*.

Political parties: The *Rassemblement du Peuple Togolais* (RPT) is the ruling party. Since March 1991, approved opposition parties are being registered.

Heads of state since independ.:		Coups d'état:
Sylvanus Olympio	1960–63	
Nicolas Grunitzky	1963–67	1963, Sylvanus Olympio killed
Gen. Étienne Gnassingbé		
Eyadéma	1967–	1967, Nicolas Grunitzky overthrown

Ethnic composition (1981): Ewe-Adja 43.1%; Tem-Kabre 26.7%; Gurma 16.1%; Kebu-Akposo 3.8%; Ana-Ife (Yoruba) 3.2%; non-African 0.3%; other 6.8%.

Religious affiliation (1991): Animistic beliefs 50.0%; Christian 35.0% (Roman Catholic 26.0%; Protestant 9.0%); Moslem 15.0%.

Exports (1987): Calcium phosphates 45.8%; coffee 12.6%; cotton (ginned) 11.8%; cocoa beans 11.4%; machinery and transport equipment 6.2%. *Major export destinations* (1987): the Netherlands 14.8%; France 7.7%; Spain 7.4%; United States 7.3%; Italy 7.0%; Canada 5.7%; United Kingdom 5.5%.

Imports (1987): Machinery and transport equipment 27.2%; food products 14.6%; cotton yarn and fabrics 11.3%; chemicals 10.5%; refined crude oil products 7.3%. *Major import sources* (1987): France 32.7%; the Netherlands 9.3%; United Kingdom 7.1%; Ivory Coast 5.5%; Japan 5.0%; United States 3.6%.

NOTE

The information in this section has been compiled from the following sources: *Rapport Annuel Mondial sur le Système Économique et les Stratégies (RAMSES) 1992*, Institut français de relations internationales, Thierry de Montbrial, ed. (Paris: Dunod, 1991). *Annuaire Statistique de la France 1990*, vol. 95, no. 37 (Paris: Institut National d'Études Démographiques (INSEE), 1990). *Panorama Mondial des Événements*, Encyclopédie permanente (Bâle: Éditions Académiques, 1968–90). *Britannica Book of the Year, 1979–1993* (Chicago: Encyclopaedia Britannica,

1979–93).   *Quid 1992: tout pour tous,* Dominique Frémy, and Michèle Frémy, eds. (Paris: Laffont, 1991).   *Africa Review 1991/992,* 15th ed. (Saffron Walden: World of Information, 1992).   *Problèmes économiques* (Paris: la Documen-tation française). *Journal officiel de la République française* (Paris).   *Notes et études documentaires* (Paris: la Documentation française).   *Le Mois en Afrique: études politiques, économiques & sociologiques africaines* (Paris).   *Le Nouvel-Observateur* (Paris).   *Le Monde* (Paris).   *Le Figaro-Magazine* (Paris).

Bibliography

BOOKS AND REPORTS

Abelin, Pierre. *Rapport sur la politique française de coopération.* Ministre de Coopération. Paris: la Documentation française, 1975.

Africa Review 1991/92. 15th ed. Saffron Walden: World of Information, 1991.

Akle, Moïse M. K. "Sécheresses récurrentes de l'Afrique contemporaine et analyse critique de quelques programmes internationaux de lutte: le cas des grands bassins fluviaux de l'Afrique de l'ouest soudano-sahélienne." Thèse de doctorat, Univ. Louis Pasteur, Strasbourg, 1988.

Altbach, Philip G., and Gail P. Kelly. *Education and Colonialism.* London: Longman, 1978.

Amegboh, Joseph. *Rabah: le conquérant des pays tchadiens.* Paris: Afrique biblio club, 1980.

Amondji, Marcel. *Félix Houphouët et la Côte-d'Ivoire: l'envers d'une légende.* Paris: Karthala, 1984.

————. *Côte-d'Ivoire: le P.D.C.I. et la vie politique de 1945 à 1985.* Paris: Harmattan, 1986.

Annuaire Statistique de la France, 1990, 95(37). Paris: Institut National d'Études Démographiques (INSEE), 1990.

Ardagh, John. *France Today.* New York: Penguin, 1988.

Atkinson, Geoffroy. *Les Nouveaux Horizons de la Renaissance française.* Paris: Droz, 1935.

Baba, Kaké Ibrahima. *L'Afrique coloniale: de la Conférence de Berlin (1885) aux indépendances.* Paris: ABC, 1977.

————. *Sékou Touré: le héros et le tyran.* Paris: Jeune Afrique, 1987.

Balous, Suzanne. *L'Action culturelle de la France dans le monde.* Paris: PUF, 1970.

Baumgart, Winfried. *Imperialism: The Idea and Reality of British and French Colonial Expansion, 1880–1914*. Oxford: Oxford University Press, 1982.

Bayart, Jean-François. *La Politique africaine de François Mitterrand*. Paris: Karthala, 1984.

Becker, Jean-Jacques. *Histoire politique de la France depuis 1945*. Paris: Colin, 1988.

Benoist, Joseph-Roger de. *La Balkanisation de l'Afrique occidentale française*. Dakar: Nouvelles Éditions africaines, 1979.

Betts, Raymond F. *Assimilation and Association in French Colonial Theory, 1890–1914*. New York: Columbia University Press, 1961.

Biarnes, Pierre. *Les Français en Afrique noire de Richelieu à Mitterrand*. Paris: Colin, 1987.

Blanchet, André. *L'Itinéraire des partis africains depuis Bamako*. Paris: Plon, 1958.

Bourgi, Albert. *La Politique française de coopération en Afrique: le cas du Sénégal*. Paris et Dakar: Bibliothèque africaine et malgache, 1979.

Bourgi, Robert. *Le Général de Gaulle et l'Afrique noire: 1940–1969*. Paris et Dakar: Bibliothèque africaine et malgache, 1980.

Britannica Book of the Year, 1979–1991. Chicago: Encyclopaedia Britannica, 1979–91.

Brunschwig, Henri. "French Exploration and Conquest in Africa." In L. H. Gann and Peter Duignan, eds., *Colonialism in Africa: 1870–1960*, Vol. 1. New York: Cambridge University Press, 1969.

———. *Le Partage de l'Afrique*. Paris: Flammarion, 1971.

Cadenat, Patrick. *La France et le Tiers Monde: vingt ans de coopération bilatérale*. Paris: la Documentation française, 1983.

Cambridge History of Africa, 8 vols. New York: Cambridge University Press, 1975 (Vol. 4), 1977 (Vols. 3, 5), 1984 (Vol. 8), 1985 (Vol. 6), 1986 (Vol. 7). [Vol. 3, *From c. 1050–c. 1600*, R. Oliver, ed.; Vol. 4, *From c. 1600–c. 1790*, R. Gray, ed.; Vol. 5, *From c. 1790–c. 1870*, J. E. Flint, ed.; Vol. 6, *From c. 1870–c. 1905*, R. Oliver and G. N. Sanderson, eds.; Vol. 7, *From 1905–1940*, A. Roberts, ed.; Vol. 8, *From c. 1940–c. 1975*, M. Crowder, ed.]

Capet, Marcel. *Traité d'économie tropicale, les économies d'A.O.F.* Paris: Librairie générale de droit et de jurisprudence, 1958.

Carbett, Edward M. *The French Presence in Black Africa*. Washington, DC: Black Orpheus Press, 1972.

Carmoy, Guy de. *Les Politiques étrangères de la France, 1944–1966*. Paris: La Table ronde, 1967.

Cohen, Samy. *Les Conseilleurs du président; de Charles de Gaulle à Valéry Giscard d'Estaing*. Paris: PUF, 1980.

Cohen, William B. *Rulers of Empire: The French Colonial Service in Africa*. Stanford, CA: Hoover Institution Press, 1971.

————. *The French Encounter with Africans: White Response to Blacks, 1530–1880.* Bloomington: Indiana University Press, 1980.

Coquery-Vidrovitch, Catherine, and Henri Moniot. *L'Afrique noire de 1800 à nos jours.* Paris: PUF, 1974.

Cornevin, Robert. *Le Togo.* Paris: PUF, 1967.

————. *L'Afrique noire de 1919 à nos jours.* Paris: PUF, 1973.

Cot, Jean-Pierre. *À l'épreuve du pouvoir: le tiers-mondisme, pour quoi faire?* Paris: Seuil, 1984.

Couste, P. B. *L'Association des pays d'outre-mer à la Communauté Économique Européenne.* Paris: Librairie technique, 1959.

Dagut, Jean-Luc. "Les Sommets franco-africains: un instrument de la présence française en Afrique." In *Année africaine 1980.* Bordeaux: Centre d'étude d'Afrique noire, 1981.

Delafosse, Maurice. *Civilisations négro-africaines.* Paris: Librairie Stock, 1925.

————. *Les Nègres.* Paris: Rieder, 1927.

Delcourt, Jean. *L'Île de Gorée.* Paris: Clairafrique, 1984.

Denis, Jacques. *L'Afrique centrale et orientale.* Paris: PUF, 1971.

Deschamps, Hubert. "France in Black Africa and Madagascar Between 1920 and 1945." In L. H. Gann and Peter Duignan, eds., *Colonialism in Africa, 1870–1960,* Vol. 3. London: Cambridge University Press, 1971.

Devillers, Philippe, et al. *Indépendance et relations internationales: quelques études de cas.* Paris: Centre d'étude des relations internationales, 1961.

Diagne, Amady Aly. *Blaise Diagne: premier député africain.* Paris: Africa, 1990.

Dumont, René. *L'Afrique noire est mal partie.* Paris: Seuil, 1973.

————. *Paysans écrasés, terres massacrées: Équateur . . .* Paris: Laffont, 1978.

————. "Impérialisme français et sous-développement africain." In François Maspéro, ed., *Tricontinental: la France contre l'Afrique.* Paris: PCM/Petite Collection Maspéro, 1981.

Dumont, René, and Marie-France Mottin. *L'Afrique étranglée.* Paris: Seuil, 1980.

Favier, Pierre, and Michel Martin-Roland. *La Décennie Mitterrand,* 2 vols. Paris: Seuil, 1990, 1991. [Vol. 1, *Les Ruptures (1981–1984);* Vol. 2, *Les Épreuves (1984–1988).*]

Fieffé, Eugène. *Histoire des troupes étrangères au service de France depuis leur origine jusqu'à nos jours, et de tous les régiments levés dans les pays conquis sous la Première République et l'Empire,* 2 vols. Paris: Dumaine, 1854.

Gann, L. H., and Peter Duignan, eds. *Colonialism in Africa, 1870–1960,* 5 vols. New York: Cambridge University Press (for the Hoover Institution), 1971 (Vol. 3), 1974 (Vol. 5), 1975 (Vol. 4), 1982 (Vols. 1, 2). [Vol. 1, *The History and Politics of Colonialism, 1870–1914;* Vol. 2, *The History and Politics of Colonialism, 1914–1960;* Vol. 3,

Profiles of Change: African Society and Colonial Rule; Vol. 4, *The Economics of Colonialism;* Vol. 5, *A Bibliographical Guide to Colonialism in Sub-Saharan Africa.*]

Gbenou, Jacques-Henry. *Urbanisation et colonisation en Afrique occidentale française, 1900–1940.* Lille: A.N.R.T., Univ. de Lille III, 1986.

Gergen, Kenneth J. "The Significance of Skin Color in Human Relations." In John Hope Franklin, ed., *Color and Race.* Boston: Houghton Mifflin, 1968.

Girardet, Raoul. *L'Idée coloniale en France: 1871–1962.* Paris: La Table Ronde, 1972.

Gonidec, Pierre François. *L'Évolution des territoires d'outre-mer depuis 1946.* Paris: Librairie générale de droit et de jurisprudence, 1958.

———. *L'État africain: évolution, fédéralisme, centralisation et décentralisation, panafricanisme.* Paris: Librairie générale de droit et de jurisprudence, 1970.

Grenier, Isabelle. *Résistances et messianismes: l'Afrique centrale au XIXe et au XXe siècle.* Paris: ABC, 1977.

Grimal, Henri. "Les Deux Propositions politiques des Africains." In René Rémond, ed., *La Décolonisation, 1919–1963.* Paris: Colin, 1965.

Grosser Alfred. *Affaires extérieures: la politique de la France, 1944–1984.* Paris: Flammarion, 1984.

Guillaume, Pierre. *Le Monde colonial: XIXe–XXe siècle.* Paris: Colin, 1974.

Guillen, Pierre. *L'Expansion: 1881–1898.* Paris: Imprimerie Nationale, 1984.

Guillou, Michel. *Une Politique africaine pour la France.* Paris: Albatros, 1985.

Hailey, Lord, GCSI, GCIE. *An African Survey: A Study of Problems Arising in Africa South of the Sahara.* London: Oxford University Press, 1938.

Hamon, Léo. *Introduction à l'étude des partis politiques de l'Afrique française.* Paris: Librairie générale de droit et de jurisprudence, 1959. [Excerpt from *Revue juridique et politique d'outre-mer* 2 (Apr.–June 1959), 150–96.]

———. *Les Partis politiques africains (II).* Paris: Librairie générale de droit et de jurisprudence, 1961.

Harshé, Rajen. *Pervasive Entente: France and Ivory Coast in African Affairs.* Atlantic Highlands, NJ: Humanities Press, 1984.

Hayter, Teresa. *French Aid.* London: Overseas Development Institution, 1966.

Hoffmann, Léon-François. *Le Nègre romantique: personnage littéraire et obsession collective.* Paris: Payot, 1973.

Imbert, Jean. *Le Cameroun.* Paris: PUF, 1982.

Jeanneney, Jean-Marcel. *Rapport.* Ministère dÉtat chargé de la réforme administrative. Commission d'études de la politique de coopération avec les pays en voie de développement. Paris, July 1, 1963.

Jeudy, André. *Administrateur des colonies: essai d'autobiographie critique.* Lille: A.N.R.T., Univ. de Lille III, 1988.

Johnson, Wesley G., ed. *Double Impact: France and Africa in the Age of Imperialism*. Westport, CT: Greenwood Press, 1985.

Kergoat, Jacques. *La France du Front populaire*. Paris: La Découverte, 1986.

Kolodziej, Edward A. *French International Policy Under de Gaulle and Pompidou: The Politics of Grandeur*. New York: Cornell University Press, 1974.

Lacoutre, Jean. *De Gaulle: le rébelle, le politique, le souverain*, 3 vols. Paris: Seuil, 1985.

La Gorce, Paul-Marie de, and Bruno Moschetto. *La Cinquième République*. Paris: PUF, 1979.

La Roche, Jean de. *Le Gouverneur-général Félix Éboué, 1884–1944*. Paris: Hachette, 1957.

Leduc, Michel. *Les Institutions monétaires africaines: pays francophones*. Paris: Pedone, 1965.

Legum, Colin. *Pan-Africanism: A Short Political Guide*. New York: Praeger, 1965.

Ligot, Maurice. *Les Accords de coopération entre la France et les états africains et malgache d'expression française*. Paris: la Documentation française, 1964.

Lombard, Jacques. *Autorités traditionnelles et pouvoir européens en Afrique Noire*. Paris: Presses de la Fondation nationale des sciences politiques, 1967.

Lutte contre le racisme et la xénophobie. Rapport de la Commission nationale consultative des droits de l'Homme, présidée par Paul Bouchet, conseiller d'État. Paris: la Documentation française, 1992.

Mabileau, Albert, and Jean Meyriat. *Décolonisation et régimes politiques en Afrique noire*. Paris: Presses de la Fondation nationale des sciences politiques, 1967.

Machel, Samora. *Establishing the People's Power to Serve the Masses*. Dar Es Salaam: Tanzania Publishing House, 1980.

McNamara, Francis Terry. *France in Black Africa*. Washington, DC: National Defense University, 1989.

Manessy, Gabriel, and Paul Wald. *Le français en Afrique noire: tel qu'on le parle, tel qu'on le dit*. Paris: Harmattan, 1984.

Markovitz, Irving Leonard. *Léopold Sédar Senghor and the Politics of Négritude*. New York: Atheneum, 1969.

Maspéro, François, ed. *Tricontinental: la France contre l'Afrique*. Paris: Maspéro, 1981.

Masson, Paul. *L'Aide bilatérale: assistance, commerce ou stratégie?* Paris: PUF, 1967.

"Mauritania." In *Africa Review 1986*, 10th ed. Saffron Walden: World of Information, 1986.

Méker, Maurice. *Le Temps colonial*. Dakar: Nouvelles éditions africaines, 1980.

Memmi, Albert. *Portrait du colonisé, précédé du portrait du colonisateur.* Paris: Payot, 1973.

Mezu, Sébastien-Okechukwu. *Léopold Sédar Senghor et la défense et illustration de la civilisation noire.* Paris: Didier-Érudition, 1968.

Miège, Jean-Louis. *Expansion européenne et décolonisation de 1870 à nos jours.* Paris: PUF, 1973.

Milcent, Ernest, and Monique Sordet. *Léopold Sédar Senghor et la naissance de l'Afrique moderne.* Paris: Seghers, 1969.

Mitterrand, François. *Présence française et abandon.* Paris: Plon, 1957.

———. *Réflexions sur la politique extérieure de la France: introduction à vingt-cinq discours (1981–1985).* Paris: Fayard, 1986.

Mus, P. *Le Destin de l'Union Française, de l'Indochine à l'Afrique.* Paris: Seuil, 1954.

Ndiaye, Guédel. *L'Échec de la Fédération du Mali.* Dakar: Nouvelles Éditions africaines, 1981.

Ney, Napoléon, ed. *Conférences et lettres de P. Savorgnan de Brazza sur ses trois explorations dans l'Ouest africain de 1975 à 1886.* Brazzaville: Bantoues, 1984.

Nkrumah, Kwame. *Neo-Colonialism: The Last Stage of Imperialism.* London: Heinemann, 1965.

———. *Africa Must Unite.* London: Banaf Books, 1970.

———. "I Speak for Freedom." In G.C.M. Mutiso and S. W. Rohio, eds., *Readings in African Political Thought.* London: Oxford University Press, 1975.

Nouaille-Degorce, Brigitte. *La Politique française de coopération avec les états africain et malgache au sud du Sahara, 1958–1978.* Bordeaux: Centre d'étude d'Afrique noire, Institut d'études politiques, 1982.

Panorama Mondial des Événements. Encyclopédie permanente. Bâle: Éditions Académiques, 1968–1990.

Passeron, André. *De Gaulle parle des Institutions, de l'Algérie, de l'armée, des affaires étrangères, de la Communauté, de l'économie et des questions sociales.* Paris: Plon, 1962.

Pickles, Dorothy. *The Fifth French Republic.* New York: Praeger, 1965.

———. *France: The Fourth Republic.* Westport, CT: Greenwood Press, 1976.

Pierce, Roy. *French Politics and Political Institutions.* New York: Harper and Row, 1973.

Projet socialiste pour la France des années 80. Paris: Club socialiste du livre, 1980.

Quermonne, Jean-Louis. *Le Gouvernement de la France sous la Ve République.* Paris: Dalloz, 1980.

Quid 1990, 1992: tout pour tous. Dominique Frémy, and Michèle Frémy, eds. Paris: Laffont, 1989, 1991.

Racine, Nicole, and Louis Bodin. *Le Parti communiste français pendant l'entre-deux-guerres*. Paris: Presses de la Fondation nationale des sciences politiques, 1972.

Rapport Annuel Mondial sur le Système Économique et les Stratégies (RAMSES) 1992. Institut français de relations internationales. Thierry de Montbrial, ed. Paris: Dunod, 1991.

Rigaud, Jacques. *Les Relations culturelles extérieures*. Paris: la Documentation française, 1980.

Rioux, Jean-Pierre. *La France de la IVe République*, 2 vols. Paris: Seuil, 1980, 1983. [Vol. 1, *L'Ardeur et la nécessité, 1944–1952;* Vol. 2, *L'Expression et l'impuissance, 1952–1958.*]

Rivkin, Arnold. *Africa and the Common Market: A Perspective*. Denver: Denver University Press, 1966.

Sabatier, Peggy. "Did Africans Really Learn to Be French? The Francophone Elite of the École William Ponty." In G. Wesley Johnson, ed., *Double Impact: France and Africa in the Age of Imperialism*. Westport, CT: Greenwood Press, 1985.

Siriex, Paul Henri. *Félix Houphouët-Boigny, l'homme de la paix*. Paris: Seghers, 1975.

Snowden, Frank M. *Blacks in Antiquity*. Cambridge: Cambridge University Press, 1969.

Thompson, Virginia. "Niger." In *National Unity and Regionalism in Eight African States*. New York: Cornell University Press, 1966.

Thompson, Virginia, and Richard Adloff. *French West Africa*. London: Greenwood Press, 1958.

———. "French Economic Policy in Tropical Africa." In L. H. Gann and Peter Duignan, eds., *Colonialism in Africa, 1870–1960*, Vol. 4. New York: Cambridge University Press (for the Hoover Institution), 1975.

Touré, Abdou. *La Civilisation quotidienne en Côte-d'Ivoire: procès d'occidentalisation*. Paris: Karthala, 1981.

Touré, Sékou. *Expérience guinéenne et unité africaine*. Paris: Présence africaine, 1960.

Tudesq, André-Jean. *La Radio en Afrique noire*. Paris: Pedone, 1983.

Vaillant, Janet G. "African Deputies in Paris: The Political Role of Léopold Senghor in the Fourth Republic." In G. Wesley Johnson, ed., *Double Impact: France and Africa in the Age of Imperialism*. Westport, CT: Greenwood Press, 1985.

Vennetier, Pierre. *L'Afrique équatoriale*. Paris: PUF, 1972.

Weinstein, Brian. *Éboué*. New York: Oxford University Press, 1972.

Williams, Philip M. *Crisis and Compromise*. Garden City, NY: Anchor Books, 1966.

World Development Report 1989. Washington, DC: World Bank, 1990.

Ziegler, Jean. *Sociologie de la Nouvelle Afrique*. Paris: Gallimard, 1964.

JOURNAL ARTICLES

"Afrique: un partenaire indispensable." *Actuel Développement* (Paris) 36 (May–June 1980), 39–40.

"Aide publique bilatérale de la France en faveur de l'Afrique: orientations et instruments." *Problèmes économiques* (Paris: la Documentation française) 2.217 (Mar. 20, 1991), 1–8.

Amalric, Jacques. "L'Entretien télévisé du chef de l'État: j'exclus le retour à l'OTAN et le retour au colonialisme." *Le Monde*, Jan. 29, 1981, 17–20.

"Après quatre jours d'émeutes violemment réprimées, l'armée a pris le pouvoir au Mali et arrêté le président Traoré." *Le Monde*, Mar. 27, 1991, 1a, 2.

"Association des États africains et malgache à la Communauté Économique Européenne." *Notes et études documentaires* (Paris). Secrétariat général du gouvernement 3327 (Oct. 15, 1966), 1–67.

Auverny-Bennetot, Philippe. "La Dette du Tiers monde: mécanismes et enjeux." *Notes et études documentaires* (Paris) 4940, 1–129.

Barrin, Jacques de. "Le Sommet franco-africain de La Baule: M. Mitterrand lie l'octroi de l'aide française aux efforts de démocratisation." *Le Monde*, June 23, 1990, 3a.

———. "Fronde africaine." *Le Monde*, June 23, 1990, 1a.

———. "Passage d'un régime militaire à une démocratie 'islamique': les intégristes en terre de mission." *Le Monde*, Apr. 18, 1992, 6a.

Beauregard, E. E. "Toucouleur Resistance to French Imperialism." *Présence Africaine* (Paris) 131 (1984), 144–54.

Boggio, Philippe. "Soleil noir sur Gorée." *Le Monde*, Mar. 21, 1992, 25, 27.

Broca, Paul. "Documents relatifs au croisement des races très différentes." *Bulletin de la Société d'Anthropologie de Paris (BSAP)* 1 (May 1860), 255–68.

———. "Sur le volume et la forme du cerveau suivant les individus et suivant les races." *BSAP* 2 (1861), 139–207.

———. "Sur les proportions relatifs du bras, de l'avant-bras et de la clavicule chez les nègres et les Européens." *BSAP* 3 (Apr. 1862), 162–72.

Bulletin de l'Afrique noire (Paris) 67 (Sept. 30, 1958), 1210–11.

"Business Briefs, West Africa," *Africa Report* 37 (1) (Jan.–Feb. 1992), 12.

Cohen, William B. "Literature and Race: 19th Century French Fiction, Blacks and Africa." *Race and Class* (London) 16 (Oct. 1974), 181–205.

"Convention de Yaoundé—analyse et commentaires." *Notes et études documentaires* (Paris). Secrétariat général du gouvernement 3327 (Oct. 15, 1966), 19–28.

"Convention Protocols, Final Act and Agreement." *Lomé Dossier*. Reprinted in *Courier* 13 (Mar. 1975), Special Issue.

"Coopération entre la France, l'Afrique noire d'expression française et le Madagascar." *Notes et études documentaires* (Paris). Secrétariat général du gouvernement 3330 (Oct. 25, 1966), 1–47.

"Coopération française en direction de l'Afrique: ses différentes formes, recherches de complémentarités." Étude présentée par la Section des relations extérieures, Avis et rapports du Conseil économique et social. *Journal Officiel de la République française* (Paris) 4 (Mar. 8, 1991), 1–135.

Coquery-Vidrovitch, Catherine. "Le Travail forcé en Afrique." *L'Histoire* (Paris) 69 (1984), 100–105.

Crowder, M. "The Impact of Two World Wars on Africa." *History Today* (London) 34 (Jan. 1984), 11–18.

Dagut, Jean-Luc. "L'Afrique, la France et le monde dans le discours giscardien." *Politique africaine* (Paris) 2 (5) (Feb. 1982), 19–27.

Daniel, Jean. "Comment on devient raciste." *Le Nouvel Observateur* (Paris), Sept. 16–22, 1983, 20–23.

Decraene, Philippe. "Problèmes et tensions entre états d'Afrique noire." *Études internationales* (Quebec) 4 (Dec. 1970), 10–16.

"Démocratie et développement au Sud." *Problèmes économiques* (Paris: la Documentation française) 2.266 (Mar. 11, 1992), 1–5.

Ekwalanga, Michel. "Une Solution à l'immigration." *Le Monde,* Mar. 5, 1992, 2c.

Fortier, Jacques. Des Étudiants de plus en plus nombreux; contrastes Nord-Sud." *Le Monde,* July 4, 1991, 14c.

Fottorino, Eric. "Le Gouvernement encourage les sociétés françaises à investir en Afrique." *Le Monde,* Feb. 23, 1990, 30a.

———. "Plaies d'Afrique." *Le Monde,* May 30, 1990, 4a.

———. "Les Syndicats africains ont du mal à rompre leurs liens avec le pouvoir." *Le Monde,* Aug. 7, 1991, 13b.

———. "La Côte-d'Ivoire reste le principal bénéficiaire de l'aide français." *Le Monde,* Apr. 11, 1992, 21a.

"Freemasonry: The French Connection." *Africa Confidential* (London) 28 (2) (May 27, 1987), 1–2.

Fritscher, Frédéric. "Un Cris d'alarme de la FAO: le continent subit l'une des pires sécheresses du siècle." *Le Monde,* Apr. 16, 1992, 6a.

Gobineau, Arthur-Joseph de. "Essai sur l'inégalité des races humaines." *Revue des Deux Mondes* (Paris) 2 (8) (Mar. 1, 1857), 159–88.

Hippolyte, Mirlande. "De Nouakchott à Niamey: l'itinéraire de l'O.C.A.M." *Revue française d'études politiques africaines* (Paris) 34 (Oct. 1968), 34–55.

Humblot, Catherine. "Canal France International à Yamoussoukro." *Le Monde,* Feb. 25, 1991, (RT) 25.

Journal Officiel de la République française (Paris) 4 (Mar. 8, 1991), 9–12.

Konaré, Alpha Oumar. "Floraison de journaux indépendants en Afrique francophone." *Le Monde,* Feb. 12, 1991, 23d.

Langellier, Jean-Pierre, and Catherine Simon. "La France n'entend pas 'donner des leçons' à l'Afrique." *Le Monde*, Mar. 22, 1992, 1b, 5.

Le Bon, Gustave. "Recherches anatomiques et mathématiques sur les lois des variations du volume du cerveau et du crâne." *Revue d'anthropologie* 2 (2) (1879), 103–04.

"Loi no 56-619 du 23 juin 1956." *Recueil Dalloz* (Paris) 27 (1956), législation, 215–17.

Luvai, A. I. "Négritude: A Redefinition." *Busara* (Nairobi) 6 (2) (1974), 79–90.

Macrum, John. "How Wide Is the Gap Between Casablanca and Monrovia?" *Africa Report* (Washington, DC) 7 (1) (Jan. 1962), 3–18.

Martin, Guy. "Les Fondements historiques, économiques et politiques de la politique africaine de la France: du colonialisme au néo-colonialisme." *Genève-Afrique* 21 (2) (1983), 39–68.

———. "The Historical, Economic, and Political Bases of France's African Policy." *Modern African Studies* 23 (1) (June 1985), 189–208.

———. "The Franc Zone, Underdevelopment and Dependency in Francophone Africa." *Third World Quarterly* 8 (1) (Jan. 1986), 205–35.

Owen, A. D. "The World Uranium Industry." *Raw Materials Report* (Stockholm) 2 (4) (1984), 6–23.

Peyrot, Maurice. "L'Affaire 'carrefour du développement' devant la cour d'assises de Paris: M. Christian Nucci au banc des victimes." *Le Monde*, Mar. 25, 1992, 18e.

Pick, Hella. "The Brazzaville Twelve and How They Came to Be." *Africa Report* (Washington, DC) 6 (5) (May 1961), 2–15.

"Politique africaine de la France: les orientations de M. Pelletier, nouveau ministre de la coopération." *Le Monde*, July 9, 1988, 4a.

"Pour ou contre le franc fort." *Problèmes économiques* (Paris: la Documentation française) 2.263 (Feb. 19, 1992), 23–26.

Robinson, Kenneth E. "Constitutional Reform in French Tropical Africa." *Political Studies* (London) 6 (1) (Feb.1958), 45–64.

———. "Colonialism French-Style, 1945–55: A Backward Glance." *Journal of Imperial and Commonwealth History* (London) 12 (2) (1984), 24–41.

Simon, Catherine. "Les Balbutiements du multipartisme en Afrique." *Le Monde*, Mar. 13, 1991, 1b, 6.

———. "Un Nouvel Acteur: le premier ministre." *Le Monde*, June 8, 1991, 4c.

———. "Afrique: la démocratie à tâtons; des élections libres auront lieu cette année dans une vingtaine de pays mais les régimes en place s'accrochent au pouvoir." *Le Monde*, Apr. 25, 1992, 1a, 6.

Simonnot, Philippe. "De Bonnes Raisons de dévaluer le franc." *Le Monde*, Mar. 10, 1992, 41a.

Solé, Robert. "Lancinante immigration: alors que le sujet préoccupe de plus en plus les Français, le pouvoir n'a pas encore trouvé les mots pour en parler." *Le Monde*, Nov. 5, 1991, 1d.

Subtil, Marie-Pierre. "Les Déçus de la démocratie au Mali: un an après le renversement du président Moussa Traoré, tous les problèmes—chômage, rébellion touareg, etc.—demeurent sans solution." *Le Monde*, Mar. 25, 1992, 6a.

Touscoz, Jean. "Document: le rapport Gorse sur la coopération de la France avec les pays en voie de développement." *Esprit* (Paris) 418 (Nov. 1972), 682–705.

————. "La *Normalisation* de la coopération bilatérale de la France avec les pays africains francophones." *Études internationales* (Quebec) 5 (June 1974), 208–25.

Vinay, Bernard. "La Zone franc d'aujourd'hui." *Marchés Tropicaux et Méditerranéens* (Paris), Nov. 28, 1986, 2979–87.

Whiteman, Kaye. "President Mitterrand and Africa." *African Affairs* (Oxford, England) 82 (1983), 329–43.

Zecchini, Laurent. "Recentrage de la politique de coopération, MM. Aurillac, Penne, Foccart et la *famille. Le Monde*, Apr. 5, 1986, 2a.

Index

About the Author

ANTON ANDEREGGEN is Professor of French at Lewis and Clark College in Portland, Oregon.